D0229651

Holocaust Child

Holocaust Child

Lalechka
An Inspirational Story of Survival

Amira Keidar

AD LIB

First published in 2021 by Ad Lib Publishers Ltd
15 Church Road
London, SW13 9HE
www.adlibpublishers.com

Text © 2021 Amira Keidar
This Edition is published by arrangement with The eBook-Pro Agency

Paperback ISBN 978-1-913543-07-5

All rights reserved. No part of this publication may be reproduced in any form or by any means — electronic, mechanical, photocopying, recording, or otherwise — or stored in any retrieval system of any nature without prior written permission from the copyright holders. Amira Keidar has asserted her moral right to be identified as the author of this work in accordance with the Copyright, Designs and Patents Act of 1988.

A CIP catalogue record for this book is available from the British Library.

Every reasonable effort has been made to trace copyright-holders of material reproduced in this book, but if any have been inadvertently overlooked the publishers would be glad to hear from them.

Printed in the UK
10 9 8 7 6 5 4 3 2

CONTENTS

Prologue

IRENA

The night between August 24 and 25 was hot. Scorching. The air was stifling and oppressive, without the slightest ripple of a breeze. I was 27, living with my mother and my older brother Kazimir in Shedlitz (Siedlce), a small, colorless town some 40 miles east of Warsaw. Mother and I were alone in the house since my brother had left for the country with his wife and son to stay with our Aunt Felicia and help with the farm. Felicia's husband, Uncle Valente, was still in a German POW camp, and save for a single postcard more than a year before, we hadn't heard from him.

I was drowsy, but the thoughts were running endlessly in my head, keeping me from the sleep I so yearned for. It had been many months since the last time I managed to sleep a full, satisfying night. The street outside was very quiet. Unlike the previous few days, there were no gunshots, no thundering boots that shake the walls—and the cries of distress of the past nights from the Jewish quarter had ceased as well.

Suddenly I heard a knock on our rear window, quiet but decisive. I immediately knew who it was.

I had known Zipora Jablon since the first grade. From the start, she, Sophia and I had become close friends. "My parents and my friends call me Zippa," she told us, and from that day on our paths never parted: we spent our childhood years together in

Shedlitz, and then our high school. Zippa and I even registered in the same department at Warsaw University, but she was forced to quit unexpectedly. It was the war that finally separated us; Zippa remained on one side of the barbed wire fence and I on the other.

Mother and I hopped out of bed at almost the same time and rushed to the back entrance. Zippa was standing on our doorstep and in her arms she was holding a small, sleeping child wrapped in a frayed blanket. A few months earlier, I learned that Zippa gave birth to a baby girl she named Rachel, but I never saw her. Since the ghetto had been put under quarantine the year before, Zippa was not permitted to leave, and we could not enter. Despite the relentless heat that night, Zippa's entire body was shivering. "Come in," I told her, scanning the street before closing the door behind her.

"My dear, dear Zippa, I've been waiting for you day and night, I knew you were coming," Mother told her and hugged her and the child, who remained fast asleep.

Zippa had no need to explain anything; we knew why she had come. Over the past few days, there were horrifying rumors in the town about the goings on inside the Jewish ghetto. Mother became distraught by those stories and found them hard to believe. "I can't understand how they let this happen," she told me a day or two before Zippa arrived. Faint echoes of gunshots and anguished voices from the direction of the ghetto reverberated all the way to our neighborhood; the endless running steps of soldiers and ceaseless movement of motorized vehicles could be heard in the town streets all day and all night.

"We're not the ones that let this happen, what can we do against them?" I asked her, not expecting an answer.

"We're a weak nation," she mused, as if to herself. "Always letting others rule our lives. We never took our fate in our own hands."

Those days my mother wasn't blaming only the Polish nation. Despite being a devoted Catholic, she never stopped wondering aloud how the good God could permit things to deteriorate so much. My mother's way of coping with the situation was to go on praying day and night. I, on the other hand, was so confused and distressed, I was barely functioning. The gut wrenching cries that rose for two whole days from the direction of the Jewish ghetto continued to reverberate in my brain well after I stopped hearing them. We had no reliable news about what was happening inside the ghetto, and there was no way to find out. All we knew were rumors. An atmosphere of terror and fear permeated the entire town.

We went into the kitchen, the only spot in the house where we used a small kerosene lamp. Mother signaled with her hand for me not to light it this time. The moon's pale light emerged through the window. Because of petrol shortages we didn't light, and in winter didn't heat the rest of the rooms in the house. We spent most of the day hours in our little kitchen. Zippa was wearing a torn dress, through which we could detect how thin she had become. She sat down wearily on one of the heavy chairs my father built from cherry wood many years ago. He also built with his two hands the oak table around which those chairs stood. Recently we had been feeling my father's absence more than ever—he passed away from an illness before the war began. Since my brother moved to the village, Mother and I were taking care of getting our food and other household needs, forced to spend hours standing in line. And the fact that there were only women in our household increased our already oppressive sense of insecurity.

Zippa cradled the girl in her arms and for a moment appeared remote and removed from the goings on. She told us nothing about the events in the place from which she just arrived, but there was no need. Her big eyes told us more than her mouth ever could. My mother gently took little Rachel out of her hands, and the baby continued to sleep peacefully despite the storm around her. Zippa followed Rachel with her gaze. She could not remove her eyes from the sleeping child. I handed her a glass of water, and she drank it in huge gulps. I handed her another glass and sat down beside her. She held my hand, and the two of us remained silent. I caressed her hair, which used to be soft as linen and now had become tough and tangled. Also gone without a trace were the luxurious dresses from her past. I wanted to inquire about her parents, about Jacob, but I felt I couldn't bear to hear her answers.

"I must go back," she said a short time later and stood up. She knew she couldn't stay with us for too long.

"Stay and sleep," suggested my mother. "In the morning we'll think of something."

"Tomorrow we'll try to talk to Zosha, she'll know what to do," I said in a broken voice and hoped that Sophia would really come up with a solution. I couldn't accept the notion that Zippa would return to the ghetto. If she did, I knew we couldn't ever help her.

Zippa didn't have the strength to resist. When my mother picked up the baby to put her to bed, Zippa followed her with her eyes until she disappeared into the bedroom. I led Zippa up to the attic, where I spread a clean sheet over a mattress. She lay down heavily. I covered her with a thin blanket even though her entire body was sweating.

Very early the next morning, Sophia arrived. I don't know how she found out that Zippa had come to us in the middle of the night, but it seemed completely natural that our Zosha would show up precisely at the moment we needed her. Zippa was still sleeping. Rachel hadn't made a sound since their arrival. It appeared that a good night's sleep was what they both missed most of all.

"Zippa and Rachel came last night," I whispered to Sophia, fearing that my words might reach alien ears. I showed her Rachel—my mother was seated next to her, delicately caressing her tiny body.

"I'll find them a hiding place," Sophia said immediately. She was always practical and efficient, and I knew I could count on her now as well.

"Fine," I told her, "but Rachel stays here."

Then I went and lay down next to Rachel. "Rochele," I whispered to her, "What's going to happen?" She was breathing heavily in her sleep. I patted her dark hair and tried to keep my ears shut; Sophia was sitting in the kitchen, telling my mother what she knew about events inside the Jewish ghetto. I wasn't able to listen, but bits of words and phrases out of Sophia's mouth reached me and sounded incomprehensible. I was overcome by limitless terror. If I could, I would have sung to Rachel so that none of the things I heard would reach her, but my throat was choked.

Rachel woke up around noon and immediately began to scream in hunger. My mother gave her some milk and prepared an oatmeal porridge. Rachel devoured the porridge through her tears, but after she had her fill she calmed down and stopped crying. For most of the day she was sleepy, her motions slow and clumsy. But when she was wide awake she'd grab my hand and lead me with her very first steps into the kitchen. Feed me, her big eyes were begging. I gave her porridge and some potato, and she fell asleep while drinking the warm milk I prepared for her. I climbed up to the attic to bring Zippa her meal. She stayed in bed the entire day and only once asked me to bring Rachel to her. I left them alone and when I returned discovered the two of them sleeping on the mattress, wrapped in one another.

Sophia returned only in the evening, after roaming the streets trying to collect clothes and a few provisions for Rachel. She managed with a great deal of effort to find shelter for Zippa. Now the three of us were sitting together in the attic. Sophia and I couldn't come up with words to comfort Zippa or cheer her up. And after Zosha said, "She'll be in good hands," Zippa began crying bitterly, with me following right along. We waited for nightfall, and then I packed food and some clothing for Zippa.

Toward midnight, Sophia said, "We must go." The night was dark and gloomy despite the almost full moon. Not a streetlight was on, no light shimmered in windows of nearby houses, and no sound was heard in the deserted streets. Only faint echoes of gunshots reverberated now and again from the direction of the ghetto. Sophia did not say where they were headed, and I did not ask.

We stood in the kitchen, too distraught to say anything. My mother held Rachel, who had just fallen asleep in her arms. Zippa did not attempt to hug or kiss the baby, knowing that if she did she might not have the strength to let her be saved. Her eyes caressed for a long time the soft infant that slept so peacefully in my mother's arms. Then Zippa's eyes welled up with tears, and she turned around and walked decisively to the door.

I followed both my childhood girlfriends to the back door. Before leaving, Zippa took an envelope out of her dress pocket and handed it to me. "It's for your mother," she told me quietly. She followed my movements as I inserted the envelope into my nightgown pocket. We embraced quickly, and she disappeared into the dark night the same way she first appeared, like a silent shadow.

I knew this could be the last time I saw her.

Chapter 1

ZIPPA

I was born in Shedlitz in 1915, during the Great War. Poland was not an independent state at the time, violated and sliced up by her emerging, stronger neighbors. When I turned three, the war—of which I recall very little, mostly the intense noises coming from the streets—was over, and Poland received independence, for the first time in its history.

From my childhood I remember Shedlitz as a peaceful, but still vivacious and colorful town. When I walked the streets, usually accompanied by my mother, my hand in her warm hand, she'd point to the little shops and say, "You see, this man repairs shoes, and this man sews clothes, and here is the baker who buys his flour from your father." I loved passing by the artisans, snug in their little shops, and guessing what it was they were making. I remember once standing for a really long time in front of the glass door of a particularly tiny store, observing the elderly man who was bent over a short, wooden table, unable to guess what he did. He sat there for a very long time and for a moment appeared completely motionless. "This man is a scribe," said my mother. "What's he scribing?" I asked innocently. "He's writing a Torah scroll," she explained.

We almost always concluded our trip in my father's flour shop on Pickna Street, one of the big commercial centers of Shedlitz. My father, Aaron Jablon, owned a flour and grain wholesale business, and he enjoyed reminding me and my elder brother Shimon that the grain trade had been in our family since the beginning of time. In previous generations, the family tradesmen would travel from one place to another to purchase the goods and then sell them. My grandfather Chaim Shlomo Jablon was actually the first in our family to establish a store in town, and it supported the entire great Jablon clan. Like his five brothers and his sister, my father worked from a very young age in his father's store. When Grandpa Chaim passed away, just shy of eighty, right after the end of the Great War, the youngest, most aggressive son, Yechiel, took over running the store and attempted to buy out his siblings. Two brothers and their sister took their share and went to seek their fortunes in America; one brother moved to Warsaw, where he opened his own flour shop; Israel, the eldest of the brothers who remained in Poland, opened a camping equipment shop in Shedlitz; and Menachem, the middle brother, died at a young age, so Yechiel agreed, under pressure from all his other siblings, to include Menachem's invalid son in the buyout. My father, who spent his entire life among sacks of wheat and rye, never considered leaving Shedlitz or the sacks. A peaceful man who avoided a quarrel at all cost, he saw no point in confrontation with his brother Yechiel and used his buyout money to purchase a smaller store, at a distance from the family business. Thanks to his good connections with his father's clients, many of them, Jews and Poles, switched to him.

I loved visiting the store with my mother, filling up my nostrils with the delicate and sweet fragrance of fresh flour already wafting from the entrance. The floor was sprinkled with a mix of rye, sesame, poppy, wheat berries that weren't yet milled and other species of grain, which I began to recognize by name in later years. My father loved explaining to me at length how each grain grew and what could be made from it. At the end of the visit he would give me a small, brown paper bag in which I collected different seeds from the floor, so that on our way home I could spread them in the great square, the Stary Rynek, and watch as within seconds flocks of gray pigeons came landing from every which way to peck lustily at the seeds from the cracks between the cobblestones.

Like many other middle-class Jewish women, my mother Josepha was a housewife. Occasionally she would take in sewing and garment repair jobs, but she did it mainly to keep busy and not because she needed to help with the family's finances. My father refused vehemently to let her work. He treated her like a queen, and my mother in response used to joke that he was surely doing it because he feared her father.

Avraham Rinezky, my mother's father, was a renowned bookbinder in Shedlitz. Unlike most of the Jablon family, who were completely secular and even had Socialist tendencies, Grandfather Avraham was a devout, observant Jew. To his chagrin, his wife Rachel and he beget only girls, and he regarded carefully picking their suitors to be his holy task. Indeed, the two elder sisters were matched with boys from the town's well-known, devout Jewish families. Leah, the eldest, who married Akiva Zuker, and Chaya, who married Joel Ringlebaum, both lived near their parents' house and were very attached to one another. Most of their neighbors were Ultra Orthodox Jews, and each time I would visit them with my mother, she derived more grief than pleasure. As we'd get closer to the neighborhood, my mother would tighten her hand around mine and broaden her steps, eager to be done with this difficult assignment. "Sometimes I don't know what to say to them," she told me once, on our way back home. "And, anyway, whenever I start talking, another toddler shows up, demanding attention."

My mother, the youngest of Avraham and Rachel Rinezky's daughters, refused to be married through a matchmaker. For one whole year, until she turned twenty, she didn't exchange one word with her father because he wanted to marry her off to an Ultra Orthodox boy, the son of the sexton of the butchers' synagogue. When her mother, Rachel, supported her decision, her father understood the war was lost and permitted her to marry her beloved, Aaron Jablon, brother of her best girlfriend. My mother once told me, in a rare moment of candor, that she had been in love with him from the age of ten, and when she turned sixteen, she knew he would be her husband. My father, Aaron, didn't live up to the religious standards of his future father-in-law, but he belonged to a respectable family whose flour shop was renowned all over Shedlitz, a fact that finally convinced Grandpa Avraham to approve of the wedding.

Aaron Jablon made a commitment to Avraham Rinezky that as long as he was able to work, Rinezky's youngest daughter would want for nothing, and so it was. Even though we were not among the town's wealthy, we never lacked anything, and my mother was never heard to complain about our economic situation, even during rough times. She always received whatever she asked for, whether fabric for dressmaking or fish for gefilte-fish, and now and then she received what she hadn't thought to ask for, like the long, wool coat with the mink collar my father bought her in Warsaw for their tenth anniversary.

Like many of the town Jews, we, too, lived on a small, quiet street, one of those narrow streets and little alleys that circled the town's center from every direction. Compared with the wide, splendid avenues and magnificent public edifices of the civic center, the humble residential Jewish neighborhoods of Shedlitz looked almost shabby. Here, too, many artisans were working on the ground floors: tailors, shoemakers, carpenters, and blacksmiths populated the tiny, cramped shops, but the houses were made of wood, the streets narrow and neglected, no cherry or chestnut tree adorned the sidewalks and the stench of the sewer frequently assaulted passersby. These neighborhoods were home to the smaller houses of worship, like the tailors' and the butchers' synagogues. The Grand Synagogue stood, properly enough, in the civic center.

We lived above Mr. Goldschmidt's barbershop. Once in a while, before going upstairs to our flat, I would stop by and he would halt whatever he was doing, ask me to shut my eyes tight, open a secret drawer behind the small counter at the corner of his shop and dig out a caramel lollipop on a wooden stick. Mr. Goldschmidt's candy tasted like faraway countries.

Perhaps because she was unable to conceive a third time, my mother became overly worried and anxious. She was the one who insisted on registering us in the Polish state educational system, despite the high tuition, and not in the Jewish system. She knew that no college in Poland would accept us if we attended a Jewish school. Also, she wanted us to absorb some Polish culture—into which, back then, she and my father were still hoping to be accepted.

Until I turned six, I thought only Jews lived in Shedlitz. My visits to my aunts and grandparents taught me to easily notice the difference between religious and secular Jews, and the Polish customers in my father's store looked and sounded to me like they were from another town. The first time I realized that Shedlitz had Polish residents as well was when I started attending grammar school. I was amazed at the sheer number of blonde hair, blue-eyed girls gathered in the big playground, and I searched for any girl from my neighborhood; I would have greeted joyously any Jewish girl. After the first day of school, I was begging my mother to move me to a different school, but the great distress was soon replaced by great happiness when, during one of the breaks on the second or third day of school, my only acquaintance in class, Chaya Luterman, and I were approached by two Polish girls who asked if we wanted to play. They called two other friends over, and every break we played hide and seek. Of the five friends who now comprised our gang—a well-consolidated group that filled my days in school and many hours after the school day—Sophia and Irena were the closest to me. Since that day, our paths never parted.

From a young age, Sophia proved how much her name, which in Greek means Wisdom, fit her. She was an exceptionally smart and mature girl, and although she invented most of our acts of mischief, she was always careful not to do anything forbidden or truly dangerous. When she wasn't busy making up a trick or a new game, she would usually attach herself to a book. "Zosha will be a teacher when she grows up," Jadja told me on one of those occasions when Sophia chose to stay in class and read during the break, instead of going out to the playground. Sophia raised her blue eyes, which since a young age had been hidden behind big, square-framed glasses, emphasizing her mature and responsible character, and said apologetically, "I'm sorry, I just can't stop reading this book, it's a book by Jules Verne that's just been translated into Polish." It was still the time when she used to knot her pale hair into two long braids. Only when we started high school did she change her hairdo. "Braids are for little girls," she told me and Irena one day, while Irena's mother was teaching her how to collect her hair in a bun behind her neck, "and I want the grownups to take me seriously." Sophia didn't understand that even if she walked in a clown dress, the grownups would still take her seriously. All the teachers in elementary school, and later in high school, would approach her when there was a need to pass a message to the rest of the girls. It wasn't made official by anyone, but Sophia was—starting in the first grade—the leader. It was just fine with us, since if ever there was a need for a leader for our group, Zosha would probably have been voted unanimously.

Sophia always preferred to let her rational mind guide her actions, and even if back then I didn't know enough to define it that way, I understood that she was an independent child with original ideas. Unlike most children, she was never swept up by other people's opinions and was never dragged into acting unlawfully. On one vacation, when we were eight or nine, we had gone on a walk and while deep in conversation we suddenly found ourselves outside the city limits. When we passed by a small cherry orchard whose fruits at the time were at their ripest, Irena and I suggested we climb up one of the trees and pick a few shiny, black cherries. Jadzia, Hanka, and Chaya were debating aloud whether or not to join us, and only Sophia objected vehemently.

"If you fall off the tree, there won't be anyone to take care of you out here," she told us, "the hospital is far away, and besides, these trees probably belong to someone." Her logical argument persuaded us, and we decided to give up the temptation and walked back home. I think it was that event that finally crowned Sophia our leader.

Without any connection to her being the strongest and most dominant member of our group, Sophia's parents' house was our preferred spot year-round, winter or summer, vacation or regular weekday. The Olszakowsky family resided in a suburb that was considered the most affluent in Shedlitz in the twenties and thirties. When I first came to their house, I couldn't believe that this two-story stone structure with the wide veranda was home to one family of four. The well-maintained garden surrounding the house looked to me as big as the park where I played with my Jewish girlfriends. Sophia's mother was a big lover of plants, and even in the living room stood large pots where Stephania Olsakowska grew many plants, which she used to groom for hours on end. As small children, we especially loved playing hide and seek in Sophia's house, which provided us with endless hidden corners. More than anything, we loved hiding behind Mrs. Olszakowsky's great big plants until she'd walk in, sooner or later, to remind us it was time to return home. I always thought she was worried about us destroying her planters. I once asked Sophie how her mother found the time and strength to keep the whole house clean and to care for the planting pots and the huge yard. "The planters and the yard are the love of her life," Sophia told me, and I thought I heard some scorn in her voice, "the cleaning she leaves to the maid." That was the first time I found out that people had maids.

Sophia's father, Oleg Olszakowsky, was a renowned pharmacist who owned his own drugstore in Shedlitz. He was an educated and progressive man, who had arrived alone from Poznan at the turn of the century and made Shedlitz his home. When I would visit his pharmacy, normally on an errand for my mother (because, to the best of my recollection, my father was never sick), Mr. Olszakowsky always made me feel that I was his only customer. Even though my parents were not socially connected to him or to his wife, each time the need would arise, they preferred to consult with him before going to see a doctor. Mr. Olszakowsky was also one of my father's regular customers, and although he was member of the National-Democratic party, which openly supported placing limits on Jews in Poland and reducing their economic influence, I was accepted in his home just like all his daughter Sophia's other girlfriends.

In many ways, Irena, the softest and most fragile in our group, was the exact opposite of Sophia. The first thing I noticed when I met Irena was her straight, perfect nose. More than Jadzia's and Sophia's blue eyes, or Hanka's straw blonde hair, Irena's classical nose was the first thing I dreamed I would copy if I could change the way I looked. It was the exact opposite of my own typically Jewish nose, which I inherited from my mother. As a child, Irena was already tall and slim, and her light brown and almost golden eyes, often filled with tears. Her honey-colored hair was silky soft, and unlike most of the Polish girls who took pride in their long, blonde hair, Irena preferred the short haircuts favored by the movie actresses we saw on posters or in magazines. Despite her fragile and delicate appearance, Irena was a friend you could count on, any time, any place. If I told her something in confidence, I could absolutely be sure she'd keep the secret. She loved reading even more than Sophia did, and unlike the adventure stories and biographies that attracted Sophia, Irena was attached as early as the fourth or fifth grade to thick French and Russian novels.

Irena's father, Jerzy Zawadzky, was a born farmer. He was tall and silent, and on my first visits to their house, I was afraid to speak in his presence. He reminded me of the Russian Czars described at such length in our study books, and I always had the feeling he saw and knew everything. Jerzy Zawadzky inherited from his father agricultural lands on the outskirts of

Shedlitz, from which he made his livelihood. In his free time, he loved to build furniture from the wood he cut in the forests that surrounded our town in every direction. On occasion, he'd bring in from those same forests some wild animals he hunted, and sold the skins and furs in the Jewish market. Sabina, Irena's mother, would cook the meat, and the aroma of her cooking wafted throughout the neighborhood. I was hoping not to be visiting Irena on such a hunt day because I knew that avoiding that appetizing food would be impossible for me. Even though my parents were secular, they still kept a few commandments, including the laws of kashrut. Jerzy Zawadzky's game meat did not belong on our menu.

One time I visited Irena's house while her father was busy skinning an animal—could have been a rabbit or a fox, I didn't know and didn't dare to ask. Irena and I stood for a long time, staring at him tearing the skin off the poor animal with the same indifference and ease one would peel an onion for soup. A short while after he was finished, an Ultra Orthodox Jew showed up to purchase the fur. "The Jews always appreciate good merchandize," said Mr. Zawadzky after his customer had left. I couldn't figure out from the tone of his voice whether he meant it as a negative or positive thing. Even when Jerzy Zawadzky became a clerk working for the town of Shedlitz, in the thirties, when toiling the land became too hard for him, his manner remained that of a farmer, unpolished and silent—and espousing right-wing views, which he never made a secret.

Like her husband, Sabina Zawadzka was also a tall and somber woman. Her face was square, her eyes narrow, and her mouth clenched. Her silky hair was always collected in a perfect bun behind her neck. But despite her austere appearance, she was a generous and hospitable woman, a devout Catholic who visited Church any chance she got. On many occasions, I saw her sitting and reading her little prayer book, which she carried everywhere.

During the early years of our friendship, I worried about going to Irena's house. Unlike Sophia's bourgeois neighborhood, the

Zawadzkys' neighbors were only lower middle-class and working class Poles, many of whom did not approve of one of their own befriending a Jewish girl. Once in a while I heard this or that neighbor mouthing something at me, but I always ignored them and the topic never came up between me and my girlfriend. Only with the passing years did I learn that Irena's parents, who seemed at first to be so grim and silent, were actually polite and pleasant folks who always treated me with warmth and love. Only Irena's older brother, Kazimir, maintained his hostile silence, and I kept my presence there to a minimum when he was at home.

Irena and Sophia became my second family. Almost every day after school we'd meet and spend time together until the evening hours, occasionally with the other girls, but mostly just the three of us. At school, there were girls who disapproved of our tight friendship. One of them, a tall, light-haired lass named Ivona, knew that Irena came from a devout Catholic home and decided to take advantage of her delicate and fragile personality. During Passover—we were ten or eleven at the time—Irena was a guest in my house, and when my mother offered her a matzo, Irena refused it. "What happened to you?" I later asked her. Irena had never before refused to eat anything in my house, she loved all the food my mother prepared, and every year she ate matzos in our house on Passover. Besides, if she disliked something she always declined politely. This time she refused adamantly to eat the matzo.

"Is it true what they say about the Jews?" she asked, her eyes lowered.

"What do they say about us?" I asked her.

"I heard that the Jews kidnap Christian children to use their blood for baking matzos on Passover," she said in a trembling voice.

"Who told you this?" I demanded. It wasn't the first time I'd heard such a story, especially from children, but I was surprised to hear it from Irena.

With great emotion and tears, Irena related all the stories she'd heard from Ivona, stories that many Poles had passed from one generation to the next for hundreds of years. I was choked by anger and humiliation. "Ivona also says the Jews killed Jesus," said Irena. "My mother believes in Jesus, but she never told me the Jews murdered him."

Ivona's tales sounded so ridiculous to me, I couldn't understand why Irena became so excited over them. "Those are just libels people made up about the Jews because we've always been a little different and eccentric," I told her in a soothing voice, but at that moment, I felt that I could wring Ivona's neck. This was the first time I had spoken with my close girlfriend as a Jew, and not as Zippa.

That night I dreamed that I was standing by myself in the town square, when suddenly I was accosted by a band of Polish school girls, and they were all screaming in unison: "You murdered Jesus! You murdered Jesus!" I tried to identify any of my close girlfriends among the approaching students, and at the very moment their faces became clearer I woke up.

When Sophia found out about the Ivona incident, she decided to take care of it in her own way. One day, a little after Passover, she approached Ivona and told her, "If you don't want me to tell the Headmistress what you do in the market after school, I suggest you leave Irena alone." Ivona and a few of her friends would go to the Shedlitz market, and when no one was paying attention, they'd steal stuff from the booths and run away. Sophia found out about it from her mother, who saw them in the act, but Sophia decided not to report them to the school principal. Maybe she decided back then to use this information as a bargaining chip.

Indeed, we never again heard from Ivona any smart comments about Jews. Very often she and her girlfriends would whisper behind our backs, but they no longer dared to come near Irena or the rest of us. Many years later we still rolled in laughter every time Sophia would imitate Ivona's frightened face as she comprehended that she'd been caught stealing from the market. Ever since then we nicknamed her Ivona the Terrible, after the Russian Czar.

There was no shortage of boys and girls who hated Jews in Shedlitz. I used to hear from my brother Shimon stories that made me shiver and made me wonder time and again how I managed to become so well integrated with my Polish girlfriends. But I was convinced that those stories about children like Ivona—refusing to sit near a fellow Jewish student, or spitting every time they passed by a Jewish child—represented only a minority. But while my own relationship with my Christian girlfriends became tighter, Shimon's relationships with his fellow Polish students became ever cooler. One time I heard him tell my father that the Jewish students in school were thinking of starting their own committee since no Jewish student succeeded in getting elected to the student council. It appeared that those events had an effect on him, so that when Shimon was attending the 11th grade at the business department of the government-run Boleslaw Prus boys' high school, he joined the Shedlitz Zionist youth clubs and went out every night on activities that he loved sharing with my father whenever he had the chance. By the end of the nineteen-twenties, when he enlisted in the Polish army, my brother's views had already been formed, and his attitudes were obvious. He knew exactly how to go about achieving his dreams. He didn't manage to complete his studies at the University of Warsaw because he had already decided to enroll in Zionist training in Ostrolenka, north of Shedlitz, on his way to making aliyah to Eretz Israel.

Life in Shedlitz was never easy for Jews. Ever since I started school and realized there were others living in the town besides us, I learned more and more from my father about the hardships the Jewish nation had endured since it settled in Poland, probably as early as the Thirteenth Century. Waves of anti-Semitism were a permanent component of Jewish life. Yankel, the son of my father's eldest brother, Eliezer, who at the time was leader of the local Bund, was murdered, along with tens of other innocent Jews, in the pogrom that took place in our town at the turn of the century. At the time, it was the Cossacks who rioted against the Jewish community of Shedlitz, followed by the Germans and then, once more, the Russians who returned to rule the town. There was always a foreign occupier in Poland—Russian, Prussian, or Austrian—who made Jewish life hell, with no particular objection on the part of the Polish residents, who were quick to adjust themselves to the demands of each new, temporary conqueror.

Thus, when Poland had finally gained its independence at the end of the Great War, the town's Jews were seized by an enormous gush of excitement. My father shared with me and my brother that he was convinced then that independence and the new constitution would usher in a new relationship between Poles and Jews. But his hope and the hopes of the entire Polish Jewish community soon evaporated, as new waves of anti-Semitism began to sweep the land. The post-war anti-Semitism did not skip over Shedlitz, although the town retained its peaceful and friendly appearance. But scattering the meetings of local Jewish organizations, beatings of Jewish citizens, arrests and other, similar harassments, turned out to be only the precursor to the events of the Russo-Polish war. In the spring of 1920, the Polish army Chief of Staff published a list of regulations against the Jews of Shedlitz, and all their political and cultural organizations were ordered to cease their activities. In August of that year, the Russian army seized Shedlitz, and two weeks later, upon exiting Shedlitz, the Polish military arrested about one thousand Jews suspected of collaborating with the Communists. Close to twenty of them were tried and executed; others were sentenced to long prison terms. Polish citizens took an active part in this hate campaign and looted Jewish homes and businesses. The town was suffused with an atmosphere of fear and loathing. Even though I was just five at the time, I remembered it well, and my father reminded me with his stories time and again, how I wasn't allowed back then to leave the house at any hour of the day.

One evening, when I was seven, my father entered the house all excited. After finishing his workday at the store, he told us, he went to visit his parents' gravesite in the local Jewish cemetery. He tried to share with us in his trembling voice what his eyes had witnessed: tens of gravestones were smashed and completely destroyed, others were defaced with offensive writing, and the entire place was covered with trash and filth.

Attacks on Jews were commonplace in those days. The economic policy instituted by the Polish government in the early nineteen-twenties—levying heavy taxes on Jews and limiting Jewish financial freedoms—caused heavy damage to the Jewish middle class, greatly reducing the number of Jewish-owned small businesses. Many local Jews were on the brink of bankruptcy. To my father's fortune, the tough situation did not hurt his business. He would come home from work every day, hang his hat on the hook by the front door, sit down heavily in a chair in the kitchen and say, "Blessed be my forefathers for choosing the flour business."

My father loved to tell us what he called "Shedlitz tales." Especially on Hanukkah nights, when darkness fell early and snowflakes began to cover the streets, we would gather in the small living room, eat my mother's potato latkes, and immediately following the candle lighting we'd sit and listen eagerly to Dad's stories. Shimon and I would be sitting on the rug at his feet, begging for a Shedlitz Hanukkah story, and then my father would wrinkle his forehead as if struggling to dig up a new tale from memory. He would sit down comfortably in the brown armchair whose velvet upholstery started to unravel at the corners, light up the pipe his father left him (for some reason, my father smoked only on Hanukkah, as if the pipe became part of the service), and every year would tell a new yarn. I loved listening to his quiet, low voice, and even though his stories weren't always happy, his voice filled the house with a pleasant sense of security. My father's tales offered a great deal of information about the history of the Jews of Shedlitz. Pogroms, riots and other harassments appeared frequently in those tales, and he would often lose himself in his memories of one pogrom or another, at which point my mother would tense up and say, "Aaron, enough now, the children don't have to hear this every year." Then he would stop, suck on his pipe, give her a warm smile, and switch to fables of the Jablon-Rinezky family—which often made my mother's cheeks blush lightly.

Chapter 2

IRENA

I nagged Zippa for many, long weeks to invite me to her parents' house, but every time she would come up with a new excuse and continued to refuse me. One time she said she had to get permission from her parents, another time she said her mother wasn't feeling well, and all the other times she just avoided the issue. "It's so much nicer at Zosha's," she told me one day after school when I asked her one more time to visit her house.

"We've been to Sophia's many times; I want to see *your* house, the neighborhood where you live. Don't you want me to come to you?"

She wouldn't answer.

Until I met Zippa and Chaya Luterman, I used to think all the Jews in Shedlitz spoke a different language and even looked different from us. At the girls' elementary school on May 1st Street, I suddenly met Jewish girls who looked like me, spoke my language and played the same games I did. It surprised me very much, but I had no one to share the experience with—my mother was always busy doing this or that and showed no willingness to listen to my stories. In my neighborhood, they spoke of Jews only as shrewd merchants and wily businessmen, the kind of folks who've taken over the civic center and were actually running Shedlitz. Zippa was my first Jewish girlfriend, and even though I was a bit leery of entering the Jewish quarter, I was curious to see these wily people up close.

One early autumn Friday our last two classes were canceled unexpectedly, and our homeroom teacher decided to send us home to prepare for the Polish Independence Day ceremony the following week. "Want to come to my place?" Zippa asked as we were leaving school, "my mother is baking challahs for Shabbat." The rest of the girls had already run home, and Zippa stayed back with me in the classroom and helped me arrange my notebooks, which always fell apart when I was in the worst hurry.

"Sure I want," I said immediately, before she could change her mind. I was glad we were just the two of us; I had the feeling that this visit with Zippa would be very special, and I didn't want it to be spoiled, not by Jadzia's endless giggles, and not by Sophia's solemnity. I wanted it to be my and Zippa's secret.

We walked along The 1st of May Street; a cold wind was blowing at us, and brown, red, orange and gold leaves covered the sidewalks. The books my mother read to me at bedtime occasionally mentioned inclement days, and I felt that I was in the midst of one such inclement day. It had been a few months since the war with Russia ended, and the atmosphere in town was festive. New stores were opening every day in my parents' quarter, and new houses were being built or old ones renovated on every block.

It was my first time in the Jewish quarter. Many people were walking on either side of the wide Warsaw Road, coming in and out of the little stores, passing among the booths that were spread on the sidewalks, feeling up the merchandise and yelling words in a language I did not understand. Most of the men wore hats and dark, long suits, and many had long beards that sometimes reached down to their chest. For some reason, they seemed to me to be poor, but not sad. The women wore long dresses with wool scarves on their shoulders and some tied colorful handkerchiefs around their head. The mixed aromas of sweet baked goods, fresh fish, and ripe fruits assaulted my nostrils. And as if all the stores and all the booths and the peddlers with their carts that circled them on the left and on the right were not enough, a few of the peddlers stood up on their horse-drawn wagons and from up high offered their goods to the passersby. "These must be those shrewd merchants that are taking over the civic center," I surmised.

I was beginning to feel regrets. I feared that if something bad were to happen to me, no one would understand what I was saying, and they'd refuse to help me. I was sorry I asked Zippa so many times to let me come to her house because now I was afraid to hurt her feelings if I asked to go home. Zippa grabbed my elbow and pointed to a booth that was laden with colorful scarves. As we were beginning to approach it, suddenly a peddler emerged out of nowhere dragging a cart full of merchandise and almost hit us. His flowing speech while bending down to collect the goods that fell off his carts made Zippa blush, but when I asked her what he was saying she answered, "What difference does it make, he's just a *meshugene*." She didn't even notice that I didn't understand what she meant by that word.

The ruckus subsided when we entered a quiet street, and Zippa said, "This is where I live." Asha Street was short, more alley than street, connecting the two main drags, Pulasky to the south and Warsaw Road to the north. Two-story wood houses, crowded and stacked up against one another, stood on either side of this narrow street. They looked so completely different from the tall and ornate houses on the main street, and I was hoping Zippa wouldn't notice my reaction to the humbleness of her block. I suddenly understood why she'd been rejecting my pleas to visit her home and regretted pressuring her. "It's nice here," I said but knew she didn't believe me.

We entered the back yard of the house at number 3 and climbed up to the Jablon family apartment. The staircase was so narrow and dilapidated that I had to hold on to the railing with all my might. Zippa's mother, Josepha, received us at the entrance as if she had been expecting us. When she shook my hand, I recalled my first day of school. It was hard not to notice the dark haired girl and her elegant mother who stood out among the dozens of Polish girls and their mothers. Zippa was wearing a light blue dress and was holding on to her mother, a swarthy woman with a grave expression on her face, not particularly tall but standing erect and determined. The mother, dressed in a dark suit, was looking around suspiciously, wouldn't let go of her daughter's hand for even a moment, and was the very last of all the mothers to say goodbye to her daughter. Before she left, I saw her kneeling before Zippa, hugging her with great force and kissing both her cheeks. I had never before seen such a show of affection, not from my own and not from my girlfriends' parents.

Now Josepha led us into the warm kitchen. A large, black coal stove stood in one corner, spreading a pleasant fragrance. The warmth in the kitchen, along with the perfect order and cleanliness, was in absolute contrast to the wretchedness of the outside. We sat down on heavy, wooden chairs upholstered in brown leather that stood around the large wooden table at the center of the kitchen. On one of the kitchen walls hung a large oil painting, showing a sailboat anchored by a golden beach against a bright, blue seascape. I had never seen the ocean with my own eyes, and since then every time I came back to visit Zippa's house, I loved to gaze at that picture, which I used as my anchor in moments of confusion or shyness. The table was covered with a bright, white, lace tablecloth, with a china plate in which rested a fresh, bright bread they called "challah" spreading a sugary aroma. Josepha served us a slice of challah and sweet tea. I'll never forget the sweet taste of Josepha Jablon's challah.

At noon, Josepha and Zippa walked me back to my parents' home. "I had a great time," I told them but felt that I wasn't able to express my feelings adequately.

"Me too," said Zippa and hugged me.

"Very glad to have met you," said Josepha and shook my hand warmly. She and Zippa walked away, and I stood and stared at Josepha, who was embracing Zippa's shoulders in a manner I had never seen before. When I entered my house, there was no one waiting for me. I sat down in the empty kitchen, confused and excited about my visit, waiting for my mother to return from Church.

A short while later, Zippa invited me once again to visit her. This time she invited Sophia, too, and so the two of us began visiting Zippa's house from time to time. Most often it was only Sophia and me because Chaya lived on the other side of town, and Jadzia and Hanka were forbidden to hang around after school. Whenever we'd get to the Jablon family home—most often on Fridays and on Jewish holidays—the atmosphere there was unlike anything else I was familiar with. They often conducted some kind of casual rite there, which nevertheless bore a sense of sacredness. Josepha would serve us the holiday's special goodies and Zippa's father, if he wasn't working at the store, would explain the holiday's customs and their origins. Zippa told me her parents were not religious, but they kept part of the Jewish commandments and celebrated all the holidays according to the tradition. We learned from Mrs. Jablon that Mr. Jablon was well known and respected in the Jewish community, and although he wasn't religious, there was a regular seat kept for him in the Grand Synagogue. I loved watching the bright, silver candle holders that stood on the kitchen table, loved tasting the Shabbat challah and the special holiday food, and most of all I loved following Josepha's expert, gentle movements with my eyes.

The first time we came to visit on Passover, she served us a cold, grayish meatball, which at first I refused to taste.

"You should taste it, it's gefilte fish," said Josepha, laughing.

"Gefilte what?" I asked.

"Gefilte fish. It means a stuffed fish in Yiddish," said Zippa.

"If it's in Yiddish then I want to taste it," I told them and cut myself a piece of the meatball. The sound of Zippa's family's language was pleasant, soft and rolling, like a lullaby. I liked the taste of the gefilte fish right away. Ever since that first Passover in their house, Josepha made sure to send me a bit of that delicacy every year. Josepha Jablon was not a cheerful woman, she kept a serious and quiet expression on most of the time, but nevertheless I felt welcome in her house. I sensed that hospitality was one of her sacred values. She always wore an elegant, modern dress or suit. "I wish my mother had such beautiful dresses," I dared tell her on one of my visits. Sophia wasn't with us that time and Josepha, Zippa and I were sitting in the living room, playing gin rummy. I don't know if I would have dared speak so directly to Josepha had Sophia been there. Zosha was always so polite and mature that sometimes I felt stupid compared to her and didn't dare say what was on my mind. Even though we were the same age, I felt more than once as if Zosha was my older sister. "My mother always wears dresses that used to belong to her own mother, and I think even her grandmother," I continued.

Josepha laughed, and I hoped I didn't insult her. "I sew by myself all of my dresses and Zippa's clothes." She smiled at me as if she just revealed a great secret, and added, "This way I get exactly what I want."

"My mother keeps all her beautiful dresses in crates in the attic," I answered, disappointed.

Zippa's father stayed home only very infrequently—he spent most of his time in his grain store, and every once in a while we'd go visit him at work. He was a short man, and almost as serious as his wife, and in the store I often saw him carrying on his back heavy flour sacks that made him seem even shorter. Most of the time his clothes were dusted with flour, and even his mustache was white. I secretly nicknamed him the Snow Man, but I didn't dare share it with my girlfriends, and certainly not Zippa. I was afraid to hurt her feelings, her relationship with her parents was so close and warm that sometimes I felt a pang of jealousy seeing them hugging and kissing her. Once, when I saw her father kissing her gently on her forehead before we left the store, I tried to recall the last time I got a kiss from my father.

Piekna Street, where Aaron Jablon had his store, was my favorite in the entire Jewish quarter. When I was wandering around there with Zippa, I was no longer afraid as I had been my first time there. There were Yiddish signs in the store windows and Zippa would translate them for me: "Here is the tanner, here a carpentry, and here it says, Usurer."

"What's a usurer?" I asked.

"I don't know; I'll have to ask my father."

Slowly but surely, I learned who owned which store, and Zippa loved testing my memory. Near Mr. Jablon's store there was a savings bank that opened ten years before we were born—that's what Mr. Jablon told us on one of our first visits to his store. All week long the Jewish quarter sizzled with activity. "Only on Shabbat there's perfect quiet here," Zippa told us. "Nobody works, and everybody goes to synagogue."

Like myself, Zippa also had an elder brother, and just like my brother Kazimir, Shimon also didn't like being at home when his sister brought her girlfriends over. He would always find an excuse to leave, or retreated into his room. Zippa didn't have her own room, she slept on a fold up bed in the pantry, and so we spent our time together in the kitchen or the living room. Zippa told us that her brother liked to call us a band of clucking chickens. I assume he had good reason, since we always had something to say, endlessly. We were six and something when we started visiting Zippa's house, and Shimon, who was ten back then, appeared thin and short, exactly like his father. A few years later, Sophia and I were already taller than him, and I assume this made him uncomfortable. He spoke to us only very rarely, and spoke only Yiddish with his family, even in our presence.

Zippa, without any doubt, was the driving force in her family. Unlike her parents and her brother, she was giggly, mischievous, joyous and vivacious, but she could also be serious and balanced when she had to. From the start of school, she stood out as a clever and talented student. She was good at math, Polish, and history, and always earned the highest marks in class. But even the best marks couldn't compensate for one blemish: she always complained that she couldn't stand the big nose she inherited from her mother. "No one is going to want to marry me," she once told me, after examining her own face for a long time in the small mirror in my room.

Zippa was not my only Jewish girlfriend, but she was the closest. She was also much more Jewish than Chaya Luterman, whose parents didn't keep any of the commandments and celebrated only some of the holidays. Chaya's father was a famous tailor in Shedlitz, and once, a little before Christmas—I was about eight at the time—I managed to persuade my mother to take me to him for a holiday dress. After weeks of pleading she conceded—and she never paid attention to trivial things like a new dress—so, naturally, I was very excited. The Lutermans lived outside the Jewish quarter, and Mr. Luterman worked in a relatively small room on the first floor of their building. His cast iron sewing machine, black and brilliant, stood on top of a big, wooden table. Next to it, waited large piles of fabrics of all colors and textures. I stood and stared at Mr. Luterman as he straightened the selected material under the needle, turned the wheel with his right hand, lowered his head to the cloth, and in mere minutes produced a new skirt from his sewing machine. After he was done measuring me from every direction with a long measuring tape, he invited us to come upstairs and visit Chaya and her mother. When we entered their apartment, I was surprised to see a small, decorated fir tree in the corner of the living room. In another corner stood a gorgeous menorah with flickering candles. When Mr. Luterman noticed my gaze moving from the menorah to the fir and back, he said, "My daughter enjoys both Hanukkah and Christmas." He laughed out loud and then explained to me in short the meaning of Hanukkah for Jews. Some of what he said I had already heard from Mr. Jablon, but coming from Mr. Luterman they sounded a little different as if he didn't take the whole thing too seriously. When Mr. Jablon spoke about his tradition and the Jewish holidays, his eyes glistened.

"It's true," Chaya merrily confirmed her father's words. "For Hanukkah I get pocket money and dreidels, and for Christmas I get gifts in stockings."

When we left their house, I asked my mother, a devout Catholic, if she could buy me a menorah.

"What do you need a menorah for?" she asked.

"Because it's so pretty," I answered innocently.

"Hanukkah is a Jewish holiday," my mother told me.

"Right, and Christmas is Christian," I retorted, "but Chaya still keeps a fir tree in her house."

My mother didn't answer. She never bought me a menorah.

Chapter 3
SOPHIA

The Queen Jadwiga government-run girls' high school was the most prestigious school in Shedlitz. It resided in a grandiose, three-story, Seventeenth Century building on Stanislaw Konarski Street. In the past, the building served to lodge visiting VIPs. The dark, heavy, wooden entrance door was lavishly ornamented in flamboyant reliefs. Irena said it reminded her of the entrance to a cathedral. To me, it mostly spoke volumes about the megalomaniacs (most notably Duchess Alexandra) who built this edifice and many similar, grotesque structures in Shedlitz. The megalomania of Duchess Alexandra, who ruled the town in the Eighteenth Century and made it what it was now, did not end with the high school's wooden front door. It stretched into the building, expressing itself in the ceilings that were far too high, making everyone entering the school feel so small. Maybe Irena was right, and the high school really resembled a cathedral. My visits to cathedrals in those days were few and far between, so I wasn't certain the comparison was accurate. Enormous chandeliers hung down from the tall ceiling above the entrance hall, and a special worker was hired to light them when the day began and put them out when it ended. The chandeliers' intense light reflected in the bright marble floor, always reminding me of an ice rink. After our first day of school, I told my girlfriends we should come to school with ice skates the next day.

Despite my loathing for the place that didn't make anyone entering it feel worthwhile, I was greatly comforted when all my best girlfriends from grammar school also moved on to that high school. In the beginning, I worried that Zippa's parents wouldn't be able to afford the high tuition—my father told me the cost of attending Queen Jadwiga High School was particularly high—but early on in the summer vacation Zippa told us her father had been saving since the day she was born to pay for her studies. Indeed, Mr. Jablon was a deliberate and wise man, and the longer I knew him, the more I admired him. When he would tell us about the Jewish holidays and tradition he always made sure to describe everything logically, and I adored his learned explanations.

The classrooms in our high school were large and spacious, exactly like the rest of the building. Soft, pleasant light always shone through the large, glass windows, so pleasant that many times I noticed one of the girls napping lightly, until she was awakened in panic by her neighbor's elbow or the teacher's ruler. To my great delight, my spot was in the last row of desks, from which I could easily gawk at Mayeski Park, which spread out from the foot of the school almost to the horizon. We spent many days in that park when we were children, first playing tag among the trees and later in exciting volleyball matches. Zippa was the best at any ball game, and I always used to tell her, "You're not just smart, you're a good athlete, too; it's not fair." Even now, in high school, the park was our favorite destination after school, but now mostly so we could have long conversations without the fear of being overheard by unwanted ears.

During our first year of school the students were forbidden to go out to the park on our breaks, so we had to make up games and activities within the school walls. Most of the time it snowed anyway, so that on our first winter in high school, the size of the place started to look advantageous. The game loved the most by

Jadzia and Hanka—I think it was Jadzia who made it up—was Queens and Baronesses. We would imagine ourselves as queens, baronesses or duchesses who arrive in Shedlitz and award the town treasures and valuable gifts we brought from faraway lands. Jadzia almost always played Queen Jadwiga, and never neglected to mention that she herself was named after her. In my opinion, this was a stupid game, but I didn't want to insult Jadzia and Hanka, who loved playing it so much. Sometimes I would make an effort and play, and sometimes I was able to come up with an excuse and avoid it. I preferred playing Twenty Questions, a game where each girl in her turn would pick a figure from Polish history, and the rest of the girls had to guess who it was with twenty yes or no questions. You could learn something from this game because each girl told something new about the person she chose. That was my own addition to the game, which I was quite proud of, but, save for Zippa, none of the girls were thrilled by the idea, because it forced them to open a book and learn about the character, whereas Zippa and I got by well without having to research the books.

On weekends, we loved going dancing at the youth center near City Hall. It was the only public activity we could all take part in. Only Irena and Jadzia went to church events—I never liked those seminars and trips, which came across too missionary for my taste. Hanka, who did attend church every Sunday, once told me that the church youth activities were too hard for her. She didn't particularly like to exert herself, but despite her being so flippant and frivolous, I loved her good heart and her devotion.

The dance soirees on the weekends would sometimes last into the night, and the atmosphere there was good. It was possibly the only place in town where you couldn't tell the differences between Jews and Christians. Everybody danced with everybody else, spoke to each other and felt equal. No other place or institution in town offered such an ambiance. Zippa was the most sought after among us; many boys wanted to dance with her. Her smarts and gifts were well known in our circle. But it always seemed to me that she was not excited about any of her suitors. It was as if she was always anticipating someone who hadn't yet arrived at the party.

In the beginning of 1933, we started studying for our matriculation exams. We spent the long winter nights mostly in my parents' house, which was bigger than my girlfriends' homes. My father got me a private tutor to help us prepare for science and math. It was a Jewish guy named David Berger who taught in one of the local high schools. The principal there was a friend of my father's and recommended David. David's dream was to teach at Warsaw University, but every time he submitted his candidacy, it was rejected. We found him exceptionally brilliant, and his teaching was clear and easy, even for Jadzia and Hanka, who were not very good at the hard sciences. We had good math and science teachers in high school, but it always seemed like they were only doing a perfunctory job of teaching. They were not nearly as bright as David and preferred focusing on history, sociology and the rest of the humanities. Most of them were socialists, and some even communists, who loved to conduct lengthy philosophical debates about political theory and the world's social movements. These discussions were boring and exhausting for most of the girls, but for me they were like flashes of light that opened my eyes and made me see the world in new colors.

Zippa bested all of us in all the subjects, most notably in math and science. She understood in an instant what took the rest of us minutes or even hours. It looked like her wisdom, as well as her beauty, did not escape the attention of our private tutor, David. He was totally charmed by her and had a hard time keeping his eyes off of her. When I told her one evening at the end of a session that I thought he liked her, she kept silent and a light blush spread on her cheeks. It was the first time I saw Zippa be ill at ease. Usually, she was decisive and self-assured, and this time it looked like she wasn't sure how exactly she was supposed to act. I thought she might want to talk about it, but she kept silent. In those days, even though we were almost eighteen, only Hanka had a boyfriend, and they already announced their wedding, which was to take place that summer, after the end of school. Jadzia said she only had "friends." She wasn't ready to commit to any one of them and mostly enjoyed the attention she was receiving. She loved being at the center of things, but when it came time to choose, she couldn't. On the other hand, she was extremely loyal to her girlfriends and would walk through fire and water for each one of us. We, too, were ready to do the same for her. Chaya Luterman didn't like letting us into her private affairs, and we respected it, and Irena was too shy and reserved every time the subject came up.

One winter evening near the end of January, we were seated, as was our habit, around the kitchen table in my parents' house. It snowed outside, but inside was warm and quiet. My mother prepared for us cinnamon tea and butter cookies with almonds, and after she had finished arranging the kitchen a bit, she sat down by the coal stove and started knitting. Every few minutes she'd come over to see if we needed anything. My father was sitting in the living room, reading, faint sounds emanating from his radio. We were preparing for a grammar exam, which was one of the first on the schedule.

We were immersed in reading a newspaper passage we were supposed to analyze when I saw my father come over to my mother and whisper something in her ear. She put down her knitting, got up from her seat and followed him into the living room. They raised the radio volume a bit, but I still didn't manage to hear the words coming out.

"What do you think they're listening to?" I asked my girlfriends, and my curiosity rose, what could it possibly be?

"Maybe Pilsudski resigned?" said Zippa.

"That couldn't be, but maybe he died?" said Jadzia and we all burst into laughter. Marshal Jozef Pilsudski rose to power in Poland through a military coup when we were about twelve. For us, he remained always this angry, severe man with a mustache, riding his white horse with a panoply of medals decorating his chest.

After all the girls had left, I asked my father what he heard on the radio, and he told me that Adolf Hitler had taken power in Germany. I had heard in school about the German Nazi party, but at the same time, I knew very little about its leader. "He is known as a big anti-Semite and as a leader with very extreme views," my father said quietly. "But you have nothing to worry about; I suggest you go to sleep."

We all passed the matriculation exams with flying colors. Maybe it was thanks to the good preparation we received from David, and maybe it was the illuminations and comments we received from Zippa throughout the preparation. Zippa, as was to be expected, received the highest marks among us.

After I had received my matriculation results, I registered to study Commerce and Economics at Warsaw University. I had no hesitation regarding which department to sign up for, I had known what I wanted to study as early as my last year of high school. The teachers at the high school—even though many of them were socialists and idealists—as well as the conversations I had from time to time with my father, led me to understand that I needed to acquire a practical subject.

One evening, a few months after the exams, I invited Zippa and Irena to my house. The three of us hadn't gotten together since the end of school, and I wanted to see them before we parted company, and each one of us followed her own path. It was the beginning of winter, it was very cold, and a prickly rain was coming down incessantly for days. Winter in Shedlitz was always long and cold, and each year I waited impatiently for it to end. That particular winter, marked by my anticipation of a letter of acceptance from the university, seemed like it would last for eternity. My mother was home and since she hadn't seen my girlfriends since we finished preparing for the exams, she asked that we spend some time sitting in the kitchen before we locked ourselves up in my room as we always did.

"I heard that you, too, are planning to enroll in university," my mother said to Zippa. Irena and I had long known what we wanted to study.

"Yes, I'm planning to enroll, but I'm not certain yet what I want to study," Zippa answered.

"What are you most interested in?" my mother asked.

Zippa always excelled at math and economics. As long as I had known her she was the best student in those areas. Her parents, too, were hoping she would pick that direction, maybe because they wanted her to work in her father's store. The matriculation marks that she received recently would have allowed her to get into any university and any department she desired, but Zippa wasn't quick to decide, and in conversations we had after school had ended, she suggested a few times trying somcthing new and different from everyone's expectations.

"But what do you most want to study?" my mother demanded.

"I'd like to study something more spiritual," she said with an almost dreamy look, "something to enrich my soul. I know I'm good at math and science, but that's exactly why I want to try something else, something I'm not so sure I'm good at.

"Maybe you should study French with me?" Irena suggested, and I was wondering for a moment when she'd gotten herself a sense of humor. Zippa kept quiet and stared at her. It seemed that she, too, was asking herself the same question. "You always told me how much you love French authors; don't you remember how much you loved reading Victor Hugo?" Irena whispered something into Zippa's ear, and the two of them blushed a little.

"It's true," said Zippa, "but I don't think my father would be happy about this idea."

"I think your father would be happy if you study something that makes you happy," my mother told her, and I wondered if she was able to say the same phrase to one of her own daughters. She never really openly criticized my decisions or actions, but often her words would imply a certain dissatisfaction regarding my choices.

After Zippa and Irena had left, my mother told me, "What a wonderful woman your friend is. It's hard to believe she's not Polish."

For a moment, I wasn't sure I heard her right. "What do you mean, not Polish?" I asked angrily. "Of course she's Polish." This was the only time my mother made any kind of comment about Zippa's Jewishness.

In the end, Zippa enrolled in the department of French literature. That's who she was, always ready to take on new challenges and try different things. She was never among those who gave up or opted for the easy path; she was always eager to prove her ability. She dared do those things that others only talked about. That was one of the many reasons I appreciated her so much.

Chapter 4
IRENA

My parents were ecstatic when I was accepted into university, the first in my immediate family to enter academic learning. Other than my uncle Valente the doctor, my extended family had no academicians. My brother Kazimir informed my parents years ago that he had no intention of attending university. He only finished high school because of intense pressure from our parents. He always said he already knew everything he needed to know, and what he didn't know no one could teach him. After he graduated high school, he found a job in a small glass factory outside town, where he continued to work for many years.

"University is an excellent place for girls," my father told me the day I received my letter of acceptance from Warsaw University. "You'll acquire a profession, you'll meet new people and, hopefully, you'll also come back with a husband in tow."

"I'm not going to university to find a husband," I responded angrily.

"Marija Skłodowska also didn't go to university to find a husband, but, still, she found one," said my father, laughing.

"Just to remind you, she had to leave Poland to be accepted into university, and she did a few other things while there, besides finding herself a husband," I told my father, feeling the tears climbing up my throat and threatening to choke me. "Besides, her name was Marie Curie, not Marija Skłodowska," I added and left the house in a huff, slamming the door behind me. I was eighteen and didn't understand why my father thought it was so urgent for me to find a husband, why couldn't he just be happy that I was accepted into university, without adding a needless jibe in the end.

Even though they lived in town, my parents were basically peasants. They were both born in a small village near Mordi, not far from Shedlitz, met at a young age and married when they were nineteen. After the wedding, they moved to the neighborhood of Novo Shedlitza, to a house that belonged to my father's family. Even after my father sold his holdings outside town and became a clerk for the city of Shedlitz, he never abandoned his true love for the land. He would often travel to his brother's village home, walk among the local farmers and breathe in the fragrance of the open fields. He knew exactly when it was time to plant and harvest, and when every fruit and vegetable ripened in our area.

The fact that I was going to Warsaw to study in university made my mother enormously excited, but it also made her very anxious. She wasn't convinced that I could get by on my own in a big city like Warsaw, and, truthfully, I wasn't sure at the time either and was hoping for more encouragement from my parents. Except for the Church summer camps I used to attend as a girl, I never left home for an extended period of time. My mother was afraid, for some reason, that once I went away to study in university I would leave home forever, and she'd never see me again.

Shortly before the beginning of the academic year, in October of 1934, Zippa and I found a flat at the center of Warsaw, not far from campus. It was a small apartment on the second floor of a tall residential building, the likes of which did not exist in Shedlitz. The flat had a small kitchen, a bathroom, and two small but pleasant bedrooms. The landlady was an old Jewish widow who lived on the first floor and was delighted to take in the two excitable young women we used to be back then.

Studying at Warsaw University was a dream come true for me, and in the days before school started I was nervous and impatient. I believed studying would make me a stronger person, more mature and ready for life. My biggest dream was to be a French teacher. I had admired the French language since I was a child. When I first entered the university, I felt as if I was stepping on sacred ground. A long and wide corridor opened up behind the heavy, wooden front doors, and brilliant chandeliers hung from the tall ceiling. A multitude of students were hurrying in every direction, with the reverberating echoes of their footsteps clip-clopping on the bright marble floor. Despite this perpetual tumult, I sensed that I arrived at the very place I had been yearning to be.

Most of the freshman year courses were conducted in large, packed lecture halls. The lector's podium stood on a stage, facing long rows of wooden chairs. The first day of school was devoted mainly to organization and registration. On the second day, Zippa and I entered the lecture hall where the Introduction to Philology was taught. It was a first-year prerequisite, and the two of us took it together.

At the lecture hall entrance, we noticed two students who were standing on the lector's stage and were yelling out instructions in every direction. Both were tall and blonde, with broad jaws and crystal eyes, and they were directing the active traffic in the hall with vigorous gestures, but in relative calm. I watched Zippa, who was staring in disbelief at the proceedings in the hall and said nothing. On the right side of the hall sat Polish students, who filled up most of the seats in the house and seemed oblivious to what was going on. On the left sat a smaller group of students who looked Jewish and who sat in quiet bewilderment. The Philology professor was nowhere in sight.

Since we wanted to sit together but didn't wish to attract needless attention, we sat down at the center of one of the last rows, between the groups of Jewish students and Polish students. When the professor—a short, bespectacled, middle-aged man in a chestnut-brown three-piece suit—arrived, he took one look at the class, chose to ignore the situation and immediately started the lecture. I didn't get one word out of what this bespectacled professor in the snazzy suit said in that opening lecture. I couldn't understand how all those hundreds of Polish students sitting with me in that lecture hall would agree to this embarrassing segregation of Jews from Poles. Back in Shedlitz there would be occasional anti-Jewish events, and some girls in high school never exchanged one word with the Jewish students, but I had never before witnessed such a demonstration of hatred and ignorance.

Zippa opted to concentrate on her studies. She didn't speak about what was happening around us, even when, later on, we witnessed harassments like throwing books or notebooks belonging to Jewish students on the floor or out the window. She naturally had no problem with the material. She avoided raising her hand in class or participating in discussions, which was very atypical, but she prepared the homework and exercises quickly and effortlessly. Once more, it seemed that studying was too easy for her and demanded little exertion.

We didn't take all our classes together, but every morning we walked to school side by side and at the end of the day we met and went back to our small flat, where we studied until the wee hours of the morning. On weekends we usually took long trips along the banks of the River Wisla, or walks in the wide parks out in the suburbs. Sometimes we'd walk aimlessly along the main streets, staring in astonishment at the tall buildings, the colorful store windows, and the women, who always appeared more elegant as well as more intelligent than the women of Shedlitz. But more than any other pastime, I loved accompanying Zippa to the bustling Jewish quarter.

Next door to the spectacular churches with their tall towers resided humble synagogues, and next to them there were dozens of stores and businesses. Even though she had never visited there before, it seemed that Zippa was feeling at home there, among the Yiddish-speaking peddlers and merchants. On Sundays, the main square would fill up with a multitude of sellers and buyers haggling so eagerly over the goods it was hard to tell who was buying and who was selling. Dozens of peddlers spread out their merchandise on tiny tables or over a blanket on the ground, and offered passersby fruits, vegetables, meat, fish, used clothes and shoelaces, each trying to out-shout the others. It reminded me of my first visit with Zippa to the Jewish quarter of Shedlitz, except here everything was more plentiful and also more noisy. Here, too, all the many stores would close under lock and key on the Sabbath, the peddlers and shoppers would vacate the main square, and the streets would be filled with families in their holiday garments, on their way to one of the many synagogues in the city.

The incidents of anti-Semitism in university were increasing, and after a few inquiries it became clear to me that the administration was not planning to take a position regarding the segregation of Polish and Jewish students, and that the professors—all of them Polish—had no intention of confronting those student activists in the lecture halls. This is when I finally understood why Mr. Berger, our private tutor back in Shedlitz, was rejected time again when he applied to teach at Warsaw University. David was rejected simply because he was Jewish.

The Introduction to Philology course was one of the hotbeds of the most overt and blatant anti-Semitic activity, although other classes had no shortage of a variety of similar phenomena. The two students who were in charge during the first day of class belonged to a small and noisy band of Polish kids for whom studying was not exactly their highest priority. They used to interrupt the lectures and yell out nationalistic and occasionally violent taunts. The professor, in his elegant suits, continued to ignore what was happening under his nose during the course, made sure to arrive a bit late, teach the lecture reading from a written text, and leave immediately at the end.

One morning, just before the All Saints Day vacation, the Philology professor was tardier than usual. The lecture hall became filled with the typical noise of young students who suddenly discovered they were not being watched. Zippa and I were conversing quietly when, suddenly, one of those two students who directed traffic on the first day and now looked like the indubitable leader of that noisy group, got up to the lecture's podium. On many previous occasions before the professor would enter the hall, this young man would stand in front of the Polish students' section and lecture them on various topics, which from our seats in the higher rows we couldn't—and didn't wish to—hear or follow. The rest of the students, especially the girls, would listen to him eagerly, applauding from time to time. Now the leader stood on the professor's stage as if this were his natural spot, and gazed with great satisfaction at the lecture hall, divided as it was into two sections. "You up there!" I heard him call out. He had a low and clear voice. I raised my head and saw that he was staring in my direction. "Are you Jewish?" he asked. The number of students at the Philology lectures had been diminishing since the beginning of the year, the hall was not nearly as packed as it used to be, and each lecture I found myself being drawn closer to the Jewish students' section and farther from the Polish section.

"I'm a student," I answered him. I was afraid that my voice would betray the storm raging inside me.

"A Jewish or a Polish student?" he continued.

"A French student," I said.

"The Polish students sit on the right side," he said, looking like he was about to lose his patience.

There was perfect silence in the hall; all the eyes were trained on me, and I felt that I was becoming pale. I didn't dare look at Zippa, but from the corner of my eye I could see her head bowed down, and I guessed that her eyes were focused on the notebook before her. I had no intention of giving up my principles and moving to sit down with the Poles, but I knew that getting on the wrong side of this student's ilk could get me in a heap of trouble. I remained in my seat.

"You don't exactly look to me like someone who..." he didn't manage to complete the sentence. That moment the door opened, and the Philology professor came in. I breathed a sigh of relief. The gang leader returned to his seat with cocksure steps. The students in the front rows shook his hand, and a few even slapped him on the back. I don't know whether the professor noticed what had been going on in the hall. As was his habit, he began his lecture and left the hall as soon as he was finished.

I looked at Zippa. Her face did not reveal her emotions. Throughout that day, she said very little. When we reached our apartment in the evening, we each went to our rooms to pack our suitcases for the trip to Shedlitz the next day, for the holiday vacation. It was our first vacation since school started, and I was very excited, eager to tell my parents about the university, about the thrilling studies, about Warsaw. I put a few clothes and my toiletry into the suitcase and went over to Zippa's room. She was just wrapping her family picture, which used to stand on her nightstand by the bed, and placed it among her clothes, which were already packed. Then she packed the few books she brought from Shedlitz in a small wooden trunk, folded up the bedclothes and put them, too, inside the suitcase. The wardrobe doors were wide open, and the wardrobe was completely empty.

"I'm not coming back to school after the vacation," she said quietly.

"I know," I answered. "I wish I could do something."

The next day we boarded the morning train to Shedlitz. The moment the train started going, we began to talk about our girlfriends we'd be seeing soon, our families, and everything we planned to do in Shedlitz during the vacation. The university incident was not mentioned even once.

Chapter 5

ZIPPA

Everything looked different when I returned home at the beginning of November 1934, only one month after I had left. Shedlitz suddenly looked small and uninteresting. I was nineteen and my biggest life's dream, studying in university, had just been smashed in front of my eyes.

My best girlfriends, whom I used to see almost every day in recent years, had been dispersed everywhere since the end of high school. At the end of All Saints Day, Irena returned to school in Warsaw. During the vacation, we got together once or twice, always with Jadzia or Hanka. We didn't discuss explicitly the reasons that led me to terminate my academic studies, but I had the feeling Irena returned to Warsaw feeling uncomfortable, or even guilty. Sophia, who was studying Commerce at Warsaw University, lived in the student dorms in town and very seldom made it back to Shedlitz. Hanka married her sweetheart of many years, a little after high school and was about to give birth to their first son. Jadzia worked in her father's clothing store, and I loved visiting her at the store and even helping when it was needed. During that period, I spent a lot of time with her and discovered many things about her I had not known in all the years we were friends. Since I spent most of my time with Sophia and Irena, it seemed that I missed out on the real Jadzia, and the days I now spent in her company were enjoyable and free from anxiety. Jadzia could be light-hearted and happy, and when her father released her from the store, we would go on walks in the park or drink coffee in one of the small cafés near his store. Chaya Luterman left with her family to Grodno, where her father inherited his father's thriving sewing workshop, which left me the only Jew in our group and made me feel a bit strange.

On the mornings I didn't spend with Jadzia, I would go do a little work in my father's store—he was always glad to get help with his bookkeeping. Our Polish customers did not frequent the store all that much during that period, they didn't bother to explain or apologize, they simply stopped showing up, one after the other. Luckily, there were many Jews in Shedlitz who still considered my father's merchandise to be the best in town. Many bakeries purchased only from him, and quite a number of private customers were making the effort to come to us from the other side of town.

My parents didn't ask me why I decided to leave my university studies, but one day, a few weeks after I had come back from Warsaw, while I was helping my mother with the house chores, she gave me an elongated look and said, "When you wish to tell me, I would like to hear."

I was debating how exactly I should tell her about the segregation of Poles from Jews in the lecture halls, about the hostile looks that followed me wherever I went, about the whispering behind my back, about all the daily harassments and insults the Jewish students, and I among them, suffered. I was concerned about the pain she would feel if she knew about those times when I went to university without Irena, and Polish students who learned with me in the same class together would ignore me demonstrably and then insult me in different ways. I never told Irena about it, but after those occurrences I avoided going to university without her. In Shedlitz, too, I used to feel the hostility, I recall students like Ivona the Terrible and others who stayed away from the Jewish students, and would sometimes whisper to each other when we'd pass by, or say a bad word, but they never attacked me or any of the other Jewish students in such a frontal manner.

"You know something, Mom," I told her, "Most of the Poles will never accept us and will never treat us as equals."

"It's true," she answered quietly. "But we must go on living our lives as we have done until now. We have nowhere else to go."

"Really? We have nowhere else?" I asked. "Aunt Sarah and Uncle Maurice have lived in America for many years, and, judging by the gifts they send us, they don't seem to want for anything."

"You really think we belong over there?" she asked me with an astonished look.

"And what about Palestine?" I demanded.

"And what am I to do there, on the dunes? I'm a woman with a weak heart. Stop talking nonsense and come prepare the Shabbat challah with me."

I was busy reading the first issue of the *Shedlitzer Leben* when Shimon came into the house and asked me to do a little errand for him. In those days of the fall of 1934, he was busy most of the time planning his aliyah to Eretz Israel as part of the Dror movement, which he joined in high school. Several Zionist youth groups were active in Shedlitz, but my brother never had any doubt which one of them he should join. Dror was the only movement with its own sports club, and as a cycling fan it was clear to Shimon that he belonged there. As a boy, Shimon participated in long tracks with the cycling club and engaged in movement activities that included summer camps and seminars. After his military service, he went for training in Ostrolenka, and when he came back, he informed my parents: "The minute I receive my certificate of entry, I'm leaving for Eretz Israel. One group of cyclists from the Hapoel Shedlitz club had already cycled its way to Eretz Israel in 1932, and Shimon was supposed to be in the group that left at the beginning of 1935.

"Can you please bring me a package from Zonshein's print shop?" he requested. "I ordered it a week ago, it should be ready, and I have to run someplace." Staring at the newspaper I was holding, the first edition of the Po'aley Zion (Workers of Zion) publication, he added with a snide, "Another newspaper with nothing in it? Every day they just sit and write, instead of getting up and doing something." Shimon was not a man of words; he was naturally quiet and shy. The only one he was able to open up to was my father, and the two of them would sometimes spend hours in quiet conversation about politics, the economy, and Zionism. Shimon was driven crazy by the dozens of Yiddish and Hebrew newspapers that were being published in Poland in those years. "What's there to write so much about?" he used to cry every time he saw me or my father reading one of the new papers, which had just begun publishing. "We must do instead of talk."

The Zonshein and Son print shop stood in Kozia Alley, a narrow, crowded passageway that was host to many artisans. Shoemakers, tailors, tinsmiths, carpenters and all kinds of repairmen worked right next to one another. The noisy and colorful alley was very close to Asha Street where we lived, but so very different from our quiet and tranquil block. Above the entrance to the printing place hung a big, wooden sign with the heading Zonshein and Son carved in curly, stylish letters. Obviously, the owners related enormous value to the written word.

"Hello," I said to the man standing with his back to me, typesetting on a wide board. "I'm here to pick up a package for Shimon Jablon."

He turned around, gave me a long look and then he said, "You must be Zippa." His voice was low and his speech slow and soft. He was very tall, his skin swarthy and smooth, his straight nose immediately brought to my mind the faces of the gods I saw in textbooks on Greek mythology. His eyes were light brown, and when he straightened his gaze at me, I could feel my cheeks blushing. I tried to answer him, but the words remained stuck in my throat.

"I'm Jacob," he extended his left hand—his right was still holding a tiny lead letter. The palm of his hand was large and paternal, and the fingertips were black with ink. I shook his hand—it was warm and soft. I quickly released my hand from his hold and stared at my now slightly blackened palm.

"Don't worry, it comes off with water," he laughed. "I'll get you your package right away," he added and turned toward the back of the shop. He returned a minute later with the package in his hands and said, in a tone that was mixed with rebuke, "Please tell Shimon that it's starting to be dangerous distributing around town all these posters they keep printing. I have to work at night because all I need is for the Polish cops to see Zionist posters in my place and right away they'll shut me down."

"I'll tell him," I said and took the package. "How did you know my name?" I dared to ask before leaving.

He smiled and said, "You're Shimon's sister. Everybody knows Zippa Jablon is the smartest girl in Shedlitz." I hurried out of the print shop before he would notice that my cheeks were on fire.

When I came back, Shimon wasn't home, as was his habit in those days. I waited for him impatiently and only by evening time did he return and quickly sat down to eat.

"Jacob Zonshein says the material you print with him is dangerous." My voice shook a little when I mentioned Jacob's name, and I was hoping Shimon didn't notice.

"Zonshein? That communist? He himself is dangerous material."

"Why is he dangerous?" I asked. I didn't know that Jacob was a communist and the information made my heart beat faster. After coming back from university, I went one time to a gathering of Po'aley Zion Smol (Left-wing Workers of Zion). Public gatherings of communist groups were illegal in Poland at the time, which is why I didn't tell anyone in my family about it.

"The communists are a danger to the Zionist movement," said Shimon, "and, besides, they're also wrong." he gathered the package I brought him and again was about to leave the house.

"Jacob Zonshein is the handsomest man in Shedlitz!" my mother joined our conversation. "I know his mother, Sarah Leah; we both get our hair done by Shoshana Goldberg. Sarah Leah just can't stop talking about Jacob, as if he were her only son."

Shimon left the house, slamming the door behind him.

Over the next few days, I was restless. I continued to get together with Jadzia and helped my father in the store, but my thoughts kept wandering to the print shop in Kozia Alley. I was hoping Shimon would ask me to go there again, but he didn't. One morning, while I was sitting in the store, preparing monthly summaries for my father, I suddenly heard a low voice by the counter: "They say you sell the best flour in town over here." It was Jacob. I hadn't noticed him coming into the store and in my excitement dropped my pencil.

"It's true," I said, bending down to pick it up, "but we only sell wholesale." It wasn't completely accurate, my father did sell mostly wholesale, but he kept a few private customers as well. I felt foolish as soon as I said it and didn't know how to get out of this embarrassing situation.

"Fine, then I'd like fifty kilograms," he said and laughed.

"The truth is that we sometimes sell to private customers, too," I retracted immediately, afraid that he would go away, and I'd never see him again.

"Stop being so serious, I only came to see you."

His words reached my ears, but I didn't fully comprehend. "To see me?" I asked and couldn't recognize my own voice.

"Yes. Maybe you'd like to go for a walk after work?"

Over the following weeks, Jacob and I would meet almost every afternoon after he finished his work at the print shop. Usually we'd take a walk in the public park, where I used to play with my girlfriends when I was a child, we'd sit down on the old bench under the chestnut tree and feel the cool evening breeze blowing among the trees. Jacob loved to walk slowly around the little lake at the center of the park and count the ducks. He told me that when he was a little boy he used to count and recount all the ducks swimming in the lake and that's how he learned to count.

Sometimes we'd sit in the small café on The 3rd of May Street, outside the Jewish quarter. I told him a little bit about myself, but mostly I loved listening to his warm and soothing voice, which sounded close and familiar to me. He told me mostly about the work at the print shop, which in our neighborhood was known as one of the best in town, and people from all over Shedlitz would come to him. He also talked about his family and about his childhood, which he said was long and boring. Jacob was the eldest son of Aaron and Sarah Leah Zonshein. He had two younger sisters, around my age, but since we didn't attend the same schools, I only knew them superficially. He was Shimon's age but appeared older, maybe because he was very tall, and many girls used to twirl around him even as a young boy. Although we were neighbors, I couldn't recall when the last time I had seen him was.

In our lengthy conversations, we discovered that both our fathers were named Aaron, and both our paternal grandfathers were named Shlomo. Shlomo Zonshein established the family print shop on Kozia Alley almost fifty years earlier. In addition, my uncle Yechiel, the same uncle who had taken over my grandfather's store after his passing, was married to Henia Zonshein, Aaron Zonshein's second cousin. These discoveries amused Jacob, who was quick to point out that he did not believe in mysticism or fate. Even though I never believed in them myself, in my heart of hearts I knew that something must surely be hidden in these small and seemingly insignificant revelations.

One evening in early 1935, Shimon came home all excited and told me: "Tomorrow night at six there's a meeting at Nachum Goldstein's house, you should go." Being my older brother, he had a tendency to think that he knew what was good for me. "An emissary arrived from Eretz Israel; I think it's important that you hear what he has to say."

Since I met Jacob, the topic of Eretz Israel almost never entered my thoughts. In the past, Shimon succeeded in infecting me with the germ of making aliyah to Eretz Israel, and when I came back from Warsaw, after my miserable time in university, I even began to engage in practical planning around the idea. But from the moment Jacob entered my life, my plans were pushed aside, and I hardly dealt with them. Shimon, on the other hand, already managed to purchase a new bike and was practicing riding it every day.

"I'm not so sure if I want to make aliyah to Eretz Israel," I told Shimon. "I haven't finished university yet, and I can't leave without a profession."

"It's all because of Zonshein, that communist!" Shimon muttered. He sounded hurt. "If not for him, you'd be running to this meeting."

I didn't answer him. Even though Jacob hadn't yet been to our house, and I told only my mother about our relationship, I knew that Shimon knew and that he was not pleased by it. The differences between Jacob and Shimon were massive. While Shimon was serving in the military, Jacob was hobnobbing with girls at Jewish youth dances; while Shimon attended meetings with his Zionist friends at the Dror movement, Jacob was meeting with his pals from the Communist Party; while Shimon was in training for aliyah, Jacob was already carrying the entire print shop of Zonshein and Son on his shoulders. But despite the great differences, they were also very much alike: their views were not the same, but it was a known fact that both had chosen ideological paths that were considered daring and even radical at the time. The Communist Party had already been outlawed, and the Jews who chose to belong to it were taking a double risk. The Zionist groups were never well liked in Poland either, and they were outlawed more than once, but, of course, continued their activities underground.

And so, on the one hand I didn't want to disappoint Shimon—and the incidents at Warsaw University were also fresh and burning in my memory—but on the other hand, the ideas Jacob spoke about had a magical effect on me. The dilemma was resolved when the next night Jacob was obligated to stay late working at the print shop, and I took advantage of the opportunity to attend the meeting at the Goldsteins'.

I arrived at a little after six at Nachum Goldstein's parents' home. Nachum was Shimon's classmate in the boys' high school, and as early as age fifteen or sixteen the two of them started attending the meetings of the Dror movement. Nachum's father owned a bookstore on The 1st of May Street, not far from the Grand Synagogue. Yitzhak Goldstein was one of the leaders of HaShomer HaTzair in Shedlitz, and he was the organizer of the meeting between the Dror youth and the emissary from Eretz Israel. When I reached the home of Yitzhak and Chana Goldstein, the emissary was already engaged in lively conversation with a number of guys, some of whom I identified as Shimon's friends from the cycling club. Nachum's mother, Chana, offered me a seat and went to the kitchen to bring a pastry she baked. Even though it was the middle of winter, the emissary from Eretz Israel had a deep tan, and the ends of his brown hair were sunburned. He told us about what was going on in Eretz Israel, about thousands of newcomers arriving from all across Europe every month, about the towns and villages being built, about the thrust of kibbutz settlements and the developing agriculture. His tales were received with enthusiasm and with great excitement and Shimon and his friends appeared enchanted and mesmerized. To my surprise, my feeling was that everything he said bore no relevance whatsoever to my own life and plans.

At the end of the evening, Shimon approached me with sparkling eyes. "I didn't believe you would come," he told me. "What do you think?"

"It was... very interesting," I stammered.

"Interesting?" he asked, and I sensed a note of disappointment in his voice. "This was the most fascinating thing I ever heard in my life. The newcomers, the thriving settlements, there's so much to do and to build. Don't you understand that over there is where we belong? Not here, with all these anti-Semites."

"Who's this beautiful girl you're yelling at?" the emissary from Eretz Israel came and stood next to us. He was born in Poland but looked completely different from all the other guys who filled up the Goldsteins' small living room.

"Meet my sister, Zippa," Shimon said to him.

"Your sister?" the emissary asked, "So why aren't you introducing us?"

Even though Yehuda Artzi was only twenty-eight when he visited Poland on a mission from the Halutz movement, it looked like he had accomplished a lot in his life. He immigrated to Israel by himself almost ten years earlier, as Leib Grinshpan. A short while after immigrating, he changed his name to Yehuda Artzi, enrolled in medical studies in Jerusalem, but by the end of his studies chose to work in agriculture and joined an HaShomer HaTzair kibbutz up north. On the kibbutz, Yehuda met a guy from Shedlitz who told him a lot about the Zionist groups in town. The Shedlitzer's tales aroused Yehuda's curiosity and led him to cancel some scheduled meetings in Warsaw in favor of coming to Shedlitz for a few days. He was hosted at the home of the Goldsteins, who were acquaintances of his parents, and they introduced him to the leaders of the Zionist groups in town and to young people planning to make aliyah. While he was telling me about himself, Shimon stood a short distance from us, talking to his friends. Every once in a while he'd give us a look, and an expression of satisfaction would spread across his face.

By the end of that evening, Yehuda decided to extend his stay in Shedlitz by a few days and cancel all his previous obligations. He explained that in Shedlitz he discovered the true Zionists, and with a little bit of effort he could bring half of them to Eretz Israel. He met with young people so full of enthusiasm, like Shimon and his friends, met the leaders of all the Zionist groups in town and spoke with anyone who wished to speak with him. Shimon became his best friend. They would arrive at my parents' home almost every evening, sit in the living room till late at night and conduct lengthy and on occasion vociferous debates. Every time I would walk in, Yehuda would become silent, stand up, extend his hand to me and make room for me next to him on the sofa. I didn't like his exaggerated airs, nor his sweaty palm, nor his servile manner of speech when he addressed me. Each time he came by I would look for reasons to sneak out of the house, hoping he wouldn't be there when I came back. None of the flowers and the little gifts he bestowed on me each time he visited helped any; I didn't even unwrap them.

The spring of 1935 arrived suddenly, the trees in the great boulevards were in full bloom and my walks with Jacob lasted longer because of the later sunsets. Meanwhile, the closer Shimon's trip to Eretz Israel came, the more nervous and impatient he was becoming. My mother didn't stop twirling around him, asking if he was sure he packed everything, did he forget to buy something, and was he still certain he wanted to leave everything and travel thousands of kilometers to an unknown place. I knew that more than worrying about him, she was concerned about herself, anxious over her ability to deal with saying goodbye to her eldest and only son.

One day, shortly before his departure, I went with Shimon to Herbert Shlonsky's sports and camping equipment store. My cousin Moshe Jablon worked there, and he recommended that Shimon come and stock up on everything he needed for the journey.

"What are you going to Eretz Israel for?" Mr. Shlonsky asked Shimon. "Stay here; I'll give you a job in my store. What do you have to look for in the desert?"

"Mr. Shlonsky," Shimon answered, his eyebrows squeezed and his eyes sparking, "the Jews have only one place in the world. It's time all of you understand this."

In the beginning of May, we accompanied Shimon to the square outside the Shedlitz train station, from which the cyclist group was leaving for Eretz Israel. They were facing a trip of a little more than a thousand kilometers to the Black Sea. My mother didn't stop crying the entire morning; it looked like the accumulated tension of the past few days found its release. At one point, Shimon lost his patience and asked her to stop crying, because if she didn't then this would be his last memory of her.

In the last days before his journey, Shimon had stayed up for long hours into the night with my father in the living room. Now, at the train station, they hugged for a long time and my father kept reminding him: "Don't forget to write us. Don't make your mother worry."

Shimon hugged Mother, who tried in vain to stop her tears, and before he got on his bike and disappeared from our sight, he kissed my cheek and said, "Zippa, we'll see each other in Eretz Israel."

A few days after Shimon's departure, the general with the mustache on horseback, Jozef Pilsudski, passed away. The Polish residents mourned his death and hurried to change Shedlitz's main drag from Warsaw Road to Pilsudski Street. The Prime Minister elect, General Skladkowski, was quick to declare that while it was forbidden to damage Jews physically, it was certainly permissible to conduct economic war against them. The Jewish press was quick to debate and deconstruct the quote, some of the papers doubted the veracity of the statement, but others, especially on the left, issued lengthy, learned articles whose bottom line was: "We told you so."

In the months that followed the atmosphere in town deteriorated, and tension between Poles and Jews increased. Many Jewish businessmen who worked outside the civic center moved their businesses to the Jewish neighborhoods. Those who chose to stay outside the Jewish quarter endured high municipal taxes and open hostility from the neighbors, slogans painted on their businesses and broken windows. Almost every week saw the forming of new craftsmen cooperatives whose declared goal was to deprive the Jews of their income. They didn't hesitate to launch slanderous campaigns, calling on Polish citizens to boycott Jewish businesses. A number of trade unions also began to close their doors before Jewish craftsmen.

The Polish government, followed by the Polish citizenry, applied Skladkowski's views in practice.

In the winter both of my maternal cousin Penina Grossman's sons were dropped from the education system because of the constant rise of the tuition imposed by the Polish ministry of education. Penina's husband was a yeshiva student, and the couple was unable to finance the school cost. Under the ministry's instructions, several Jewish public schools were closed down. The elementary schools, which were considered private, stopped receiving financial support from the government and some of them also had to close their doors to the many children whose parents could not afford the high tuition.

I decided to re-enroll in university and study agriculture. The thought of making aliyah to Eretz Israel became relevant for me. My parents supported me but informed me clearly that they were not planning to immigrate. Jacob, too, was beginning to understand that this would probably be our best option. We agreed that by the end of my studies we would make aliyah together.

In September, I traveled once again to Warsaw, found a small rental room in the apartment of an old, childless, elderly Jewish woman, and began my studies a second time. I didn't know how I would manage to face once again hostile students or indifferent professors. This time I was on my own, without Irena, who was studying on the other side of town. Zosha was also studying in Warsaw, but the distance between our departments was great, and I knew we wouldn't be able to keep a daily contact. To my delight, I discovered that the majority of students at the agriculture department were Jews since there was low demand for the subject among Poles. Most of the Polish students in the department were there to study and not engage in politics, and the professors were mostly young, with Socialist-Liberal tendencies, and some even

Communist, and they abhorred any expression of discrimination or anti-Semitism.

But in addition to my studies, I was very concerned about my separation from Jacob. Would he wait for me? Would he forget me? How could I stand being so far away from him? I didn't have answers, only increasing worries.

Chapter 6

SOPHIA

In the summer of 1938, I finished my studies in the Commerce department at Warsaw University, and when school was over, I was accepted to work for a large cooperative of industrial companies named PoEm. The cooperatives flourished in Poland in those years, not only in industry but in agriculture as well, and, come to think of it, in most of the productive sectors. It was this phenomenon that must have given everyone a false sense of power. Since there already was a manpower shortage (many male members in our organization were enlisted by the military), I was given the job of inspector and was traveling to factories belonging to PoEm, to review and report on their management.

A few months after I started to work for the organization, I was sent for training in the city of Uppsala, Sweden. The letters I was receiving from my girlfriends and my family bore bad omens. Jadzia told me her thirty-year-old brother, a discharged Polish Army officer, received a mobilization order for an unlimited time. Hanka, too, told me that her husband and two other friends we knew from the dance soirees received mobilization orders. Zippa was writing very little and too infrequently. Even though she was still studying in Warsaw at the time, I managed to get from her that the circumstances of the Jews of Shedlitz was getting worse and that she was concerned about the deteriorating situation and was considering immigration to Palestine immediately after graduation. Irena received a scholarship to study in Paris and wrote me from there about her school and the new friends she was making, from all around the world. Her letters were the only ones that didn't include stories of mobilization orders or anti-Semitic harassments.

My mother told me that every night you could hear from the direction of the railroad tracks the heavy echoes of vehicles and trains on their way west and north. Shedlitz was a central junction and the Polish army passed through our town on its way to the German border.

When an influx of refugees from Austria and Czechoslovakia started to reach Sweden, I realized the situation concerned more than just Poland. Even though my training period in Sweden hadn't ended, I decided to return to Poland, and in the spring of 1939 arrived in Warsaw to take up my previous job with PoEm.

At the end of August, I was sent on behalf of the organization to conduct an administrative review at a large metal factory in the town of Lubartow, north of Lublin. The organization had already lost many workers at that time, most of the men had enlisted in the army, and almost no one but women, elderly or handicapped employees remained to do the work. Every workplace I visited was mired in the harsh atmosphere of uncertainty. Labor conditions were tough, the trains did not operate in an orderly fashion, and my trips to each destination would often take days and sometimes a week.

When I reached the factory in Lubartow where I was supposed to conduct my review, on Friday, September 1, I found locked and barred doors. The big sign hanging at the front of the building left no doubt that I had indeed arrived at the right place, and I didn't understand why no one was there to greet me, as was the norm everywhere else I had visited. I circled the factory a number of times but didn't see a living soul. The management offices in the back were also shut. After a long hour in which I roamed around the deserted metal factory, I decided to return to the train station. An elderly female clerk sat behind the counter reading a newspaper. She couldn't tell me when the train to Warsaw would arrive. "Yesterday one train to Warsaw passed through; the schedules are not accurate these past few weeks." She sounded indifferent; it was obvious she didn't care.

I started to walk toward the main highway to Warsaw. I stood by the side of the road hoping a car would drive by and take me out of this bizarre town, but no vehicle appeared on the horizon. A few people were walking in the streets, and they all seemed troubled and in a hurry. I was about to return to the train station when suddenly a peasant showed up riding a horse-drawn cart.

"Where are you headed on such a day?" he asked me. He looked to be in his forties, but his face was wrinkled, and his skin sun scorched.

"I was sent to review the metal factory," I answered, "but didn't find anybody."

"Whoever sent you probably hadn't heard the news," the peasant said.

"What news?" I asked, confused.

"Germany has invaded Poland! The war has begun!" the peasant declared, sounding like someone sent to deliver bad news, which he himself had not fully digested. "Where do you need to go?"

"Warsaw."

He snorted and said, "I'm not going to Warsaw, but I'm headed north, I can take you close to Kotzk."

The peasant extended his hand to me, and I climbed on his creaking buggy. On the road he told me that as soon as he had heard about the declaration of war, he decided to leave his home and his lands and travel to his elderly parents who were living on an isolated farm not far from the village of Kotzk. He was taking along most of his possessions on the cart.

The horse carried on until just before sunset, and as soon as it began to show the first signs of fatigue, the peasant asked me to get off. We were close to the village of Kunow and walked the rest of way. A pair of peasants who saw us arriving in the village invited us into their home and offered us lodging and supper. Heavy rain started coming down early the next morning, but the peasant insisted on getting back on the road. He said that the only thing that would stop him from reaching his parents would be the German army. He covered the sacks on his cart with a sheet of burlap our hosts gave him and jumped on board. The horse seemed to regain his strength overnight and was eager to get going. The highways and dirt roads we rode on were almost deserted. Save for a few scattered carts belonging to local peasants we ran into. There was hardly any traffic, and I spotted very few pedestrians on their way here and there.

We rode for a few hours in the pouring rain and when we came close to Kotzk, the rain stopped and the peasant agreed to stretch his journey a little and accompany me to the Kotzk train station. Near the railroad, he helped me off the cart and said he had to get to his parents before it was too late.

The Kotzk railroad station was nothing more than a small ticketing stand, which was completely deserted when I arrived. Broken benches stood on either side of the track, carved with the names of boys and girls who had apparently gone there in better times. I waited for a few hours on the Kotzk platform, but nothing happened. Before dark, I decided to turn toward the village houses and look for someone who could help me.

Kotzk was a small and sleepy village, and it looks that agriculture was the residents' only source of livelihood. "It shouldn't be hard to find peasants in need of a pair of hands," I thought, and since I had no idea when the next train would reach the village, I figured it would be worth it to offer my services as a day worker. The first house I reached belonged to an older peasant woman whose husband and two sons had left the village a few weeks before the war broke, leaving her all alone with a herd of cows and sheep whose utters were bursting with milk.

I stayed with that peasant a few days. I helped her with the milking and in cleaning the cowshed and the pens, and in return for my labor she gave me food and a bed to sleep in, and she also got me a few clothes from her friends. One night the railroad guard arrived at the peasant's home to let us know that the next day a north-bound train would be passing through the village. The peasant tried to convince me to stay in her house, the news about the advancing German army was not encouraging, but I knew that I had to go on. Before I left her house, she packed me bread, cheese, and sausage and added a bottle of homemade vodka.

Very early in the morning I arrived at the station platform and after a few hours, I suddenly spotted a train emerging from the south. It approached the Kotzk station with a slow clatter, but it didn't look like it was going to stop. It slowed down by the deserted platform, and I managed to read the sign that designated it as the property of the Polish army. The doors of one of the cars were open, and without giving it another thought, I hopped on. The car was empty of cargo, and only a few soldiers were napping on its floor. I was afraid that they would throw me off the train, but fortunately they agreed to let me stay as long as I didn't come out of hiding before the last stop. Maybe the bottle of vodka I offered them helped them decide not to throw me off.

"Where are you headed?" I asked them.

"Lukow. That would be your final destination."

We reached Lukow toward evening. The soldiers helped me sneak off the train, but they had no idea about the trains going to Warsaw.

Lukow was a relatively large town compared to the villages I had been passing through. It was situated on a major junction, and one could easily proceed from it in any direction. I was hoping that in Lukow I could finally board a train that would take me to Warsaw. A few passengers were sitting at the Lukow station, but they couldn't tell me when the train to Warsaw would be leaving. The ticket counters were empty. I got out of the station and started to walk in its vicinity. A short distance from the station, down the street, I spotted a boy who looked about twelve, energetically repairing a bicycle.

"I'd be happy to buy it from you if you're interested in selling," I told him. I had some money left, which I kept stashed inside one of my boots. I had nothing to lose; the train that picked me up in Kotzk was probably the last one on my journey.

"I don't sell this one. Brother need it Saturday morning." The boy was pale skinned, with a light mop of hair, and from his manner of speech, I guessed he hadn't gone past the fifth grade. "But I have in shed another bike, if you want."

When we entered the shed to look at his other bicycle, the boy said, "My brother goes on Saturday to visit his girlfriend."

"Great," I answered indifferently. His brother's love life was not of great interest to me. I wanted to get to Warsaw, to be among civilized people and to return quickly to my job. The company of illiterate peasants was starting to drain me.

"Her name is Katarina and my brother says after the war they get married," the bike fixer continued to proudly tell me about his brother, without any encouragement from me. "Here is your bike." He pulled out of the far corner of the shed a battered frame without wheels that looked like it had been standing there for ages with no one bothering to check on it.

"Can you fix it?" I asked with concern.

"My brother's bike is even worse, and he has to get to Shedlitz. Where are you going?"

That night the bike fixer's family embraced me into their fold as if I were their long lost daughter. They were thrilled and excited to meet someone who was born and raised in Shedlitz, a place they, naturally, had never been to. The mother made me a supper, the kind of which I hadn't tasted since my last visit with my parents so many months before. She begged me to keep an eye on her eldest son, who had planned the trip to Shedlitz against her wishes. The amorous boy, a lanky sixteen-year-old with the face of a child and speech that was even more infantile than his younger brother, kept asking me about Shedlitz, he wanted to know anything I could tell him about the town. A few months before the war broke he had met a girl from Shedlitz, who came to Lukow to visit her grandparents who lived nearby. The two fell in love as only sixteen-year-olds can, and when the war broke the boy decided he had to travel to his beloved, no matter the cost. While I talked to the boy and his mother, the father was snoring noisily in the living room, the younger brother, the bike fixer, was napping on the tattered rug, and their two little sisters were sitting and staring at me indifferently.

The trip to Warsaw suddenly seemed unnecessary and stupid. Why travel to Warsaw when all my family and friends are in Shedlitz? The distance from Lukow to Shedlitz was not great, Warsaw was much farther, and I had no way of knowing what was waiting for me there.

The next day was a Friday and after a few hours of work the young bike fixer succeeded in rehabilitating the old bicycle for me. His lovesick brother and I got on our way with the first light of dawn Saturday, September 9. The roads we took were full of ditches and potholes, and the boy explained that hordes of German planes had been flying over and bombing ceaselessly, probably to slow down the retreating Polish army. We advanced slowly, the rain, which had been coming down off and on for most of the day, made thick, slimy mud that didn't make things easier, my legs hurt, and I felt that my body was going to give in. Near the village of Vishniew, some eight kilometers outside Shedlitz, both my tires exploded, forcing me, sadly, to abandon them. I had to proceed to Shedlitz on foot. Lover boy was impatient to reach his beloved Katarina but agreed to walk with me after I promised him that when we got into town I would take him to her house. Since he had never been to Shedlitz before, he accepted my offer, and I was glad not to have to walk alone. Even the company of a young peasant who probably had never been inside a school was better than walking by myself.

The boy was not mistaken regarding the retreat of the Polish army. The quiet that was typical of the first days of my journey was replaced as soon as we left Lukow with an ever increasing hum coming from the west. Large forces of the Polish army were heading east. Tanks, armored troop carriers, buses, cars, and even soldiers on foot were pouring through without any order or discipline. They looked like battalions of toy soldiers who received different commands from different operators. From the north could be heard the endless buzzing of approaching planes. The war had begun; it could be clearly felt.

Chapter 7

ZIPPA

During my first years at the Agriculture Department in Warsaw, the Jewish students were not yet segregated from the Poles, as was the case in the Liberal Arts Department, but later on the atmosphere in the former also became distant and suspicious. It was rare to see Polish students keeping company with the Jews, and toward the end of my fourth school year the separation between Jews and Poles was already complete, albeit not official.

I met Esther Munchak on the first week of school. She sat next to me during one of our first lectures, and when I first saw her, I was convinced she was a Christian Pole. She had light hair, smooth and long, and light blue eyes. When she told me she was Jewish, I was sure for a moment that she was joking with me. The Polish students, too, were convinced she was one of them and more than once shot her comments like: "What are you doing hanging with these Yids?" Esther chose to ignore them and despite her Polish appearance, she knew precisely which side she was on.

Esther's parents were educated liberals and reminded me very much of my own parents. Just like them, they, too, were not religious but observed most of the commandments and celebrated all the Jewish holidays. Esther and her younger sister Ducia attended

Polish schools and spoke Polish without an accent. Unlike my own parents, Esther's lived in a large house in a suburb of Warsaw, far from the mostly Jewish downtown area, and almost every weekend I would travel to them for Shabbat. Esther's mother's challahs were almost as delicious as my mother's, and Mrs. Munchak's cooking reminded me of my parents' home in Shedlitz. In a very short time, I became part of the family.

I kept in touch with Jacob in those years mostly through letters, since I couldn't afford to travel to Shedlitz often. I waited for his long and enchanted letters like a prisoner waiting for his furlough. His handwriting was precise and ornate. Alongside worrisome tales about the deteriorating condition of the Jewish community in Shedlitz, he always made sure to add a few words that resonated with his yearning to meet again soon. Often when I would finish reading his letters, my face would be awash in tears of happiness and longing. When I returned to Shedlitz for summer or Easter vacation, the only times I permitted myself the trip home, we would spend every evening together, one time in my parents' house, the next in his. I knew that the minute I finished my studies we would make aliyah to Eretz Israel, and I was longing for that day to come. What few letters my parents received from my brother Shimon made clear that no matter how bad things were in Palestine, they would always be better than the situation in Poland.

In one of his letters, which I received in November 1937, Jacob told me that in the past month some polish wagoners started showing up in Shedlitz with hats that read: "Christian Wagoner." It was part of an overt propaganda campaign conducted by the anti-Semitic groups in town. The propaganda bore fruit and succeeded in causing many Jewish families to lose their livelihood, as they were deserted en masse by their Polish customers. This, of course, was not the only example of cases in which Polish associations managed to drive out Jewish laborers. The deterioration of the status and economic situation of the Jews in Poland was swift. The decrees kept coming down morning and night.

Throughout the year, 1938 dozens of Jewish merchants and craftsmen lost their vending spots in the Shedlitz municipal market. Other Jews were ordered to leave the market with the excuse that it was going to be renovated, and as if that was not enough, the city government decided to move market day to Saturday, instead of Tuesday and Friday, which was an economic death sentence to the Jewish merchants. Professionals such as lawyers and doctors were also hurt badly during that period, and the authorities frequently canceled their licenses for no reason.

In those years, anti-Semitic acts were increasing across Poland. The Jewish cemetery of Shedlitz was desecrated more than once, and assaults against Jews became more and more commonplace, so much so that Jews were afraid to leave their homes after dark. The situation in Warsaw wasn't any better. After the events of Kristallnacht, about which we read detailed reports in all the papers, it was as if the Poles received a legitimization for even more extreme expressions of hatred toward us.

The Zonshein and Son print shop saw some reduction in orders, the Jews of Shedlitz were too busy just trying to survive each day to engage in printing bulletins, disseminating ideological leaflets or hanging up signs. To the Zonsheins' good fortune, while Jewish businesses were wilting, the Jewish press flourished, and in 1935 Jacob and his father were asked by the leadership of the Po'aley Zion movement, which was the Jewish group closest to Jacob's politics, to put out for them their party journal *Shedlitzer Leben*. It saved the print shop from going under.

My father's business was also experiencing a downturn, especially due to the flight of Polish customers who stopped visiting the store almost completely. Only Sophia's father, the pharmacist Mr. Olsakowsky, continued to purchase regularly from my father. I don't know if it was because he found the best merchandise in town in our place, or maybe it had to do with my friendship with Sophia. Fortunately, our Jewish customers continued to show up as usual, since flour was the most basic ingredient in the Jewish cuisine, and my father's flour was considered among the best in town.

The closer I was getting to the end of my fourth year at school, the more impatient I became. I had only one year of study left, and since I finished most of my courses and had only a few papers left to submit, I was planning to spend most of my time in Shedlitz in the coming year. I was counting the days until I could go back home, especially so I could see Jacob every day. Two days before the end of the school year he surprised me in my apartment, showing up all cheerful and beaming with smiles. "I came to help you carry the suitcases," he said. I was happy beyond belief.

When we boarded the train to Shedlitz two days later, his mood was even better. He smiled a lot and laughed at everything I said, but he was also suspiciously silent—and normally he loved to talk and regale me with lengthy tales about anything and everything in the world. A little after the train started going eastward, Jacob took out of his pocket a small wooden box, opened it gently, turned it toward me and asked, "Do you like this ring? It belonged to my grandmother."

Jacob and I got married in August 1939, a short while before my fifth year at the agriculture department was to start. Rabbi Hirsch Tenenbaum married us in the Tailors' Synagogue on The First of May Street, and after the ceremony we went to Jacob's parents' house to hold a reception for close family members and a few guests. Irena, Jadzia, and Hanka, who lived in Shedlitz, arrived to celebrate with us. Hanka, whose husband was enlisted in the army, arrived with her two small children. Only Sophia, who was spending most of her time traveling around the country, didn't manage to come. Chaya Luterman sent greetings from Grodno and apologized for being unable to attend. Esther Munchak arrived from Warsaw, along with her younger sister Ducia.

In recent years, my meetings with my Polish girlfriends had become more and more rare. It's true that Sophia and Irena, like myself, were studying in Warsaw, but our departments were far apart, and we couldn't keep daily contact. Our only meetings took place in Shedlitz when the three of us would come on vacation, and each time anew it felt as if we had never separated. Usually we'd meet in Sophia's parents' house, exactly like we had done since we were young students, and would chat for long hours about everything that happened in our lives since our last get together.

In the course of the spring and summer of 1939 there were many postings of mobilization notices on the building of city hall, and messengers on bikes or on foot would come out of the building to deliver mobilization orders. Every once in a while an emergency was declared. In the final days of August, residents began to dig shelters near their homes, fearing air raids.

Sometimes I would be flooded with a wave of guilt for the great happiness that had befallen me, at the exact time things in town were deteriorating and the tensions mounted. I would look at my husband Jacob and recall the words of my grandmother Rachel, who, whenever she tried to describe the perfect man, would say, "He's tall, he's handsome, and he's studying in university." I needed to pinch myself to make sure I wasn't dreaming that this tall and handsome man is indeed my husband. My mother's friends told her more than once, "Jacob is the most handsome man in Shedlitz and Zippa is the smartest girl."

On Friday, September 1, two weeks before Rosh Hashanah, I was awakened very early in the morning by the jarring and deafening sound of loudspeakers. The first sun rays hid behind a thick layer of clouds when the Shedlitz policemen started marching in the town streets, announcing vociferously, practically shouting, that forces of the German army had invaded Poland.

During the late morning hours, a few hours following the announcement by the country's president about the war that broke between Germany and Poland, planes began to emerge out of Shedlitz's cloudy sky. They circled the town a few times and then flew away. Opinions in the neighborhood were split regarding the identity of those planes; some argued they were Polish, others German. Jacob arrived at our house early in the morning and left with my father and a number of neighbors to stock provisions. The stores were already short of many products, and everybody bought whatever they could lay their hands on.

The next morning deafening sirens were heard throughout Shedlitz. German patrol planes resumed their circles above the town. In the coming days, German aircraft continued to fly around Shedlitz as if they were declaring their ownership of the town. Once in a while they would drop bombs over the open area outside town.

On the morning of Thursday, September 7, without any advance warning, dozens of German fighter planes burst out of the north and began a massive air raid on Shedlitz. Jacob was already inside the print shop. Since the war began, he moved in with us but continued to leave every day for work, printing special editions of the *Shedlitzer Leben*. His parents and two sisters, who lived above the printing place, were quick to get out in time and ran to the house of relatives on Krotka Street, at the end of the Jewish Quarter. Jacob left the print shop and came running home. We helped my parents go down into the cellar, where a few neighbors, the Goldschmidt family, had already found shelter, and where we remained the entire first day of the bombings. During that whole day, Luftwaffe planes dumped thousands of bombs on the town, spreading devastation and destruction everywhere. The bombs came down mercilessly on the town throughout the day and the night; we heard them falling everywhere, sometimes really close by and other times farther away.

On the morning of the second day of bombing, after a few hours of quiet, Jacob decided to come out of the cellar to check out the fate of his print shop. Despite my mother's objections, I decided to join him. Father wanted to come out and check on the store on Piekna Street, but Mother gave him one of those looks that could nail a man to his place. "You're not planning to leave me all alone at home, are you, Mr. Jablon?" she asked, positioning herself between him and the door.

"I could go later," he answered quietly and caressed her hand. They sat down on the living room sofa, looking old and exhausted.

When Jacob and I reached Kozia Alley, we were dumbfounded. Out of the crowded street which used to be crammed with businesses and homes, only rubbles of tones and ripped buildings remained. Many wood houses were on fire; some were already burnt out, with a thick smoke rising from the ashes. Many wounded were laid out in the street, and no one could help them. Furniture and houseware items, covered in thick dust, were strewn everywhere, mostly broken or burnt. The family home above the Zonshein and Son printing place, which was one of the only few stone structures on Kozia, had collapsed entirely, burying the print shop below. Jacob stood for long moments, staring at the ruins in disbelief. He paced among them, collecting in his hands Hebrew lead letters that were strewn about everywhere. He blew on them gently and cleaned them with his shirt tail. He stopped collecting the letters only when we heard once again the buzzing of approaching planes from the north.

The next day my father and Jacob went to check on the store on Piekna Street. Its fate was no different from that of the print shop. Piekna Street, which was all stone structures, had been demolished, and most of the workshops, the stores, and the homes had been destroyed completely. It used to be one of the most central and important streets in the Jewish quarter, and unlike the other streets, which were narrow and dense, Piekna was very wide: many stores and workshops resided on the ground floors of three-story buildings, and broad sidewalks stretched on either side of the street, with tall acacia, oak, and cherry trees. In springtime, these trees would bloom in all their glory, spreading intoxicating fragrances, and we nicknamed Piekna the Champs-Élysées of Shedlitz. Now there wasn't a single house standing in the boulevard, and smoke billowed from mountains of stone and plaster. My father said almost nothing could be rescued from the store, what little merchandise had survived the bombings was taken by desperate passersby. The only thing Father managed to save was the adding machine he inherited from his father. The scales and all the rest of his work tools were destroyed in the air raids. Like Kozia Alley and like many other streets in town, Piekna Street had turned into a smoking ruin.

After he'd seen his family's print shop and my father's store thoroughly destroyed, something inside Jacob was broken. Before he'd seen the calamity with his own two eyes, he was usually able to encourage all of us with his pure optimism. Now his spirit was completely crushed. He spent most of his time in silence, his gaze distant. Only the message that reached him in the late evening of the third day of bombing that none of his family members had been hurt lifted his spirits a little.

Later on that same evening Uncle Yechiel and his ten-year-old daughter Selina arrived in our house. They were hit by tragedy: Yechiel's wife, Henia, and both his sons were killed on the first day of the bombings while they were digging a protective ditch outside their house. Yechiel was forced to bury all three right outside their utterly demolished home. Yechiel's large store, the one built by Grandfather Shlomo-Chaim Jablon with his very hands, was totally destroyed. Yechiel and Selina stayed over to sleep in our living room.

The German bombs put an end to any activity that still existed in the town. Food stores stood empty, craftsmen weren't working, the main business in those days was attempting to come out of the inferno alive and to get a hold of something to eat or drink. The Polish military forces stationed in town fled for their lives when the shelling began, leaving behind them confused and frightened civilians. According to the rumors that were flying in town, thousands had been killed in the shelling, most of them Jews. The German bombs were directed with precision at the Jewish trade and residential areas.

But the true inferno of Shedlitz began only after those four days of bombings ended. On Monday, September 11, three days before Rosh Hashanah, a little before dark, we were all sitting in my parents' home when Jacob suddenly rose up and said, "Listen, can you hear?"

My mother awoke from her nap and asked in fear, "Hear what? What are you talking about?" Her hearing was getting bad recently, and the constant bombardments made her condition worse.

I went to the door with Jacob, and we peeked at the dark street. Neighbors and passers-by were standing as if frozen on Asha Street. From a distance could be heard an ever increasing noise that sounded at first like an enormous thunder rolling toward the town at a frightening pace. Those were the German army forces that were advancing quickly toward Shedlitz from the northwest. Within a few hours, the German army conquered Shedlitz, facing no resistance from the locals.

In the course of the following days thousands of German soldiers were spread around the entire town, posted at every crossroad and by every central building, and their presence was felt most distinctly in the Jewish neighborhoods. Their entrance into the town was a signal to the Poles to start looting the Jewish stores, most of all the food stores. My father and Jacob walked around during the morning hours, in a desperate attempt to acquire a few food products with which we could celebrate Rosh Hashanah.

Not only stores and workshops were robbed in those early days of the war. When the heavy shelling began, most of the Jewish residents fled in panic outside the town. The Polish residents invaded the vacant homes and looted them. Polish neighbors and colleagues turned instantaneously into enemies who found no means too despicable to derive some benefit from the Jews' flight. Every day we saw them entering the empty Jewish apartments, and coming out with their arms loaded with home appliances, furniture, blankets and whatever else they could grab.

The Germans arrested many Jews and used them for various labors, especially clearing the roads and removing the enormous amount of rubble, but also to work at the factories outside the town. Many of those who were picked for forced labor never made it back to town. On the eve of Rosh Hashanah, German soldiers entered the Grand Synagogue, forced out the people who were praying there and sent them, too, to work. They were marched on foot to the new labor camp that was erected in Wegrow, and rumors in town suggested some of them were shot to death on the way to camp.

Ten days after they had entered with great fanfare, the Germans vacated Shedlitz and were replaced by soldiers of the Red Army, who were welcomed joyously by the local Jews. Some of the business owners who were lucky enough and the source of their livelihood was not destroyed by the heavy shelling, went ahead and opened their businesses. The Red Army put an end to the molestation and the looting of the Jews, and my father returned home with a few sacks of flour acquired for us by Mr. Olsakowsky. Jacob started working at a small grocery store, one of the very few that remained whole in our neighborhood.

Our glee at the Soviets' arrival did not last long because they only stayed two weeks in town. No one knew why the Red Army replaced the Wehrmacht and no one knew why it left, but judging by the way those actions were taken, in an orderly fashion, absent any confrontation between the two armies, the residents understood that behind all that was some kind of deal between Hitler and Stalin. When the Red Army was about to leave town, a Soviet officer passed through the streets of Shedlitz announcing aloud that every citizen, Pole or Jew, was permitted to leave town along with the Soviet forces.

"We're leaving for Russia," Yechiel announced as soon as we found out about the Russians' departure. "We have nothing left here, and after the Germans come back, our situation here will be worse."

"And how will you get there?" my mother asked.

"I fetched a wagon and a horse." Yechiel was a shrewd merchant who knew how to get whatever he needed, even in a time of war. "Moshe and Genia are also leaving, with their children. We're departing to Zabinka tonight." My cousin Moshe's wife, Genia, was born in the village of Zabinka, on the banks of the Bug River, where the Russian border now stretched. Genia's parents were still living there, and I was glad to know she and Moshe had someplace to go to. Jacob also wanted to leave, but I refused vehemently because my mother was sick and unable to travel all the way to the Russian border. It didn't even occur to me to leave my parents by themselves in Shedlitz. My mother thought otherwise, and once we knew Uncle Yechiel was leaving, she pushed us to also leave town: "Save yourselves as long as it's still possible, run away from here before it gets worse," she pleaded with me.

"I can't leave without you," I answered her, "we'll all leave together."

"Zippa," my father joined her, "Please listen to your mother. We are old already. You are young, your whole future is in front of you, leave now before it's too late."

"I think they're right," said Jacob, "better to live under Soviet rule. I don't want to be here once the Russians leave, and the Germans come back."

The next morning we left home. We took a few clothes and food in a sack. Jacob went to say goodbye to his parents and sisters, and when he returned he told us with excitement that the Russians allotted to all the Jews wishing to leave town a few cars on the train that was evacuating the Red Army eastward. We ran immediately to the train station, along with thousands of residents, mostly Jews, who were also leaving town at that time. Some traveled to the small villages near the town of Shedlitz, others continued east to the Soviet-occupied territory, and others just fled, not knowing where they were going. The most important thing was to leave town; men and women on foot, the elderly and children on loaded wagons tied to emaciated horses, young people on bicycles laden with bulging sacks, and a few hundred lucky ones, like us, who managed to cram into three cargo cars in the train that was transporting Red Army soldiers to Brest-Litovsk. Jacob and I spent a week on the roads, until we found ourselves in Lvov, a major industrial city that in the past belonged to Poland and now was part of the Soviet-controlled territories. When we arrived there I understood we had no place to go and no one we could turn to in this huge city. I also realized that I had no idea when I would see my parents again.

Chapter 8

IRENA

After I had finished my studies at the University of Warsaw, I earned a scholarship from the Ministry of Education to study French Instruction in Paris. In the fall of 1938 I arrived in the French capital, the city I had read and dreamt about so many years. During the long journey on the train taking me from Warsaw to Paris, I was overcome with a wave of contradictory emotions, which were mixed with each other, causing me to cry for most of the way, until the train reached the Gare de l'Est. I was happy and ecstatic to be traveling to the city that had been the subject of my thoughts and dreams ever since I could remember myself, but also fearful and alarmed at the prospect of arriving in a large and foreign city where I didn't know a living soul. The numerous concerns I had had before the trip evaporated once I could see that all the students going to school with me were foreign and lonely just like me, and soon we created for ourselves a small island of foreign students forced into camaraderie. At the Sorbonne Foreign Students School, which I attended, Polish students were studying alongside Germans, Italians alongside Englishmen, and a lot of Spanish students who had fled the civil war over there.

The French professors were conceited intellectuals dressed in carefree elegance, who bequeath to the neophyte foreign students their great love for the French language and literature. In addition to the French professors the Sorbonne at the time employed German and Italian academicians who bestowed on us lectures about European civilization. One of the professors, a tall and handsome German with very light hair and blue eyes, taught us a course on the history of the European continent. In one of the classes, he said that he wholly believed that soon Europe would be exactly like the United States. Most of the students didn't really understand him. I, too, at the time didn't comprehend exactly what that German professor was hinting at, I refused to think of my teachers as capable of demonstrating extreme nationalistic views, in my eyes they had to be noble intellectuals. Only later on that year did it become clear to me that not only were some of the professor extreme nationalists, some were even used by their governments for propaganda purposes and to gather information. Of course, there were also leftist, socialist and communist professors, but they usually kept a low profile and preferred not to discuss politics in their classes.

After school I would go with my new friends to the small movie theaters of the Latin quarter to see American movies, or to the dark, smoke filled clubs, where they played Jazz and Swing. Sometimes we sat for hours in the cafes of the 5th Arrondissement or organizing parties with different international themes. When we were fresh out of energy for culture, we just strolled along the banks of the Seine until the wee hours of the night.

For years, I had longed for Paris and pictured it in my head. From an early age I read the books by the best French authors, admired the romantic and impressionistic painters, and more than anything loved reviewing books describing the city's beauty. And she did not disappoint me. I was dizzy from my new academic and social life, which were nothing like my life at Warsaw University, and felt like an Alice who had fallen into Wonderland.

But my happiness didn't last very long. In January 1939, my mother informed me that my father suffered a brain stroke and was staying at Shedlitz's central hospital. When I read my mother's telegram, I couldn't believe the words that floated before my eyes. My father, this tall, strong, quiet man of the land, incurred a stroke and was being hospitalized. It was inconceivable to me. I remembered him plowing the fields belonging to our family outside town, skinning the fur of the animals he hunted with his hunting rifle; I remembered his quiet voice when he spoke, and his light eyes and his piercing gaze. I couldn't imagine him lying helplessly in a narrow hospital bed.

Four months after I had arrived in Paris I packed all my belongings and boarded the first train that took me to Warsaw and from their home to Shedlitz. When I reached town, my father was already in a state of total unconsciousness, and a week later he passed away before I had a chance to say goodbye to him.

The winds of war had already begun to blow in my country at that time, but I was not aware of them or refused to internalize them into my consciousness. I was too busy with family matters to deal with politics, a topic that was never close to my heart. I tried to help my mother and my brother substitute for my father, but soon realized it was beyond my ability. My father was the pillar of the family, the central figure everyone counted on, the one taking care of all the household needs. Not only was he the main provider, but he also fixed, built and acquired whatever we needed. His death left us confused, and in the early days helpless as well. For many, long months I was unable to recover from my father's death, which landed on me as a complete surprise. Although he was a silent and closed man, with a tendency to underestimate the value of personal problems, I still loved asking for his advice when I was facing a personal indecision, and never imagined life without him. Now, when the situation in Poland had become foggy and unstable, when tens of thousands of soldiers received their mobilization orders, and the threat of war was hovering over our heads, the fact that I would not be able to rely on my father became sevenfold worse. My mother did not demonstrate her emotions, at least not in my company. She maintained the routine at home, but I knew that economic matters troubled her very much. She and my brother Kazimir sat in the kitchen entire evenings, poring over my father's documents. Mother's visits to Church became more and more frequent.

In the beginning of August my brother Kazimir let us know that he was going to marry Christina, his high school sweetheart. They set the date of their wedding for Thursday, September 7. At the same time, I also received an invitation from Zippa, who was going to marry Jacob Zonshein, her boyfriend in the past few years. Since she had left the French department at Warsaw University, the connection between us diminished a little. In the few meetings, we had we behaved as if nothing had happened, but I felt that the incident at the university was hovering like a black cloud over our friendship. Despite my best intentions, I now belonged to a different class, one from which Zippa would be forever barred.

A few days before the war broke, I went with Hanka and Jadzia to Zippa and Jacob's wedding party. Back when the two of us had been studying in Warsaw, she was already totally gaga over him and talked about him with glistening eyes. I only met him for the first time at their wedding. Jacob Zonshein reminded me of the men I read about in the great novels of the last century. He looked so handsome and noble that he made Zippa look like a little girl next to him. From the warm looks he was giving her incessantly I gathered he was just as in love with her as she was with him. Their happiness seemed almost impossible considering the events of the day.

Josepha Jablon also looked happy and excited at the wedding. She wore a dark blue dress that I guessed she sewed herself. You didn't see such perfect dresses in those days, not even in Parisian stores. Josepha moved among the few guests, making sure they were all content. I hadn't seen her for a long time and was surprised to see how vigorous and vivacious she was.

Despite all the signs and the warnings, the war caught me completely off guard. I had barely managed to digest my father's sudden death at the beginning of the year, when all of a sudden I was forced to deal with a new reality that agitated and frightened me.

My mother asked my brother to push off his wedding date. She told him we shouldn't mix such important personal affairs with wars, but he refused to listen. "Who knows how long the war will last," my brother said, "some things mustn't be postponed."

Kazimir and Christina were married on September 7, at ten in the morning, at the office of the secretariat of the district of Novo-Shedlitza where we lived. The district priest conducted a short and practical ceremony, and at the moment he was about to sign the marriage certificate we suddenly heard an enormous crash that shook all the walls of the three-story building. In the days before the wedding, many German planes had already been circling above the town, but they didn't cause any damage, and we figured they were just conducting patrolling and intelligence missions. The enormous noise we heard on the morning of September 7 at the Novo-Shedlitza secretariat was not made by a patrolling plane. Objects started falling off the walls to the floor, and bits of crumbling plaster started dropping on our heads. We rushed outside my family along with Christina's parents and sister who were with us. As soon as we left the district secretariat we saw that the office building across the street was collapsing to the ground.

Bombs continued to drop around us ceaselessly. We hid inside a nearby building that looked the most solid and waited. The bombing stopped only a few hours later, and we managed to get out of our shelter. Christina's white dress became black and dirty, her delicate makeup was now smudged on her cheeks, mixed with the plaster that landed on her during the blasts. Her long hair, which she collected before the ceremony in two braids she tied behind her head, was now messy and dirty. Even though we all looked like dusty ghosts, I couldn't take my eyes off of my sister-in-law, who maintained her noble and respectful appearance even in those circumstances. She was a tall and slim woman with a serious face; her eyebrows were designed carefully, and her lips were thin and tight. She often reminded me of my mother, not only in her serious, even severe manner but in her look, too. They say that many guys choose wives who remind them of their mothers, and in my brother's case this was probably the case.

On the way home we saw whole houses that had collapsed, burying residents who were hiding from the bombs. Many wounded were lying down on the sidewalks; others were running every which way, covered in dust and full of panic. Enormous ditches opened up in the pavements and chaos ruled the entire area.

When we arrived and saw our house standing upright, we danced and hugged one another like small children. It seemed that all of us were glad to find some way to ease the tension of the past few hours. The shelling stopped only after five days, and an eerie silence took over the town. When I found out that the areas most damaged from the shelling were the downtown neighborhoods where mostly Jews lived, I asked the Jablon family home to see how they were, but my mother forbade me to go out. She argued that as long as we didn't know what was going on, no one leaves the house.

Shedlitz changed hands over a few days. First came the Germans, followed by the Soviets, followed yet again by the Germans who returned to the town and swiftly made it their own. The residents became prisoners in their own town, which was ruined and battered, with thick smoke billowing everywhere and the scent of death emanating from all the streets. Shortly after the Germans had conquered the town a second time and forced on us a kind of artificial, harsh routine, I decided to go to Zippa's house, which was smack at the center of downtown.

I reached Warsaw Road, that same wide boulevard through which I arrived at the Jewish quarter my first time, eighteen years before. Although the street name had been changed quite a while back to Pilsudski, for me it was still Warsaw Road, the bustling, colorful street, with the mixed aromas of baked goods and autumn leaves, where so many people were engaged in mysterious and thrilling activities which to a child of six looked like they came from another world. When I arrived, I was shocked to discover that the street was no longer as wide as it used to be, and the only aroma in the air was the smell of fire, crumbling plaster and filth.

When I arrived at Zippa's parents' house, the door was closed. I knocked a few times.

"It's Irena," I cried.

After a few minutes, the door opened a crack. Zippa's mother stood at the entrance, her eyes red and her hair messy. She opened the door for me, and I followed her into the kitchen. Once again I was flooded by the memory of my first visit to 3 Asha Street, and the memory of the beautiful and elegant woman who opened the door for her daughter's Christian girlfriend, letting me peek into her world. The woman who opened the door for me on September 1939, looked nothing like the woman who opened the same door in 1921. She aged many years even since the last time I had seen her, less than a month earlier, at Zippa's wedding. She was bent over, and her face was sagging.

"Zippa and Jacob left for Russia," she said in a broken voice. I handed her the food package my mother sent, and she burst into bitter tears. I couldn't find the words to comfort her.

The kitchen was empty and gloomy; the windows shuttered. There was no white tablecloth on the table, no sizzling pots on the black coal stove, and no fragrance of cooking food in the air. It was hard to believe that this was the same kitchen in which I spent long, enchanted hours in our childhood. I was glad my mother took the trouble to prepare the food package, but I knew it would only last a short time.

My mother, brother, sister-in-law and I decided to leave town and move for the time being into the village home of my uncle and aunt. My father's younger brother, Valente Zawadzky, a retired physician, was drafted into the Polish army a few months before the war. All contacts with him were stopped once he was absorbed into General Alter's infantry division, positioned on the German border as the spearhead of the Polish army. Felicia was left all alone. She and Valente never brought children into the world, and we were their closest relatives. We moved to the village to distance ourselves from the bombarded town and to help Aunt Felicia with her different chores.

Chapter 9

ZIPPA

Jacob and I were not the only refugees arriving in Lvov in September of 1939. Tens of thousands of Jewish refugees from all over Poland were roaming the big, gray city, which until two weeks ago belonged to Poland and now was under the rule of the Red Army, probably following those pacts between the Russians and the Germans, as was the case in Shedlitz. Compared with Shedlitz, Lvov was a real city, with 350 thousand Polish, Ukrainian, and Jewish residents. The multitude of refugees filling up the city since the start of the war were forced to stay in synagogues, train stations, and sometimes on the streets, under miserable living conditions. Because of shortages, it was almost impossible to get food products at reasonable prices. Despite everything, we managed to find an apartment in one of the city slums, along with another couple we met on the train from Shedlitz. Jacob found work in a large print shop, which was owned by a wealthy Jew, and I enrolled in Lvov University to finish my studies.

Jacob said we had to stay in Lvov until things improved, Shedlitz was under German army control, and we had no reason to return anytime soon. Despite our miserable conditions in Lvov, Jacob was glad to be living in a city under Soviet rule and even joined a group of Jewish laborers, members of the Communist party, who like us fled from Poland and would meet in the evenings for long talks into the night and for stormy debates of the state of Europe.

My longings for Mom and Dad made me restless, and thoughts about them living alone in German-occupied Shedlitz wouldn't go away. My mother was a heart patient and my father, who was only 55, was physically and emotionally exhausted from the situation and from his long years of working at the store. I couldn't forgive myself for fleeing and leaving them to their fate.

In the beginning of 1940, Uncle Yechiel delivered to me a letter from Mom. Since we had left Shedlitz in September, Yechiel managed to return for a few days' visit and escaped back to Russia again.

Shedlitz, February 1940
My Dear Zippa,

I hope my letter finds you in good health and that you and Jacob are managing to get by in Lvov. I heard that you started to attend the university, and I'm very glad about it and certain that these studies will serve you well when you and Jacob make aliyah to Eretz Israel after the war.

Your father and I are enduring difficult times, and I don't know how to tell you about everything that's happening here without breaking your spirit. During the day Aaron is roaming the whole town in search of a little income and food, there's an allowance for each person, but it's far from enough. Sometimes Dad stands for hours in the food distribution line, and when his turn comes there's nothing left. Other times he can't even get to the head of the line because the Poles chase away the Jews with no intervention on the part of the German soldiers who stand and stare indifferently. The Jewish community tries to do all it can, providing the town Jews with basic products, but it's not enough.

A few days after you left, on October 10, the German army returned and conquered the town again, and since then there have been German soldiers at every crossroad and at every entrance to our town. Their uniform is polished and their weapons bright, and they look like someone who's here to settle down, not just stay a short while. They took over many buildings in town, evacuated tenants from their apartments and moved in. By the end of November the German secret police, the Gestapo, arrived in town. I can't even begin to describe to you the enormous fear that seizes me every time a Gestapo man comes toward me. The best way is not to run into them, which is nearly impossible. When you do run into them you must salute at once, otherwise they can beat you to death.

As soon as they arrived in town, the Gestapo ordered the Jewish community to elect a 25-member committee called Judenrat, and a Jewish police force whose job would be to carry out whatever orders the Gestapo drops on the community. The elected head of the committee is Yitzhak Nachum Weintraub head of the Jewish community, but Aaron told me he's very old, and the acting head of the committee is Dr. Henryk Loebel whom you know from the hospital.

On the last day of 1939 an order came out obligating every Jews aged twelve and older to wear on their right sleeve a white ribbon with a blue star of David. Failing to wear the ribbon may carry a heavy punishment including arrest and torture. I told Dad, "That's it, now they're marking us; I'm curious what will come next." Your father said, "They've marked us long ago, now they're only putting the official stamp on us."

And if all of that was not enough, all the Jews in town were ordered to mark the front of their stores and places of business with a large Star of David. The word "Jude" must be written in giant type, as if it were a sign of disgrace. Dad says he's glad our store was destroyed in the shelling, so he won't have to see it be humiliated by the Nazis, or worse, be handed over to Poles.

On the night of December 24, Christmas Eve, the Germans burnt down our beautiful Grand Synagogue. They arrived in the middle of the night, circled the building, took out all the Torah scrolls and set fire to the synagogue, and the fire spread to the study hall. Simcha Lederman, who used to be the Zonsheins' neighbor before Kozia Street was destroyed by the bombing, passed by there the next morning and saw the building all ashen and burnt almost to the ground. The Torah scrolls they took out of the synagogue they burnt in a huge bonfire. Lederman met Dad and told him about it, and he was so shaken that uncontrollable tears were streaming from his eyes. "In a place where they burn books, some day they'll burn people, too," Dad told him. Heinrich Heine wrote this more than a hundred years ago.

Why the Nazis choose to burn our synagogue on Christmas night of all times, we don't know. They probably found in it some cruel symbolism. What we do know is that inside the Grand Synagogue of this town we will no longer be able to pray for a better future. Only the small synagogues remain, the Tailors' Synagogue where you got married, and the Butchers' study hall. When will they get to them, too? No way to know.

The Zonsheins are in an even worse state than us. Since their house was destroyed, they've been staying with relatives, without work or property. Their extensive family is trying to help them. We, too, host them once in a while, despite our poor circumstance, and try our best to ease their suffering. Tell Jacob that his younger sister Rosa is also planning to travel east, Aaron and Sarah-Leah will probably update you soon.

I hope the situation will improve and that soon they'll allow us to live our lives quietly once again. We have no control over our situation, and all that's left to do is bow our head until the storm passes.

Dad and I are praying for your peace and miss you with all our heart.

With love, Mom

After I had finished reading the letter, I felt that I could no longer bear my longing for my parents. My conscience didn't stop tormenting me for leaving them alone in occupied Shedlitz. That very evening, when Jacob came back from work, I told him I wished to return home.

"Are you mad?" he cried, and for the first time since we've known each other I heard a note of anger in his voice. "The bloody Nazis are sitting in Shedlitz; half the town is bombed and ruined, the Jews barely have anything to live on, and you want to go back? As long as the Germans are still there, we have no chance for a normal life over there. His dark eyes flashed with fury. Those were not the same eyes I had met the first time I entered the print shop on Kozia Street.

"And here we have a normal life?" I asked him. "Look at us, we, too, are barely making it. The city is full of refugees with nowhere to live or to go. The apartment is crowded and the mattresses full of fleas and lice. We don't even have heat in the house."

"Here at least we have the Russians, maybe they don't love the Jews any more than the Nazis do, but at least they let us live our lives and they don't torture us."

I knew he was right, but I could no longer stand the longing and the thoughts about my parents who were left all alone. Since Shimon made aliyah to Eretz Israel, I had been the only child at home, and my mother was dependent on me. Even if she didn't specify it in her letters, I knew that more than anything she was suffering from longing, just like me.

"Jacob, please, I can't stay here any longer," I begged him in tears. "We don't know what will happen here in the future, there at least we have a home, a family, you can find work, and we'll wait until everything passes."

"First finish your studies and only then will we figure out what to do. It's not good to make hasty decisions." His voice calmed down a little, and he hugged me strongly. My whole body was trembling. I was no longer able to stay in this big and foreign city. "If you don't come with me, I'm going back there by myself," I told him, crying.

"You know I'll follow wherever you go, please stop crying, I can't see you like this." Now his voice was soft and gentle. His big palms caressed my hair.

At the end of February 1940, Jacob and I left for Shedlitz. I was sorry I was unable to finish my university studies, but I was glad to leave the filthy city that was so packed with refugees. If things in Shedlitz weren't any better, at least I would be with my family, we'd have a roof over our heads and we wouldn't have to live hand to mouth as we did in Lvov. When we left Shedlitz, five months before, the roads east were full of refugees fleeing for their lives in fear of the German occupation. From the Soviet train taking us to Brest-Litovsk, we saw on the side of the tracks thousands of people traveling on foot, on horse-drawn buggies or on bicycles. Now, on our way back, the roads were deserted, and it was so cold that you couldn't see even Polish peasants anywhere.

On our way to the Polish border, we passed through Moshe and Genia's home in Zabinka, and we stayed there a few days. Moshe found a Polish peasant who agreed to help us cross the border, now patrolled by German soldiers, and take us to the village of Mordi, some twenty kilometers east of Shedlitz. The Bug River was completely frozen at the time, and Moshe was forced to pay a substantial sum to the peasant, for whom smuggling refugees to either side of the river was his only livelihood. If not for Moshe's help and if not for the two pairs of old leather shoes and a few warm clothes that Genia got for us, I'm not sure we would have survived our journey.

The town I had left at the end of September 1939, was shelled and in ruins, but the town I returned to at the beginning of 1940 looked like a nightmare. I couldn't believe how accurate my mother's descriptions had been.

The streets were neglected and dirty; half the houses were destroyed by the shelling early on in the war, and no one bothered to clean the debris. The few Jewish stores still left standing were marked by large stars of David, and everywhere it said Jude in large type as if it was some incurable disease everyone should stay away from. The few Jews roaming the streets were marked the way you mark animals going to slaughter.

Both my parents burst into tears when Jacob and I walked into the house, which looked like no one had lived in it for years. The windows were shuttered, the shelves empty and the cabinets smelled of mildew. My parents had aged terribly. It was hard to believe we had only just parted company five months before.

A short while after returning to Shedlitz, Jacob and I joined up with a group of friends we had known from the Communist party and the Po'aley Zion movement, and together attempted to get and distribute food to the town's needy. The number of needy families was growing all the time, and we had plenty of work.

Toward Hanukkah of 1940 I began to feel like a prisoner in my own home. "I'm feeling trapped," I told Jacob and my parents one holiday night. "We can't go on living here, and we have nowhere else in the world to go to." We couldn't even find candles to light the menorah; we'd used them all for light. Even though we tried to instill a holiday atmosphere in the house—Dad sat down like he used to and tried to tell stories of the past, and Mom fried latkes of a dubious nature—depression was deep, and none of us felt any reason to celebrate. The year which was about to end was characterized by a tormented and frustrating adjustment to the German occupation rule and its multiple whims.

"Maybe you'll go out of town for a while?" my mother suggested. "Irena has relatives living in a village; I'm sure they're not staying there this time of the year. The Poles like celebrating New Year in town, with the whole family." To my surprise, Jacob accepted the suggestion and the very next morning I went over to the Zawadzky family in the Novo-Shedlitza neighborhood.

I had met Irena a few times since our return from Lvov. She lived with her mother, brother and sister-in-law in their house, after a certain period in which they lived with their aunt in the village. The last time we met had been a few weeks earlier, in Jadzia's father's fabric store. I came over to sell him some of my mother's jewelry, from which she was forced to part with a heavy heart and against her will because we needed money for food. The encounters with my girlfriends were not easy, it was clear they felt guilty, I felt they were ashamed of what was happening to the Jews of Shedlitz, and mostly they were ashamed of the way many of the Polish residents treated the Jews. They didn't ask much about our situation, but they nevertheless brought me food and clothes each time, even though I never asked. The last time we met, Jadzia's father had bought all the jewelry I brought for a higher price than I was asking. It was all he could do for me.

Irena and her mother were happy to see me. I hadn't seen Sabina Zawadzka since the war broke out, and she had aged by many years. Their small apartment was being lit with a weak gasoline lamp, there was no heat, and although the Christian holidays were coming soon, there was no feeling of celebration in the house. In my childhood days I loved coming to Irena's during the holidays, when the apartment was full of lights, a fir stood proudly in the living room, and the aroma of cooking and baking emanated from the kitchen and filled up the place.

I was relieved by the absence of Irena's brother, Kazimir. Since we were children, I felt uncomfortable in his company. He never addressed me or looked at me, and when I arrived he usually exited. Aunt Felicia was staying at the time in the Zawadzky apartment and agreed without hesitation to let me borrow her house for a few days.

Early the next morning we packed a little food and rode out on a horse drawn buggy Jacob was able to borrow from relatives. I was happy to disconnect from the city, from the despair, the humiliation, the fear and the endless search for food and water. When we arrived in the village, we followed Felicia's instructions to feed the few animals she still kept on her farm. I was surprised to see Jacob, who had never lived out of town, merrily caring for her cows and sheep. Milking was being taken care of by one of her Polish neighbors, who brought us fresh milk every morning.

"When we move to Eretz Israel," I told Jacob one morning, "I'll buy you a herd of cows and sheep."

"When we move to Eretz Israel," he answered, "you'll raise our children in the palace I'll build you and I will leave every morning to work in my print shop, which will be the most magnificent and successful in the entire Middle East."

We stayed and dreamed for three days and three nights in the house of Felicia and Valente Zawadzky.

At the beginning of March, there was a pogrom in the Jewish quarter. The German authorities informed the Judenrat that, following a Molotov cocktail that had been thrown at German soldiers, which they claimed was done by Jews, the entire Jewish community would be punished. One night toward midnight Gestapo soldiers arrived in our house. They yelled and raised hell, breaking dishes and tearing pictures off the walls, but to our great fortune did not harm us. Gestapo soldiers entered many Jewish homes, broke doors and windows, shot in all directions, beat up men, women, and even small children, and left behind many dead and severely injured. Only after three days of destruction and ruin were the members of the Judenrat able to persuade the Germans to stop. Interrupting the pogrom cost the Judenrat, so we heard, hundreds of thousands of zloti.

After the German soldiers had left our house, I couldn't get any shut-eye. The much yearned for sleep didn't arrive, even though I was tired, frightened and exhausted. I got out of bed at first light feeling very nauseous and dizzy. Mom heard me and right away got up to see how I was doing. "I think you're pregnant," she told me when I mentioned my endless fatigue, the nausea and the dizziness I had experienced recently.

Jacob was ecstatic. A broad smile spread across his face for the first time since we came back from Felicia's village. My parents, too, were excited and happy to receive their first grandchild. Only I was less excited than they were, I didn't know how we could care for a baby when we could barely care for ourselves. I wasn't sure that this was exactly what I wanted or needed right then and there. This was not the world into which I had dreamed of bringing my first child. I was overcome by a terrible sense of uncertainty.

Chapter 10

IRENA

One after the other the countries of Europe surrendered to Nazi occupation during the spring of 1940. First to fall were Denmark and Norway, followed by Belgium, Luxembourg and Holland. England was being bombed ceaselessly. My own psychological state was not good at the time. My father's death, our uncertain economic future, and above all the ongoing war—dealing with all these events was beyond my capacity. When I heard that France, too, surrendered to Germany, I collapsed. France was the country I believed in the most and counted on more than the rest of the countries of Europe, and its quick capitulation was a great disappointment to me. For many days I couldn't stop crying, I hardly ate, and I couldn't perform even the lightest daily chores. Mom went to Mr. Olsakowsky's pharmacy and returned with a brown paper bag with medicine that was supposed to lift my spirits. They didn't help, and I stayed in bed for a whole week.

I met Zippa only very infrequently in that period. After she came back from Lvov, we'd meet now and then at Jadzia's father's fabric store. It was hard to tell what exactly was happening to her and to her family since she didn't tell much, and we were afraid to ask. The whole time she talked only about Jacob, her eyes sparkling and her pale cheeks suddenly turning pink. I was still not used to seeing the serious, intellectual, even tempered Zippa blush and become excited like a child every time she spoke of her fresh husband.

Every time she came into the fabric store she'd bring along something that she asked Jadzia's father to try and sell to the Poles. Sometimes they were kitchen appliances, silver utensils, Polish books, anything of value, no matter how little. Jadzia's father would buy from her everything she brought. The last time we had met she brought a small box with her mother's jewelry. I knew how much Josepha Jablon cherished those jewels, which went from mother to daughter in her family, and my heart broke when I thought about her and how she had to part with them forever. Now and then Zippa would also ask to purchase something from us, especially food or warm clothes. We always made sure to get her whatever she asked, and when we couldn't we'd send it to her later. At the beginning of the war she would bring over every once in a while some food that Josepha had prepared, once a sweet challah and once she even brought gefilte fish because she remembered how much we all liked it. But those deliveries grew few and far between and over time Zippa became more and more isolated. Her visits to the store became shorter, and so did our conversations.

One day, in the spring of 1941, she reached the store with a big smile on her face. Her cheeks, which over the past year had become pale, took on a pinkish hue. "I hope you can help me this time," she told us with bright eyes, "I have a bit of an unusual request." I didn't understand why she looked so happy since over the previous year and a half the lives of the Jewish residents had become unbearable. I myself was avoiding going into the Jewish quarter because I was afraid of the sights I might see, and when I needed to get to the south side of town I used to bypass the Jewish quarter just so I wouldn't be walking through the streets I recalled from my childhood years.

"I'm pregnant," she told us with a big smile, "and I need a few baby clothes."

At first the news of Zippa's pregnancy flooded me with warm feelings. I hugged her with all my might and immediately started to cry, as usually is the case when I get excited. Only after she left, and I remained with Hanka and Jadzia in the store, did I begin to digest what she had told us and my feelings of joy became mixed with worry and concern. How could Zippa raise a baby under the conditions imposed on her and her family, and how much longer would this situation last? Is it even right to bring a baby into such a difficult reality? The more I thought about it, the more I was overcome by feelings of sadness and pity, but despite all that I was still hoping that the birth of the baby would bring a bit of happiness into the home of Zippa and Jacob.

Things were not easy for Poles, either. Many men were enlisted in the army, and many of them were captured by the Germans, men and women alike were taken as forced laborers in Germany, there was little food in the stores and in the streets there was an atmosphere of malaise and despair. There was no one to turn to with our troubles, government institutions were nonexistent, City Hall was not functioning, all the municipal departments were subservient to the Nazi regime.

Down the street where we lived, a few doors from our house, the Gestapo created one of its Shedlitz commands. Before the war, this gorgeous house belonged to a Polish land dealer, but the Germans kicked the family out to the street, confiscated the house and made it their own, as they had done elsewhere. Many families, particularly ones from the wealthier neighborhoods, were being thrown out of their homes by the Germans in those days. Zosha was lucky the Germans didn't reach her neighborhood, which was one of the more modern in town, probably because it wasn't close enough to downtown.

Even the children of the Gestapo soldiers, who were living with them in the neighborhood command center, nearly caused us heart attacks. One of their favorite hobbies was to throw rocks at the residents' windows along the street. Almost every morning we'd hear them competing who would hit more windows. My mother was not afraid of them; she used to come out of the house and chase them away like alley cats. But this did not deter those

German kids, who would move to the house next door, and the following day we'd hear them throwing rocks once again, and once again my mother would chase them away.

The Germans did whatever they wished in Shedlitz, and to my great sorrow I realized that many Poles, including some I knew personally, chose to collaborate. In most cases, this paid off, and they received many perks, the most desired of which was a home or a store that belonged to a Jew before the war.

In the summer of 1941 the Gestapo ordered all the town residents to turn in their radios. The Germans must have feared that our leaders in exile would send us nationalistic messages over the air, to give us a little hope and revive our fighting spirit, which had been lost after the quick defeat of the Polish army. Their concerns were probably justified: after two years of occupation, most Poles had become apathetic at best and desperately needed something to revive them. All that mattered to the people at that time was to get food and warm clothes for winter and to make sure there was a solid roof over their heads, since so many houses were still in a ruin. The government in exile, which sat in London, represented our only hope for a better future, but it was far away and disconnected, and after the radios had been confiscated it could lose whatever little influence it still had on the Polish nation. The only ones who dared to act in a tangible way against the German invaders were those brave and pure of heart individuals who joined the resistance, which was working underground and about which I first heard from Sophia.

In our house, there was one radio, on which we'd listen to the news from London. That receiver was our only line of communication to the free world. We knew that if the Gestapo soldiers discovered our radio it would be the end not just of the radio, but of us as well, but my brother refused to hand it over to the Germans. His wife was very afraid of keeping that instrument in the house. Now, after the birth of their eldest son, she had become a worrier, but she didn't dare argue with her husband. As soon as the order to turn in all the radios was issued, Kazimir brought a garden stake and dug a ditch in the corner of the backyard. Every day we'd listen to the news at noon from the BBC and immediately after the news my brother would return the radio, wrapped in burlap, into its hiding place and position an old armchair over it. That's how we survived several visits of the Gestapo in our house.

Toward the middle of June 1941, there was an increase in the traffic of German forces moving through Shedlitz. Long columns of tanks, trucks, cars and motorcycles crossed town at all hours of the day and night. Many planes reverberated in the Shedlitz sky, flying to and fro, east and then westbound. The sound of plane engines terrified me. Each time they passed over, I imagined they were bombing us again. One night I woke up screaming, and my entire body was covered in cold sweat. My mother and brother hurried over, but I was crying so hard I couldn't explain what happened. That night I moved my mattress next to my mother's bedside.

The morning of June 22, 1941, was warm and pleasant, the sun peeked periodically behind the clouds as German troops continued to stream through town on their way east. It was a Sunday, and my brother Kazimir hadn't gone to work at the glass factory, even though the factory operated seven days a week. My mother came back from church all worked up, but she wouldn't tell us why and quickly went into the kitchen instead and began her chores. At noon, we all entered the kitchen and my brother brought the radio out of its hiding place, to hear the news. The announcement that Germany declared war on Russia shook our entire family; it was a complete surprise none of us had anticipated. We were all terribly agitated, and we all started talking at the same time, suggesting different explanations. The broadcast lasted longer than usual, and we were so excited and so engrossed in discussion, that at first we didn't hear the knocking on our door. When my brother finally noticed, there was no time to return the radio to its hiding place. Before he managed to go open the door, we could hear the Gestapo soldiers breaking it down and entering the house.

"What shall we do with the radio?" my mother asked in terror.

My brother grabbed a box that was standing in the corner of the kitchen and placed it over the radio, dragged the tablecloth and covered the box with it in one continuous motion. “Sit,” he ordered my mother.

My mother sat down on top of the box; I brought her a large bowl of potatoes, and she began to peel them. The Gestapo men searched the entire house, not telling us what they were looking for, only barking their orders in German in every direction. They didn’t find the radio.

After that day, we decided to hide the radio in the attic. One of the walls up there was a double wall; my father built it years ago and always liked to say that some day it might be of help to us. Only my brother would climb up there to listen to the news, and I was in charge of letting him know if I heard Gestapo soldiers getting close.

Chapter 11

ZIPPA

The declaration of war on the Soviet Union and the great victories Germany won at the beginning of the campaign infused our lives, particularly Jacob's, with terrible despair. Up to that point, Jacob had been harboring some hope that the Red Army could save us, and now even that hope was fading.

In the spring of 1941, the Gestapo conducted a census of all the Jewish-owned residences in Shedlitz. The soldiers went through every street, marking all the Jewish homes and apartments with large Xs. Even though at the time we were no longer surprised by any of the actions taken by the Germans, no one was able to guess what they were going to do next. The explanation came on Friday, August 1, the eve of the 9th of Av (the Jewish fast day commemorating the destruction of the Jerusalem Temple). It was a hot and hazy summer day; the city looked even grayer than usual. Jacob managed to procure for us a kilogram of cherries from some Pole, in exchange for my mother's last silver jewels. The fruits tasted sweet and juicy, reminding me of beautiful summer days, not so long ago when I would go to the Shedlitz market and buy anything I wished. At noontime that day an order was circulated throughout the Jewish neighborhoods to establish a Jewish ghetto in Shedlitz. Until then, most of the Jewish residents were concentrated in two main quarters, and our movement through the town was still free until the evening hours when the curfew started. Now, according to the new order, the Jews were restricted to the streets of the First Quarter, including a portion of May 1st Street, as well as Jatkowa, Tragowa, Aslanowicza, the Stary Rynek and other streets. It was the poorer and more neglected of the two quarters.

The few Poles still residing in the First Quarter were ordered to evacuate their homes, but no one was pressuring them to leave. However, Jews from elsewhere in town received an urgent instruction to move into dwellings within the First Quarter. Asha and Kozia Streets were considered part of the Second Quarter, so we understood that shortly the Gestapo soldiers would arrive to remove us from our home. I was already in an advanced stage of pregnancy, and the idea of having to leave my parents' home terrified me.

Indeed, two days after the announcement, Gestapo men broke into our apartment late at night, screaming at the top of their lungs, ordering us to move out at once. They behaved in a similar manner in all the other homes in our neighborhood. Every once in a while we heard the anguished cries of Jews who refused to leave, cries which were usually followed by the sound of gunfire. We picked up what few articles we managed to pack in time and were pushed by the Nazi soldiers to our new apartment, on Aslanowicza Street. Most of our neighbors from Asha Street were also thrown out to the sidewalk, some with only the clothes they were wearing at the time.

When we reached the First Quarter, we discovered that its condition had become much worse since the beginning of the war. The streets were covered with heaps of garbage and dirt. The air was saturated with sewage odors. The apartment we were allotted was on the second floor of an old and rundown wood house. When we arrived, we realized there were two other families already residing there. Jacob and I were given one bedroom. There were three decrepit and filthy mattresses on the floor. We were lucky that Mom had insisted on hauling a few blankets and bedclothes from our house.

From that day on, all the remaining Jews of Shedlitz, about ten thousand altogether, were crammed in the quarter that became known as The Big Ghetto. Facing it was The Small Ghetto, into which some two thousand additional souls were pressed, in a triangle of streets of an even poorer neighborhood.

The dwelling places were so crowded, that many Jews preferred to sleep out on the street, at least until winter. Every day we witnessed tens of human beings who had died of hunger, illness and especially the epidemics that broke out every few weeks. The worst epidemic of all was the typhus, spread through lice and fleas that stuck to the ghetto residents. Even though the Jewish hospital was within the Big Ghetto perimeter, it did not have the necessary means to treat typhus patients, and whoever was infected knew his fate was sealed.

The piles of trash in the street grew higher with every passing day, and the smell of an open sewer permeated the air. The harsh conditions aggravated the nausea I was feeling all day anyway and increased my fatigue. Day and night I was asking myself what would be the fate of the baby I was carrying in my belly, how could I take care of it and offer it a normal life. Some days, suddenly and without any warning, my heart would swell up with feelings of sorrow and pity for the little baby I was about to bring into a world so bereft of hope. I found myself bursting into unstoppable weeping which could go on for hours.

Of my entire family, only Jacob's mother understood my predicament. When he told her I was pregnant, she told him: Who could even think of bringing children into such a world? Sarah-Leah Zonshein had always been a rational and pragmatic woman, and the war only amplified those qualities in her. When we returned from Russia, she refused to speak to us for a whole month, arguing that escaping to Russia had been the smartest thing we had ever done, and coming back the stupidest. I knew she was right, and I was sad for Jacob, who was also convinced his mother was right but gave in to my insistence that we return to Shedlitz.

The food rations given us by the Germans grew smaller every day while the restrictions forced on the Jewish population were increasing. During our first months in the ghetto, Jacob was involved in smuggling food, which was very common but also involved great risk. He had connections with a few Poles and was also getting help from some people we knew. Sophia's father and Jadzia's father were among them. But when Jacob realized that smuggling was too dangerous and didn't do much good (at that time the Poles were already very fearful of helping Jews and limited their cooperation with ghetto dwellers), he decided to take advantage of his contacts in the Jewish community and the fact that his uncle was a member of the Judenrat and asked to volunteer for the Jewish police. At first my parents' reaction to his decision was very negative. There were differences of opinion in town regarding the members of the Judenrat, as well as the Jewish policemen. We often found ourselves arguing, even within our own family, whether the Judenrat indeed improved things for the Jews, or were only looking to help themselves and their relatives. There were rumors about policemen who dealt harshly with their fellow Jews when they came to collect tax money, and even about some who were keeping for themselves food that was intended for distribution among the residents. There were also stories about a few extreme cases in which Judenrat members put collected public funds in their private pockets. Still, despite all that, their dedicated efforts were being appreciated. I also shared the concerns about Jacob's enlisting in the Jewish police, I worried especially about his being forced to act against his conscience, but he was determined that this was the only way for him to be of any use.

One early evening, a short while before Yom Kippur of 1941, Jacob arrived in our flat dressed in his ironed and starched uniform, with an officer's cap on his head, a nightstick hanging from his belt (they didn't trust a Jew with an actual firearm), and on his right arm a band that read: Judischer Ordnungsdienst—Jewish Administrators. When I saw him standing like that by the front door, dressed in his clean and orderly uniform, wearing that impressive hat, my heart ached. If not for our insane condition, I would probably have felt pride in my husband's striking appearance. But in our current condition the best I could hope for was that his new status would somehow help the baby I was carrying in my womb.

On the morning of Yom Kippur, October 1, we woke up at dawn to the sound of loud noises and pounding coming from the street. Jacob went outside at once to find out the source of the noise. He returned a while later and said in a choked voice, "They're closing us in; they're erecting a wire fence around the ghetto."

"What will happen?" my mother asked. "How will we survive?"

Apart from the rations delivered by the Jewish community, the main food providers for the ghetto residents in those days were a few brave Poles and Jews with Arian ID cards who went to work outside the ghetto, smuggling food in. On rare occasions, my Polish girlfriends managed to find ways to send me food packages, and Hanka one time even sent me a package of baby clothes. I had no idea how we'd now get the extra food I so needed. The rations that were delivered to us never sufficed, and if the ghetto gates were closed, we would all starve.

"Starting today, no one goes in or out of the Ghetto," said Jacob.

"We're finished," whispered my dad.

At that moment, I felt a pain slashing through my belly as if a long and sharp knife was stabbing and turning up my insides. I collapsed on one of the mattresses that were thrown on the floor, and Jacob quickly sat down next to me and took my hand. "Are you all right?" he asked.

"Yes, call Rivka," I told him.

Rivka Eisenberg was a good friend of my mother. Before the war she worked as a midwife, and even after the war broke out, and later on in the ghetto, she continued to assist many women in our neighborhood to give birth. She arrived with Jacob half an hour later.

Outside our flat the loudspeakers barked Gestapo announcements about locking the ghetto gates and the punishments handed down to anyone who failed to obey the law. Inside the apartment, the tenants were walking around like zombies at the sound of my increasingly louder screaming, each one of them trying to contribute some advice from his or her wealth of personal knowledge. At some point, my mother decided to clear the place of all its inhabitants and asked the tenants to find something to do outdoors. Only Jacob and my father remained sitting in what used to be the kitchen.

At one in the afternoon, the little baby girl was out. Rivka cleaned and dressed her up and immediately placed her on my chest. Her hair was black and shiny, her skin soft and delicate, and her cheeks pink. Right away she burst out crying, drowning the hollering loudspeakers outside and calming down the minute I began to nurse her. I stared at length into her tiny and wrinkled face. Even though her eyes were shut, I imagined them as dark, wise, almond eyes. Mom sat next to me, caressing the baby's miniscule hands. She was so stirred, she kept wiping her own nose ceaselessly, to the point where Rivka suggested she might leave me alone with the baby. The uncertainty and apprehension that had followed me like heavy shadows my entire pregnancy were dissolved at once, replaced by the feelings of happiness and pride, which flooded my heart. I asked Rivka to call Jacob over. When he arrived and saw the baby in my arms, his eyes welled up with tears. "I want to name her Rachel," I told him, "after my maternal grandmother." Jacob agreed immediately.

After the ghetto lockdown, the situation deteriorated quickly. As if we weren't crammed densely enough in those small apartments, in November a new shipment arrived in the ghetto—Jews who used to live in the villages surrounding Shedlitz. The food supply diminished until it became impossible to get anything to eat in a legal fashion. Grownups and children sat on the filthy sidewalks begging for handouts, but no one had anything to give them. Many diseases spread through the ghetto and every day the Jewish Administrators, with Jacob among them, were forced to remove many bodies from homes and from the streets. As the situation deteriorated, ghetto residents became more cynical. Rumors spread about Judenrat members, as well as Jewish policemen, who were willing to turn in a fellow Jew for a slice of bread or for the shadow of a promise of survival.

I never questioned Jacob about his job, knowing his heart won't allow him to squeal on a Jew or do anything else that didn't measure up to his moral standards. We were not any better off than the rest of the ghetto Jews, and only little Rachel was offering us, at long last, a drop of happiness in an ocean of despair.

My parents were in seventh heaven; my mother took care of the baby while I was sleeping, my father played with her, keeping her busy during all the times she wasn't eating or napping. It appeared that this new life that had been created under the ghetto's inhumane conditions made my parents believe we still had some hope to survive the war and to go on with our humble lives in the town we used to love so much.

But as more days passed, our hope was clearly becoming an illusion. In winter, the harshest typhus epidemic to date broke out in the ghetto. The piles of bodies mounted each morning at the entrance grew ever higher. Jacob would leave the house each day at sunrise and return well after sunset. He hardly spoke; his eyes became sunken and sad. His parents and sisters were barely surviving; they lived in one disheveled room in a miserable apartment in the Smaller Ghetto, together with both their daughters' husbands, and only thanks to his position as policeman did Jacob manage to visit them on occasion. Both his sisters' moods were so dark, they hardly ever left the house. Both had married before the war. Mina, the elder, had given birth to two girls before the ghetto was created, but her younger daughter didn't survive the harsh conditions and passed away on her second winter. Rosa, Jacob's younger sister, was supposed to head east with her husband, but after we had returned to Shedlitz in early 1940, she claimed to have no intention of going anywhere and persuaded her husband they would be better off staying. "With Jacob here, we have no reason to leave town," she said with a decisiveness she probably inherited from her mother.

Only little Rachel managed to raise a smile on Jacob's lips. He loved to hold her in his arms for long hours, telling her stories and singing her lullabies. Lalechka, he called her, Dolly. When she'd give him one of her bright smiles he would bring her toward his chest and give her a long hug. He grew ever thinner but always managed to bring me something extra to eat so that I could go on nursing the baby who, to my delight, was gaining weight. My conversations with Jacob, which once would last well into the night, were now down to a few clipped words each day, touching only on our most basic needs. The sights he saw during the day made his night's sleep fitful, and he woke up frequently with his forehead covered in cold sweat.

In December, just at the beginning of the deep cold, the Germans ordered the ghetto residents to hand over immediately all the furs and coats in their possession. Most of us had no valuables left, and handing over our furs was like being stabbed yet again in our empty stomachs. Mom grabbed the mink fur she managed to stash away when we vacated our apartment, looked at it and said: "Human scum! I hope this fur will bring you much happiness!" Even under the miserable conditions of our lives, Mom didn't lose the cynicism that so characterized her.

Many people in town, and not only the cabalists among them, were voicing great trepidation at the approaching year of 1942. They recalled the exile from Spain of 1492, believing we were embarking on a much greater catastrophe. The cynics were wondering how much worse could things become, but I was unwilling to contemplate the different implications associated with the arrival of the new year, as well as what was yet to befall us. All I was interested in at the time was my eternal concern for my little daughter, who, just like me, was born in the midst of a great war.

Chapter 12

SOPHIA

A little after I arrived in Shedlitz, in September 1939, I started to work at the main city hospital, where, for the first time, I ran into the actual consequences of the war. Thousands of injured and dead were arriving at the hospital during the first days of the shelling, and many of the injured died over my months of work there. The Jews received particularly bad treatment and often were not even allowed inside the hospital.

There were no orderly work shifts; everybody worked until they could no longer stand on their feet. Sometimes I was so exhausted at the end of a work day that I didn't have the energy to walk to my parents' house, opting to stay and sleep in the hospital. One day one of the doctors in the department where I was working approached me. "Sophia," he told me, "I notice you've been very exhausted lately, why don't you take a day off and come back to work with renewed strength?"

"It's not just because of the work, Dr. Grebski," I answered. "I'm feeling helpless, so many innocent are hurt, it's inconceivable that we do nothing."

"I think I know what you can do," said the doctor, taking me aside. "Tomorrow night at eight I'll come by to pick you up. There's a few people I'd like you to meet."

The next evening I waited for Dr. Grebski outside the hospital and from there we drove to a small village outside Shedlitz, the home of Lucina and Alexander Rychleski. On the way, Dr. Grebski told me that Lucina and Alexander were a young couple in their early thirties, who had both been, until a few months ago, lectors at the History Dept. of Warsaw University, but were fired without cause. They decided to move to Shedlitz, where Lucina's family lived, and a short while later they moved to the village outside the town where we were headed. I wondered why Dr. Grebski wanted me to meet them, but I let him tell me just what he deemed necessary.

The house where they lived belonged in the past to Lucina's grandfather and grandmother. A few stray chickens were clucking in the yard, and when we entered the living room, which wasn't very large, but still warm and cozy, we discovered there some twenty young men and women, only one of whom I recognized. They appeared like a group of young intellectuals gathered to discuss the future of the world. Later that evening I found out that this, more or less, was what they actually had in mind.

We stayed at the Rychleskis until the wee hours. At some point during the night, after hours of talking and drinking tea, Alexander took us to a forest clearing not far from their house, and showed us the weapons stash the group had been able to acquire in the previous months. Even before the group was dispersing, at dawn, I already knew that I was going to join this small underground led by Lucina and Alexander Rychleski.

One week following that meeting, Lucina arrived at the hospital where I worked. She didn't say why she was there, only asked to meet me alone. She waited outside the hospital until my shift was over, and then we went to my parents' house.

"I see an important role for you in our group," Lucina told me. I looked at her beautiful face, her lips were thick and her nose straight and thin, her long, auburn hair fell over her shoulders. At the meeting in her house, I noticed how all the men in the room were eyeing her, but it looked as though Lucina was not aware of them.

"I'd be happy to do anything, but I've never shot a weapon and I never been a distinguished athlete. I will probably require lengthy training." There were many stories circulating in the hospital where I worked, about the members of the Polish underground, but no one knew what exactly they did. Those who knew said nothing.

Lucina smiled and said, "We'll teach you all of that later on. Anyone can learn to use a weapon, it's not so complicated. I want you to start a school, grades one through twelve, you think you can do it?"

Since Poland had been occupied by the Nazis, high school and university education was outlawed, while the elementary school system was under the complete control and continuous supervision of the Germans. Study topics were chosen carefully, and many subjects, such as Civics and History disappeared completely from the curriculum. Lucina and Alexander, who had both been kicked out of university, probably for their politics, could not accept the fact that the Nazis were taking over our spiritual life as well, and so they decided to establish, in addition to the fighting troop that was engaged in tangible action against the Nazis, an underground education system. They began to set up several schools in agrarian areas, mostly in the Lublin District.

Those schools were in danger every place and every time; if even one local informed the authorities, the school would be closed down and the entire staff transported to the forced labor camps. That's why the locations for those schools were selected very carefully, because it was important to build a system of trust with the locals, to make sure that they cooperate fully, and that they have no interest in sabotaging the system.

Alexander and Lucina's main targets were the cooperatives, which were highly developed at the time in Poland's agrarian regions. They were small, agricultural settlements, organized under a common economic framework, with common interests and a common social network. The members of the cooperative were usually farmers with socialist tendencies, and many of them with clearly communist leanings. I was familiar with all of it from my work for PoEm.

The day after my meeting with Lucina I asked to meet with the head of my department and explained that I could no longer work for the hospital. He didn't ask for an explanation. Dr. Dudek had also attended that night meeting at the home of Lucina and Alexander.

At the first phase, I was sent for training in a small school that had been active for a few months in a village not far from the city of Radom. Children from the entire region arrived at the school to study in grades one through twelve. I spent two months there, trying to learn as much as I could from the local staff: my education included not just the various subjects taught at the school, but also, even more important, preparing a cover story in case of unexpected visits, how to identify stool pigeons and enemies, and how to thwart and prevent informing before it happens.

When I came back from my training period, I traveled to Warsaw to meet with Katja, my schoolmate from university. Since I knew her views well, I was hoping she would agree to become a teacher in the school I was about to establish. Katja got married right after university, and her husband, an officer in the Polish army, became a prisoner of war a few weeks after the invasion. Shortly after finding this out, Katja gave birth to their first son.

We met at the home of her husband's parents, in a small suburb of Warsaw. Her son Janek was almost a year and a half old already and waddled restlessly through all the rooms in the house. When she heard my proposition, Katja agreed at once to join me. It seemed that she was happy for this opportunity to leave the house where she wasn't feeling completely at ease. Katja hadn't been working since the start of the war, and just like me she was also unwilling to accept the situation forced on our country. Since we couldn't reveal to her husband's parents what we were about to do, we agreed that Katja would tell them we were planning to volunteer at a Catholic organization that was taking care of orphans.

In the beginning of 1941 we arrived in Zakrzówek, a small village south of Lublin, where we began to establish our first school. Over the first few days we met with the leaders of the cooperative, interviewed teachers and local workers we wanted to add to the school, and finally met with the parents and children of the area. At first we couldn't reveal to the heads of the cooperative and to the teachers our plan to also teach children from the seventh through the twelfth grades, and only after a long and careful series of interviews we clarified our exact intentions. We didn't wait for the start of the school year and began to teach in July, first the subjects offered in the government's educational plan, but later adding other subjects, which were prohibited to teach in Poland at the time. The children, especially the older ones, whose studies were terminated at the beginning of the German occupation, were thirsty for knowledge and for a learning structure, and would arrive at school with great joy.

At the end of October, Lucina came to visit the place. Her face was terribly pale, and she looked haggard and worried. "What happened?" I asked with great concern when she entered my office. She hadn't announced her visit, and it surprised me, but her presence made me happy.

"They closed down the Shedlitz ghetto," she told me quietly. "They surrounded it with barbed wire fences; there's no way to go in or out." Since the ghetto had been created, in the summer, Lucina would go in regularly, passing messages and delivering packages to many Jews. In the past, I asked her to look for Zippa and to try her best to help her, especially after I found out she was pregnant.

"Have you seen Zippa recently?" I asked.

"No, but I found out she had a baby girl named Rachel."

I decided to travel to Shedlitz as soon as I could. Almost a year had passed since I left town, and the news about the creation of the ghetto and the condition of the Jews in town worried me. Even though I didn't know how I could help, I felt the need to meet Zippa and maybe even see the baby.

In mid-December, a little before the holiday vacation, I arrived in Shedlitz. The city was dead frozen; heavy snow had been coming down for two days, and now the streets were completely covered. Gestapo soldiers, SS men, and gendarmes in long coats and shiny boots were roaming the entire city, which was a mere shadow of its former self two years earlier. Many houses were still in ruins, relics that no one bothered to rebuild, after numerous bombardments at the beginning of the war. Long lines stretched in front of food stores, even though they didn't have much to offer.

Even before I went to my parents' home, my feet carried me to Asha Street, where Zippa once lived. Nothing was left there of the bustling Jewish neighborhood that existed in the past. The few neighborhood homes still standing were inhabited by Poles, transplanted there by the Gestapo, in place of the Jewish tenants. The house at no. 3 Asha was one of the very few that remained completely intact, but it looked neglected and miserable, its windows broken and boarded with wood planks, all the paint was peeled from the walls and heaps of trash were piled by the entrance.

I left Asha and walked down Marshal Pilsudski Street. German soldiers armed with rifles were marching beside a three-meter high, barbed wire fence that stretched along the entire length of the street. I continued walking next to the fence through Jan Kochanowski Street until I reached the cathedral, which stood erect and unharmed amidst a sea of ruins and barbed wire. I debated whether I should go in and at last decided to pay a visit to Irena, who lived a short distance away.

Irena was very surprised to see me, and as I anticipated, immediately burst into tears. It took a long time before she calmed down enough to share with me what had happened in her life since the last time we met. She was not in good shape, being so sensitive and delicate to begin with, and now the war was threatening to destroy her. The string of events of the past two years were too great a burden on the fragile Irena. I tried to encourage her, but I wasn't sure I succeeded. She asked me to visit her again before returning to Zakrzówek.

Later that same day I met with Lucina and Alexander and requested that they assist me in entering the Jewish ghetto. I knew it could be dangerous, but I had to see Zippa, I had no intention of abandoning our friendship because of the war.

I was not able to enter the ghetto, but a member of the underground working on corpse removal detail at the ghetto's gates (which is how he managed to smuggle packages inside even after the lockdown), was able to send Zippa a message from me, through her husband Jacob, to get near one of the corners of the ghetto where we could meet.

Two days later, Zippa arrived at our rendezvous spot exactly at the time I requested. She looked drained and terribly skinny, but her face shone when she saw me. She was wearing a tattered overcoat, several sizes too big. She took out of the coat pocket a picture of Rachel, her baby daughter, and her eyes filled with tears. I gave her my hands and she extended her hands to me. There were freeze burns on the back of her hands. I immediately removed my leather gloves and passed them to her through the fence, and she hurriedly put them on. There were no words we could say at that moment. We stood and held hands for a long time until we noticed a Gestapo soldier walking toward us. Zippa quickly tucked her hands into her coat pockets and walked away.

Chapter 13

ZIPPA

Shabbat, August 22, 1942. Over the past two weeks, we've been living under terrifying stress. We've heard that the Jews of Warsaw were being expelled from the city. Trains full of people are leaving Radom, Kielce and other towns in our area. According to rumors, they were headed to Treblinka. We know the same fate was awaiting us, too, but continue to delude ourselves that it won't happen here.

Horror stories are flying around town about a train loaded with Jewish corpses that arrived from Radom at the Shedlitz train station, or about villages and towns whose Jewish inhabitants all disappeared on the same day. Ducia, my friend Esther Munchak's younger sister from Warsaw, is staying with us these days, and she's been telling us terrifying things about what goes on over there. Ducia came to Shedlitz about a month ago, at the beginning of the expulsion of the Jews from the Warsaw ghetto, because she was told that Shedlitz is a "labor town," where Jews won't be hurt. The only things she managed to drag along, besides a few clothes, were some notebooks and pencils and now I'm trying, in the faint light we have here, to write about the events in our lives.

Yesterday afternoon, like thunder on a clear day, we received the news that the expulsion of the Jews of Mińsk Mazowiecki, only 40 kilometers from us, would take place today. We are next in line, but continue to hope that this will "bypass" us since the local authorities have promised that we are a "labor town" in need of many working hands.

The mood in town is getting worse from one minute to the next. I comfort my beloved parents, but my eyes well up with tears. I look at the only true comfort in our possession, my gorgeous, 11 months old daughter, what has she done to deserve a life in this hell?

On Friday afternoon, a rumor spreads through the ghetto that any and all expulsion has been postponed. People on the street are kissing one another happily. May it only be the truth! To our chagrin, this is the optimist's response to every piece of bad news, as my husband so rightfully put it. When we're about to go to bed, our neighbor Ula Nussbaum, also a Jewish cop, walks in to tell us there's a chance something will happen tonight. We were informed of a meeting of the Polish police that was set for 2:00 in the morning, and that many Germans have been picking up unfinished jobs from ghetto artisans. They seem to know something we don't.

The heart starts to pound strongly, and tears are falling from our eyes. I look at my girl. I ache so much over her. In the meantime, we continue to delude ourselves: maybe it's nothing, maybe the Polish police are getting ready to chase after partisans. Ducia argues that the Polish police do not engage in these actions. One says this and another says the opposite.

At 2 in the morning, Jacob arrives and tells us to get ready. I take out of the suitcase a few things for Rachel; we wake up the neighbors who know nothing, and I comfort my dear mother.

Suddenly a shot is heard, a signal for the closing down of the ghetto. Not saying a word, I begin to dress up my girl. We remain in a horrible state of insecurity until 4 in the morning. Then a volley of gunfire is heard and Jacob storms in with the news: "We're surrounded." He tells us that SS men, and members of the Polish "blue police," as well as trucks loaded with hundreds of Ukrainians, have circled the Big Ghetto.

Both my parents burst into a frightful howl. My mother calls to me: "Save yourself and the baby, let my life's toil not be for naught." I don't respond. I finish dressing up Rachel, I wrap her in a blanket, throw a coat over my shoulders and I'm ready to roll. Where to? I don't know. And I'm not even thinking about clothes and food. Rachel wakes up and starts crying, my father approaches her and as always kisses her and me quietly. Jacob has removed his uniform and directs me to follow him. I'm so stunned and frightened, I don't even ask where to, I don't even say goodbye to my parents and Ducia. Mother accompanies us to the hallway and says, her voice drenched in tears, "Children, try to give us a proper burial." Those words of hers finally break down all my notions of balance and rationality, and I say to her in a broken voice, "Mommy, what are you saying? Do you really think I'll never see you again?" Leaving the apartment, I'm thinking, Where's the poison I asked Mr. O to give me? We could have all ended our lives.

Meanwhile, people are assembling in the streets, and wailing and weeping can be heard from inside the homes. Now and then you see a man running with a package in his hands, every once in a while a shot is fired. Leaving the neighborhood is out of the question. My husband leads us to the police headquarters and from there to the bathhouse attic, next door to the headquarters, so we'd be close by in case they give special treatment to the families of policemen, as we were told was the case in Warsaw. I walk up, handing Rachel to some stranger and she cries to me, "Mamma!"

"I'm taking you right away, my daughter," I tell her, trying to sound calm.

I make an effort to get organized comfortably in the attic, asking my acquaintances to pull a mattress down from the table to the floor for me, and I try to get the girl to fall asleep on it. What nonsense, now she should chat and play to her heart's content, better if she's sleepy later on, but who can think logically at times like this.

It's 5:30 in the morning. Every now and then more people arrive at the attic, but none of them are my relatives. Why doesn't Jacob bring over my parents and Ducia?

At 7 I can hear Ducia's voice. I'm happy, certain that my parents are following behind her. But she's saying nothing. Luckily, she has brought a few dry toasts for the baby. Jacob sent candies, too, and lemons, cherries, bread. What is it all for? I'm so bewildered; I can't assess the situation for myself, just how terrifying things are, the fact that we might have to sit here for who knows how long.

By now there are some 100 people in the attic. Time and again we hear more shots from the street. The expulsion has begun, and my parents are still not here. My mother's final words are ringing in my ears. "Why did I leave the house without them?" I mumble. Ducia calms me down. "You did it to save the baby." But I could have saved my parents instead.

It's 10 o'clock. The isolated howling and crying merge into one great cry. Later we discovered that the Jewish police received an order to vacate the apartment and send the people to a gathering spot, the umschlagplatz. For the time being we don't know the cause of those terrifying, gut-wrenching cries. Frightened and immersed in this horrible dread, I watch over the baby, amusing her so she won't be crying. For now she's delighted to receive the teat and remains quiet, but what will come later?

Later I feed her some civgali, a sedative drug one of the women in the attic has given me, to make my baby sleep. I don't want to think about anything, so I won't go mad. Where are my beloved parents? What has happened to them? I pray that they receive an easy death.

Shabbat. The noon hour approaches. From the street we can hear the footsteps of our hangmen, non-stop shots, non-stop howling. Suddenly, some terrible pounding shakes up our attic.

They're demolishing the stores next door to our hiding place. In a minute, they will reach us. God in heaven, please don't let the baby wake up. To my chagrin, the noise is just too loud, and the girl wakes up, crying bitterly. The people who have been sharing our fate all these many hours are turning ferocious. One woman leaps at my child, trying to choke down her crying, but I push her off strongly, telling her that as far as I'm concerned, if my child doesn't live—they can all perish. In order to muffle the sound of Rachel's crying they push both of us into a closet that stands there, in the attic. I give the baby a teat, sing to her, amuse her as much as I can. Every minute feels like an eternity. At last Rachel calms down, having grown accustomed to the noise, which has still not subsided. I'm drenched in sweat, the heat in the attic is excruciating; finally I lose consciousness. Ducia gives me a slice of lemon, which revives me. I walk Rachel, my little naked doll, down the length of the attic, and I can't stop weeping. If only my mother were here, it would have been easier to go through this. She would have been better at keeping Rachel entertained. Ducia forces me to eat a slice of bread and drink a bit of water. "You must get nourishment for the child," she tells me calmly. We're so lucky to have Ducia.

The noise has subsided. We found out later that the Jewish police destroyed the basement door on purpose, to prove to the Ukrainian soldiers there was no apartment down there, and they bought it and walked away. For the time being, we're saved.

I leave Rachel on the mattress with Ducia and crawl to the roof to look at the street below. Terrible desolation. My beautiful town is looking like a ghost town. From a distance, we can still hear howling, the cries of the murdered, and shots, unceasing gunshots. In the beginning we thought those shots were only meant to scare people, but later we found out every shot meant a person was killed. All day long we hear the trotting of boots in the streets, the crashing noises made by invaders of homes and businesses, and the screams to high heaven. My mother's last words and my father's calm kiss keep troubling me. What has become of them? Only half a day has passed; what if we're forced to stay here longer? Rachel is being very quiet, my golden doll, my beloved Lalechka. When I tell her, "Quiet!" and put a finger on my mouth, she looks at me with her amazing, black, wise eyes, as if she understands.

Our police are circling the attic, letting us know through different utterances that they're watching over us. The attic is unbearably hot, the baking rooftop is creaking, and every tiny sound makes our hearts race ever faster. Night is approaching. I stare at the attic window, hoping Jacob would give me a sign of life, but no one can be seen. Weary after this terrible day, I fall asleep.

An air raid siren wakes me up. Maybe fate will truly take pity on us; maybe the bombings will save us? But the siren dies down, there are no bombs, but there is, instead, a sudden asthma attack as many are coughing. Shushing them doesn't work—those wretched victims can't help it. But their coughing noise grates against the silence here, forcing me to block my ears to avoid hearing it. It's a pity the night is almost over.

Morning breaks and my poor little doll wakes up crying with hunger. My breasts are completely empty. They're so badly bitten that the slightest touch causes me terrible pain. But I control myself as best I can, just to keep the child quiet. I give her a piece of toast, dipping it in the juice Mother gave me at the last minute, and then I pour a little water into the palm of my hand. Rachel drinks eagerly and finally bites my hand—she wants more. My Lord, how can I stand and watch my child being tortured?

It remains quiet until ten o'clock, and then the terrifying noise starts anew, again we hear the horrible howling, again the gunshots. The pandemonium of the evacuation continues today, Sunday, except now they're conducting the Aktion with even greater rage. We hear the constant noise of storefronts being shattered, of shots, and the final cries of the executed: "Sh'ma Israel" and "God of Israel"—these are the words on the lips of the Jew who finds himself at a dead end, and these are the words we hear ceaselessly.

It's very hot again up in the attic; breathing is difficult. What I fear the most is repeated now: my baby is tired, and she bursts into tears. Once again I must fight the people—this time I'm depleted of energy, but Ducia keeps guard over me, pushing everyone aside, bringing me out of the closet—where they had made me go again—recruiting a few people to fan some wind on the child, and this revives her a little so that after a few minutes, which seem like hours, she slowly calms down. I breathe in relief, a little.

Down in the street the Ukrainians are "playing" alongside the Sonderdienst, the Special Service. They had broken into Shmuel Weiss's bakery at 2 Jatkowa Street, literally below us, they brought out everybody who was hiding inside and shot them all. We continued to hear the shots and the cries of the murdered. Then, after a few moments of quiet, we heard footsteps, followed by a choir singing of The Volga. I look at Ducia in horror. The Volga! The beautiful, sentimental Volga, in the face of the bestial murder of helpless men, women, and children? How cruel and sadistic can these people be?

That sight drives me absolutely insane. I've lost all sense of balance, but still, I must keep my hungry child entertained, while she's swallowing whole cherries, grabbing the dry bread I feed her and eagerly drinking water out of the palm of my hand. At the same time, I understand that I'm not allowed to complain, because what little I now have could disappear.

Suddenly we all jump with excitement. Someone is knocking on the door, calling out to us in Yiddish. I'm sure it's Jacob, but it turns out to be Ula Nussbaum, our neighbor. He brings some bread and information about the outside world. The Aktion is still on, many people have been shot, they kept 500 men for labor duty. Accordingly, they'll try to get all the young men out of here. What will become of the women? It's not known. Once he's left, a rumor is spreading that the hospital is still operational, and the women could be transferred there as caretakers. Instead of rejoicing, I'm struck with terrible despair. It means we could have saved my parents! It's my fault they died, and even if I'm among the survivors—that feeling of remorse would stay with me for the rest of my life.

Meanwhile, I don't see Jacob. Has anything happened to him? I'm looking at the street from the attic. Hospital nurses are bringing water for the people gathered at the umschlagplatz. The Jewish policemen keep bringing in cartloads of corpses, but I don't see Jacob. I'm frightened, my heart stops beating every now and again. Suddenly, in another corner of the attic, someone says he can see my husband. Ducia runs over and spots him. I'm relieved.

The heat in the attic is unbearable. My baby collapses helplessly, weeping constantly. What should I do? I force myself to write Jacob that if things stay the way they are, he should try to get poison for the child at the hospital because my heart is breaking when I look into her eyes. It's four in the afternoon. The shooting hasn't stopped for a moment, together with the howling and the screaming. My child sleeps and I stand, looking at the street.

A cart loaded with a pile of the dead is passing down below, pushed by our cops. They look horrid, pale, tortured, sweat running down their faces. I admire their courage, taking part in such an operation and not going mad at the sight of their murdered relatives! Instantly, the picture changes: a Ukrainian or a Lithuanian (same devil) is ushering a couple with a child. The child is crying in fear and can't walk. The escort kicks him along, and when that isn't helping, he hits him with his rifle butt. The miserable father jumps him, slapping his face with his last bit of strength, again and again. At the same moment, three shots are heard, and the three victims fall to the ground. The criminal walks away, whistling happily. I'm standing paralyzed with dread, and still I'm experiencing some satisfaction that this "pure Aryan" has felt on his flesh the ire of a poor Jew. There have been quite a few incidents like that. The tears are running continually from my eyes —did they beat up my dear parents? How could I leave them? Did they forgive me? I did it for the sake of their beloved grandchild!

Early in the evening Ula came to visit his cousin and brought the news that my mother-in-law, both her daughters, both my brothers-in-law and the granddaughter, Jacob's niece, had been shot. Poor Jacob, this is why he's not showing his face! Meanwhile, the rumor about the hospital is far from certainty, and we have no idea what would become of the women.

I hand Ula a letter to deliver to Jacob.

Chapter 14

IRENA

When Zippa came to my house in the midst of the Aktion to eliminate the Jews of Shedlitz, I didn't ask how she managed to flee from the ghetto. She was too frightened and agitated, and I didn't want to disturb her even more. The most I could get out of her was that her husband Jacob, being a Jewish policeman, found a way to smuggle her and the girl out of the ghetto.

The next day, after she had left with Sophia to the safe house outside the town, my mother and I laid Rachel down on the mattress in Mom's bedroom. The girl slept heavily until the morning and then woke up crying with hunger. I immediately gave her some milk and fed her, until she calmed down.

During the first few days Rachel cried a lot, she was almost one year old and it looked like she was missing her mother. But the food we provided calmed her down, and slowly she began to show some curiosity about her environment. Because the Gestapo headquarters was so close to our house, we didn't dare take her outside, not even to our back yard. Our neighbors, too, were a great menace, and we feared that they would start asking questions or inform on the girl to the Gestapo.

My mother showed no sign of conflict or hesitation regarding Rachel; she asked me no questions and raised no doubts. Just like myself, she was devoted to Rachel from the moment she arrived, as if she were family. We had to provide her with food, clothing, cloth diapers, and whatever else a year-old tot might require.

A few weeks after Rachel had come to us, my brother and his family returned from our aunt's house in the country. Now the house became awfully crowded. "What are you planning to do with the child?" my brother Kazimir asked my mother one morning while she was cooking porridge for Rachel. It wasn't hard to notice that my brother was tense and worried about the situation that was forced on him. He rarely came near the baby and most of the time he ignored her outright. His wife Christina, too, seemed bothered by the situation, but if she harbored any objection she didn't express it in words and didn't demonstrate it in my presence. She treated Rachel like a guest, with a kind of cool, distant politeness, the way she treated most people.

My brother went back to work at the out of town glass factory. I found out, even though Kazimir never told me this himself, that the factory used to belong to a Jew from our town before the war, and a little after the war started it was confiscated and handed over to Polish ownership. The fact that my brother worked in a factory that was taken from a Jew hurt my feelings very much; I was aware that many factories in Shedlitz were transferred from Jewish to Polish owners and no one protested, no one objected. Then again, how could we protest? And to whom, exactly?

The events of the past few days—the horrible wailing that emanated from the Shedlitz ghetto for whole days and nights between the 22nd and 25th of August, Zippa's sudden—albeit so very much hoped for—appearance in the middle of the night, the little girl whose presence suddenly made me the one responsible for her well being—all these things shook me up greatly, and if I weren't obligated to care for Rachel, it's quite plausible that those extreme events would have made me lose my mind. My older brother's behavior, the brother who took over for my father as the center of our family, my brother who voiced his objection to the presence among us of a year-old girl without a relative in the world, my brother who worked in a factory confiscated from a Jew —in the end it was his behavior which finally stirred me out of the emotional breakdown into which I was being swept.

"We plan to do precisely what God orders us," my mother calmly answered Kazimir.

"And what exactly does that mean?" my brother inquired. He was never among the devoted Catholics. He went to Church only on Sundays, mostly to appease my mother and maybe to quiet his own conscience a little. His wife was more devoted than him, but she never expressed an opinion that contradicted Kazimir's, whose favorite saying was that God won't saw wheat for us, nor mill flour for us, since each of us must do those things himself.

"It means that we'll take care of her as well as we would have taken care of her if she were your own child," I replied in a new, unfamiliar voice.

"Really?" he asked, his face grown long with astonishment.

"Do you even know what has taken place in the ghetto?" I asked him. The sounds of gunshots and the cries of the murdered in the Aktion still reverberated inside my head. My brother had been spared those sounds, having spent those August days in our aunt and uncle's country home.

"Does it mean that we, too, must die, because they died?" he answered with a question. Last year, the Shedlitz Gestapo headquarters published leaflets that stated explicitly that "Anyone willfully sheltering Jews or aiding them in other ways will incur the death penalty…Henceforth this rule will be executed severely and without mercy."

"If Dad were here you wouldn't have dared behave like this," I told him angrily. So many times since the war began I found myself being furious with the good Lord, who had taken my father from us just when we needed him the most. I knew my anger won't help any, but it was the only way to ease some of my pain.

"Dad is not here, and we must find a solution for this girl ourselves. I have no intention of endangering the lives of my entire family for the sake of one child who isn't even our own." He looked at me and added angrily, "And if Dad were here, he would have acted exactly the same."

My mother and I didn't attempt to protest, knowing it would only enhance his objection. I recalled the letter Zippa had left for my mother when I said goodbye to her before she went to the safe house. I climbed up to the attic and retrieved the letter from behind the ceiling beams where I stashed it, fearing the Gestapo might discover it in one of their searches. I came back downstairs and handed my brother the letter. "Read it," I told him.

My brother sat down on one of the kitchen chairs, his wife Christina, who had been standing silently on the side throughout our conversation, sat down next to him. Their son Stephan and little Rachel continued to play with the kitchen utensils, taking them in and out of the cabinets, laughing out loud. I watched my brother and his wife while they were reading the letter. I knew that in no small measure Rachel's future depended on their reaction.

Dear Madam,
Shedlitz, August 1942

As you may know, it is possible that soon there won't be any Jews left in our beloved town. Conditions in the ghetto have become untenable and every passing day brings us closer to extinction.

On Friday night, the Germans initiated the liquidation of the Jewish ghetto. According to what we've heard, the Nazis have assembled most of Shedlitz's Jews in the town square (as they have done in other places) and sent them by train to a camp, most likely Treblinka. It is possible that my beloved parents have gone with them, I still don't know for certain what has become of them. During the first night of the Aktion, my husband managed to bring me and our child to a shelter. We are staying here together with about one hundred people. Conditions here are exceedingly difficult, we hardly have any food or water, there's barely enough air to breathe, and the place is choking hot. Once a day someone brings us a pittance to eat.

One day they demolished the stores in the street below us, and the terrible noise made my daughter start screaming so much, that one Jewish woman attacked her and threatened to strangle her. To keep the child's crying down, they pushed both of us into a closet.

The sights we see from the attic window are too difficult to describe, but still, I will try and tell you the short version, so you'll comprehend our situation: the ghetto streets are completely deserted, save for the Jewish policemen who are hurrying every which way, carrying carts loaded with the dead bodies of Jews who had been executed merely for being Jews. Many corpses are still strewn in the streets, waiting to be removed. Most of the houses and the stores in the ghetto have already been completely destroyed. The sound of stomping boots in the street, the noise of destruction of homes and shops, and, foremost, a terrible fear of things to come—these are the components of my daily routine. At any moment, they are likely to break into our hiding place, too, and bring the end upon us.

I'm telling you all this so that you'll understand I had no other choice. I hope that from this letter you'll find out what the Nazis are doing to the people who used to be your neighbors and friends. My husband and I have decided to take the child out of the ghetto and bring her to you in the hope that this way we would save her from the miserable fate awaiting her here. We didn't reach this decision lightly, as you surely can imagine. My husband objected to giving away our little one, saying that if we were destined to die, let us die together. "Even if we manage to get her out of here, I'm still concerned for her fate. How can I be certain she'll live?" he asked, quite rightfully.

I responded that any solution we'd find outside the ghetto would be preferable to the fate that awaits her here, but my husband still wouldn't calm down. "There's the threat of the death penalty for any Pole who hides a Jew at home," he said, "and the Nazis are sure make good on it."

I insisted that we must save the child, no matter the cost. If I didn't save her, there would be nothing left of our family and no testimony left of the injustices committed against the Jewish community. When my husband realized that I wasn't giving in, he started to plan a way of helping both her and me escape. If the child remains sleepy over the next few days, please don't worry, as I was forced to give her a large dose of sleep medicine so that she did not wake up on the way.

Dear Madam, my little girl has committed no crime and hurt no one in her short life, and I will not permit the murderers to steal her life as they have stolen so many other lives. I've known you since I was a little girl, so I know you'll guard my beloved daughter like the apple of your eye, and I beg of you to care for her until the end of the war.

Should you find out the fate of my family, I wish that my daughter be told the whole truth, that she grow up and find out what happened to the people who loved and adored her so much. I want her to know how great was the love we gave her in the first year of her life. I hope that this love will provide her with the strength to lead her life in the best possible way, even if it is without the people who loved and adored her so much. I enclose with this letter three recent photographs, so that my daughter will know how her parents and grandmother looked, and that she'll always remember that she was the light that shone on the final months of our lives.

I ask you that after the end of the war you'll look for my brother who immigrated to Palestine and give him this small child. What has been happening to me might be my punishment for being so naïve that I didn't move to Palestine when it was still possible to do so.

Please raise my daughter according to the principles of the religion that advocates loving mankind, whoever they may be.

May God grant you and all the members of your household health and a long life.

My love and appreciation are yours eternally.

If any feelings were evoked in my brother while reading the letter, they were not evident on his face. His wife Christina kept looking at the three pictures that were attached to the letter. Her face remained blank, too. After they had finished reading, she took it out of Kazimir's hand to read it one more time. "We must invent a cover story for the girl," my brother said finally, "and start looking for a place where she can stay should the war continue a very long time. She can't stay here forever."

Chapter 15

SOPHIA

I was busy organizing the classrooms in the school at Zakrzówek, when a member of the underground came by with a letter from Lucina. It was a Sunday, August 24, a particularly hot and muggy day. The village was quiet, and it looked like all the locals were enclosed in their homes or praying in church. More than a year had passed since Katja and I began to operate the school and recently I started to feel that the place was becoming less and less safe. In the beginning everything was progressing with relative ease: the local children would arrive in school to study Math and Science, but also Polish, History, and Social Studies, subjects that the Nazis made illegal to teach. In every classroom there were books, maps and other "legal" teaching accessories, which served as a cover for the forbidden subjects we were teaching—usually only orally, with no writing, so as not to take risks. Since high school studies were absolutely prohibited, the older children sat in small groups in the same classrooms as the younger children. In case of a sudden inspection, they would disperse among the younger students and pretend to be helping them, rather than studying themselves. The fact that I was teaching the children about the true past of Poland, as I knew it and not the way the Germans dictated, made me feel that I was making a tangible contribution to the war effort. If the young children knew their country's language and its past, no enemy could defeat them. At least that's how I felt at the time.

Since the beginning of 1942, there was an increase in harassments from the multitude of Ukrainian residents living in the area. They destroyed our equipment and wrote slurs on the school walls. There were also a few cases of violent provocation of students. Visits by the Polish police became more and more frequent. One morning a black car followed by a police motorcycle arrived at the school. An SS officer and two Nazi soldiers exited the car hastily, and two Polish policemen hopped off the motorcycle and quickly attached themselves to the former. The Germans, shadowed by the Polish cops, went through all the classrooms, examined the maps, looked at the books, and left about an hour later. A few anxious parents decided to take their children out of the school. In consultation with Lucina, both Katja and I decided to leave the place in the hands of the local teachers, who would maintain it as strictly an elementary school, while we fled the moment it became possible, before being discovered.

The letter from Lucina reinforced my decision to leave Zakrzówek that same night and reach Shedlitz as quickly as I could. Katja decided to take advantage of the break and went to Warsaw with her son, Janek, to visit his grandfather and grandmother.

Early Sunday evening I arrived in Lucina's house. She brought me up to date on all that she knew regarding the events inside the Jewish ghetto. Lucina's role was to coordinate the group's activities and communication, which is why she remained in the village house throughout the war. Her husband Alexander, who coordinated field action, was roaming around all of eastern Poland, coming home for short and very infrequent visits. The combatants in the field would deliver to Lucina a letter or a message whenever possible, but at that moment she hadn't heard from her husband in many weeks.

"How can we save them?" I asked Lucina after she finished telling me about all the horrors taking place in the ghetto in recent days. I told Lucina when we first met about Zippa and Jacob, she knew that Zippa and I were close friends and that I would do anything for her. I shuddered when I recalled the last time I had seen Zippa the previous winter, how she stood behind the high barbed wire fence looking fragile and defeated. She was so thin, her clothes so worn down and her hands red and bloated. I remembered how her hands trembled from the cold when I gave her my leather gloves through the hole in the fence.

"I'm afraid it's impossible," said Lucina. "The ghetto is locked in, and you can't even get near the area. From what I've heard about what's going on in there, I find it hard to believe they're still alive." I realized that even if Zippa managed to escape somehow from the ghetto, she wouldn't stand a chance of passing by the Gestapo's ambushes and exhaustive searches that Lucina described. Zippa was swarthy, and her features were classically Jewish, she wouldn't be able to get by any Nazi soldier without being arrested. How strange, I thought, when I was a child and saw her for the first time in school, she looked to me like the most beautiful girl I had ever met. When we got older, too, I always thought she was so unique and pretty, and now her beautiful face and skin color became her death card.

I left Lucina's and Alexander's house very early Monday morning, wishing to reach Shedlitz and meet my parents as soon as possible. It was the first time since the beginning of the war that my faith was being shaken. I felt drained, without a drop of strength to keep on fighting. I started driving in the direction of Shedlitz in the old car I had purchased when I arrived in Zakrzówek, said car now sounding like it would fall apart at any moment. Even though this was the height of summer and the weather was hot and muggy, the sky was cloudy and gray, and it looked like heavy rain was coming down shortly. The fields outside the town were yellow and abandoned. It was summer vacation, not a child to be seen now in the villages and the fields.

When I reached Irena's house the next morning, Zippa was already there, together with Rachel. She was laying on the bed up in the attic, looking exhausted, her brown eyes swollen. Rachel was lying on a mattress. Mrs. Zawadzka was gently caressing her body.

Throughout the day I was working on organizing Zippa's escape. I asked Lucina to urgently help me find Zippa a safe house. Most of our underground activity took place in the small villages outside Shedlitz, and I knew there wouldn't be a problem finding a spot in one of the abandoned homes through which we moved. The only thing I didn't know was how I'd manage to move Zippa from Irena's house to the safe house, once we located one. Toward noontime, I already had in my head a detailed and consolidated plan. I had a few hours left to make sure that no element be overlooked and cause us to fail.

That evening, when we were sitting in the attic, I recalled that not so long ago we still used to climb up to this very attic, to rummage through Mrs. Zawadzka's large wooden crates. One of the crates had carefully folded dresses, shirts and long, colorful skirts that used to belong to Sabina's mother and some even to her grandmother. Another crate held shoes, scarves, and hats, and inside a third crate, organized meticulously, were all the silver and crystal services passed down from generation to generation. We'd take great pleasure in running delightful masquerade balls, trying on the old clothes, despite the slight moldy odor. "Just don't touch the crystal," Mrs. Zawadzka would yell from downstairs. "Fine, Mama," Irena would answer, pouring us imaginary champagne into the delicate crystal cups.

Now the three of us sat down and didn't dare to glance at the dusty crates in the corner, symbols of the end of our childhood. None of us was able to bring up for the others those childhood memories, but I had the feeling we were all thinking about them.

I asked Zippa not to worry about the child. "She'll be in good hands," I promised, and immediately felt how stupid it was of me to ask a young mother not to worry about her tiny daughter that she didn't know whether or when she would see again.

"I know," she told me and only then, for the first time, as if some dam had filled up to the rim and collapsed, she burst into bitter tears. Irena immediately started to cry along with her and the three of us sat hugging one another a long time.

Late that night Zippa and I left the Zawadzky home. The safe house Lucina prepared for Zippa earlier in the day was a few kilometers from town. I didn't allow my fears to overcome me. If everything worked out as I had planned, in the morning Zippa would already be safe. At the appointed hour, I took Zippa to the corner of Sokolowska and Popjeluszki Streets. Based on the information I received, the SS nightly patrols left the ghetto gates on the hour, circling the ghetto clockwise. We had sufficient time to get from Irena's house to the rendezvous point with Janusz, a member of the underground who worked in removing corpses from the ghetto, without running into the patrol. When we reached the intersection, Janusz was already waiting for us. He had arrived with a Polish co-worker who agreed to help in exchange for a large sum of money, which I was able to solicit, mostly from my father and Jadja's. Earlier, in the afternoon, Janusz and I had met and together planned how we'd smuggle Zippa. At first he refused to help, claiming the risk was too high; if we got caught we'd all be executed. I only managed to persuade him by going carefully over the details of the plan and tying all the loose ends together. I also assume that the money he was promised helped convince him. This was clearly against the instructions of Lucina and Alexander, but I felt that without a financial incentive I wouldn't be able to enlist any help.

The corpse removers were being overworked in recent days, toiling most of the hours of the day and night. The Jews who weren't transported by train to Treblinka, Janusz related, were being destroyed systematically, their bodies removed to the ghetto gates, where they were picked up by Poles for burial in the town cemetery.

The body cart Janusz was pushing was usually filled to the rim, but under cover of the late night hour he managed this time to fool the SS men guarding the Polish workers and didn't fill the cart completely. We were supposed to pack Zippa onto the cart, but when she saw the dead bodies she balked, refusing to climb onboard. Only when she understood that this was her only chance did she climb onto the cart and the two men drove her to the Jewish cemetery. From there, the plan was for Zippa to sneak into a nearby grove, meet up with another member of our group, a woman, who was waiting for her on a cart tied to a horse, to drive her to the safe house Lucina had prepared.

After bidding a quick farewell to Zippa and the two Polish guys, I walked down Sokolovska Street, alongside the barbed wire fence surrounding the now dark and silent ghetto, then sneaked into the dark cathedral. To avoid drawing needless attention, I decided to stay inside until dawn.

Three days after I parted with Zippa at the corner of Sokolovska and Popjeluszki Streets, I managed to arrive for my first visit with her. Her safe house was in a fir and cedar forest, in a completely remote area, some ten kilometers from Shedlitz, where no one had any reason to be in summer. Each early December dozens of lumberjacks would arrive in the forest to cut down firs for Christmas, but now there wasn't a soul around. She was staying in an isolated wooden house that used to belong to a ranger who abandoned the place during the first days of the war. The nearest village was about five kilometers away, and in late August there was no danger of anyone happening by. I brought Zippa food and a few clothes. I discovered her in the midst of deep depression, and throughout my visit she didn't stop crying.

"Have you heard anything from Jacob?" she asked as soon as I walked in. She was searching for the answer in my eyes, but I had none to give her. "And my parents, have you heard anything about them?"

"No," I answered. "We're constantly trying to find out what happened to them."

"I can't stay here," she told me, trying to restrain her crying.

"Zippa, you must wait a while, I promise I'll take care of you." I felt she wasn't listening to me.

"I'm going crazy here, all by myself day and night."

"There's nothing for you to do outside, they'll catch you as soon as you come out."

"I have to find out what happened to Jacob and my parents. I can't remain here while they're over there."

"You have to stay here for the sake of Rachel."

She became silent and turned her head to the window. She glared at the closed window for a long time.

The following days I tried with all the means at my disposal to find out the fate of Jacob and the fate of Aaron and Josepha Jablon. I went looking for Janusz, hoping that he would know something about Jacob, given how he ran into Jewish policemen all the time in the course of his workday. When I came near the ghetto gate, I could see the deserted streets, the house doors torn off their hinges and thrown into the street, the smashed windows and the blinds that were swinging in the wind. The wooden houses looked like they would collapse at any moment, not a single house remained undamaged. The bodies were piled up near the ghetto gate, and broken furniture and trash were rolling in the streets. The asphyxiating stench of death emanated from the place.

A Polish cop guarding the gate told me with a smile: "Once we clean up the place, it will finally belong to us."

From one of the local workmen I found out the Jews who had survived the three days of the Aktion were concentrated in the Smaller Ghetto, within the triangle of Sokolovska, Aslanovicza and Listopada 11 (November 11, 1918, Polish Declaration of Independence Day, only 24 years ago). That same workman also let me know Jausz was no longer working there. At the conclusion of the three-day Aktion, he collapsed and was rushed to the hospital. I went right away to the local hospital to see him.

I found Janusz laying in bed, pale as the wall, a distant and indifferent expression on his face. For a long time, he didn't utter one word. "I don't believe it," he finally mumbled. "I don't believe it."

"Have you heard anything about Jacob Zonshein?" I asked.

"No. It's hard to believe that anyone survived that hellfire."

A few days later I visited Zippa again. I told her everything I had seen in the ghetto. This time she was no longer asking if I knew anything about her family.

"I'm going back there," she declared.

"Zippa…" I started to say, but couldn't find the words.

"I must find Jacob. It can't be that they killed everyone, they promised to protect the Jewish cops."

"Give me a few more days to find out exactly what's going on there," I said, playing for time.

She looked at me, and I felt she was trying to say she could depend on me. "Fine," she said, finally, "I'll wait. But after you find out, I'm going back there."

I decided to enter the Smaller Ghetto. I knew that once Zippa has made up her mind, nothing could stop her, and I preferred to know what she was getting into and to try and help her as best I could. To that end, I also enlisted Hanka, who was still working for whatever was left of the Shedlitz administration. I was happily surprised to see how Hanka, who used to be such a frivolous, carefree girl, had turned in time of war into a contemplative and pragmatic woman. I was glad to have her with me that day.

We arrived at the ghetto in the morning hours. "We're from City Hall," Hanka told the Polish policeman standing at the entrance.

"And what are you looking for?" he asked indifferently.

"We were sent from the Health Dept., to conduct a thorough examination of the place for a future cleaning and purification," I answered in the most natural sounding voice I could muster. I showed him the forms Hanka brought with her from the City. "Fine," he said, "but you need to get this past him, not me," and he pointed at an SS officer standing on the side, staring at us.

I tried to dig up from memory the few words I learned in high school German language class and approached the officer. He listened without uttering a sound and finally said, "Give me your papers, I don't want to catch you saying even one word to anyone, and in one hour precisely you'll be back here." He instructed one of his soldiers to escort us.

Despite the close accompaniment, we were able, mostly with our eyes, to collect tidbits of information regarding conditions in the Smaller Ghetto. The filth and the crowding inside the houses notwithstanding, life was being run quietly, and the German soldiers were not bothering the local residents, most of whom were busy collecting artifacts and arranging them in piles, or otherwise cleaning the streets. A few Hasidic Jews were busy collecting sacred books that no one wanted any longer. Even some commerce was underway in one spot, as a few Jews stood behind small stands, selling food supplies and junk. Many gypsies could be seen in the streets as well, but none of them were working. Instead, they mostly sat down and sang, some playing with improvised instruments. The place looked as if a storm had swept through it, and now the survivors were collecting the broken pieces, picking the last crumbs of humanness. Obviously, I couldn't find out anything about Jacob, nor about Aaron and Josepha Jablon, since the SS soldier didn't budge from us throughout our tour. We made believe that we were filling up the forms we brought with us and left the place a short while later.

Chapter 16

ZIPPA

That's it. I decided to leave this safe house. I must find my husband and my parents, since I don't stand a chance of surviving here by myself anyway. The two weeks I spent in this isolated house in the middle of the forest were more terrifying than my time up in the attic in the ghetto. The thoughts keep running inside my head and I've no one to share them with, save for this notebook that Ducia gave me. Dearest Ducia, who knows what has been your fate and the fate of your beloved family? I'm also losing my mind not knowing what has become of Jacob and my parents. Even thinking about Rachel, my little daughter, isn't enough to keep me here in hiding. I must find Jacob, only hoping that being a Jewish policeman, he was able to survive even the toughest ordeals. Despite her outright objections, Zosha agreed to help me return to the ghetto. She understood I could not go on hiding in this safe house, not knowing what has befallen my loved ones.

I arrived at the ghetto, where I discovered that by the end of the Aktion the Gestapo, through the new Judenrat, distributed a promise to all the surviving Jews that no harm would come to them. Almost two thousand Jews have gathered inside the triangle of Sokolovska, Aslanovicza and November 11 Streets (What cruel irony was now attached to the gloried name of that street), a triangle containing only a few houses, which in normal times would hold not more than twenty families. The houses in the main ghetto were burned or demolished, since, their owners are no longer among the living anyway, and who would want to live in an apartment that used to belong to a Jew?

The Germans have stopped the mass killing for the time being and are spreading rumors throughout the ghetto that the worst is already over, probably in order to seduce the Jews to come out of their hiding places. I don't believe one word they're saying. I'm living here in horrible conditions, in a filthy apartment teeming with lice, in a neighborhood full of gypsies who have become our heirs. The stench of death hangs in the air. Our mood is miserable. Every day new people show up, having escaped from the trains coming from other towns: Łuków, Węgrów, Sokolow, and many others.

I've been here almost a month. Around me there are Jews who've been picked by the Nazis to stay alive after the Aktion, as well as a few who managed to flee from the death trains to Treblinka and returned to the ghetto because they had no place else to go, and they believed that the worst was behind them. Those who have been to Treblinka and managed to escape tell me about the transports going there.

The thousands of Jews who were assembled on Shabbat in the square were forced to sit for many long hours, bowed down, on the ground. It was a hot day, and the sun was beating on their heads. A member of the Judenrat who spoke good German started making his way toward the German officer who stood at the entrance to the square monitoring the entire Aktion. He was hoping to plead with the officer to give the people a little water, but he didn't manage to reach the officer, as a few shots burst and he fell dead where he stood. That moment the machine guns went into action, killing anyone who attempted to stand, or even sit upright. People were dropping like flies on the sidewalk. Here they grabbed children from their mother, there a husband from his wife, a brother from his sister. Blows became the most natural thing: they beat you because your clothes are nicer, your face more intelligent; they beat you because you're a human being. What meaning is there to the blows when murder becomes so routine and petty.

After the Nazis had assembled the town Jews in the main square, they began to send them to the train station. Those transports continued throughout Shabbat, Sunday and Monday. The Jews of Shedlitz offered no resistance, they had been living in this town for three years now without hope, humiliated, and now so exhausted emotionally that they no longer had the will to live.

On Monday, the day I was rescued, they shot the entire hospital staff: Drs. Lubel, Glazowski, Schwartz and others, all the nurses, the aids, and all the rest of the hospital workers, as well as the patients, among them a few babies. All the young women who were hiding in the hospital, the Shedlitz intelligentsia, those who wished to secure their lives that way, fell along with the nurses. For some time, we had believed that they wouldn't harm our hospital, how could they? But that, naturally, was of no help, and they destroyed the place the way one would destroy an ant hill. Afterward they amassed all the dead young people on carts, like so many animal carcasses, and transported them to the cemetery. From one corpse, they stole a suit; from another, its good shoes; from a third—valuables.

Those who were sent to the train station were piled into cargo cars. A hundred and two hundred people were pushed into a cattle car with a capacity of forty to fifty. All my information was received from those who managed to escape from those cars. The people inside each car, shocked at first, were slowly becoming deranged: "It's hot," "Water!" they screamed. But they didn't receive water. They undressed, and after a while most of them stood naked—men, women, and children. They paid no attention to one another. "It's hot, I'm choking!" they cried, and sure enough, many did choke. First the elderly and the sick, followed by small children.

People were fighting for their lives, pushing through to reach a window; they couldn't stand the suffocation. They jumped on each other's back. "Give me some air! Let me near the window!" But the small window was not enough for everybody. The young ones won out, most of the elderly did not remain alive, they didn't have any energy left to fight over a little bit of air.

The cars reached Treblinka. My source for news from there is Mr. Max Bigelman from Warsaw, who worked for two weeks (from August 27 to September 9) sorting personal articles and later was able to flee. This gentleman is living with me now and has a lot to tell. At this moment, while I'm writing, he continues to tell his tales, and another listener is Mendel, who collects documents from the Shedlitz ghetto. Bigelman relates that when the cars arrived at the Treblinka train station, they proceeded through the gate into the camp, and when they stopped they were emptied of people and articles. The people were led through the gate to a square that held two sheds. In the yard, they directed the women and children to the left and the men to the right. The women stood in front of one shed and the men in front of the other. Large posters were hanging there, saying: "Attention! You must undress in the vestibule. After the shower, each will receive a clean dormitory, clean clothes, and you will be sent to work..."

The women took off their shoes outside, then went inside and undressed. From the shed, through a corridor, the women proceeded over a pathway in the grass, until they reached a "shower" located in another shed, which was hermetically sealed. In there they crammed some four hundred women and girls and barred the door with a metal rod from the outside. Four machine guns were posted in front of the shed, to make sure none would escape. As the doors were closed, gas was delivered into the shed. After three to four minutes they had all choked to death, but they kept them inside the shed another ten minutes, and then they opened the shed from the opposite side, where some two hundred Jewish workmen were already standing, waiting to go into the shed and bring out the bodies. But the corpses would stick to one another, and they had to pour water on them to separate them. They piled the bodies on carts to lead them to the graves. Half an hour later, the shed was empty, and if anyone alive was hiding among the bodies, they would be caught and shot by the graves.

I'm writing all this in my notebook, but my heart refuses to believe the words my own hands are writing... God in Heaven—so much hypocrisy, so much sadism, so much barbarism.

The men's shed offered a similar process. At the entrance to the "shower" stood a band of Jewish musicians who accompanied their brethren to their death. The workmen who removed the "showered" victims were isolated from the ones doing the selection work in the front yard. It was forbidden for the latter to know anything, but, naturally, they knew everything. Those who worked in the front yard were young people who were picked to go through the clothes left behind by those entering the "shower." They sorted, packed, loaded on the train and immediately shipped back those packages. It was thanks to those train cars going back that the few hundred men were saved, and from them we're now collecting all this information.

Mr. Max's eyes well up with tears when he tells us about the moment his wife and their fifteen-year-old daughter got off the train. He tried to save them. Being a key employee, he approached his "manager" requesting that he let them remain as workers. But he received a negative response and had to say good-bye to his daughter, who told him, "What can we do, Daddy, don't be sad."

His wife did not know they were going to their death, but he told his daughter. What a terrible tragedy! What have these people experienced? I don't want to think about it, or I will go crazy with terror.

Two weeks later, Mr. Max got into a car with articles that were being shipped back, and saved himself.

My hair stands on end when I hear his stories. Terror surrounds all of us. Will people who didn't live near these events ever believe it? Can anyone believe that what I write here is the truth and nothing but the truth?

These are the chronicles of the Jews of Shedlitz. That's how tens of thousands of people ended their lives, among them my beloved uncles and aunts and all my family and Jacob's family and all my acquaintances and friends. I've also received accurate information regarding the fate of my dear parents, information I began gathering with concern and trepidation from the moment I arrived here.

I found out that on Shabbat my parents decided to go to the deportation square along with all their neighbors. When one of the neighbors, a close acquaintance, wanted to give my mother the heart patient some poison—my mother would not accept it. She said she had resolved to go through this entire hell together with Dad, and maybe by sacrificing her own life she would save my life and the life of her granddaughter. I found out that they went to the square, and that Ula Nussbaum gave them water and apples several times, and they kept asking about us. When they parted, my mother said to Ula, "Best of health to you, I pray that you'll be spared."

On Sunday, they were sent with the others to the train station, but there were no more cars available, and they were forced to go back and sleep in the square. What hell! By Monday, they discovered that Rachel and I had been saved, and then my beloved mother said she would go to her death as if she were going out to a dance. That same day they were shipped off. I was told that both suffocated in the car. I believe it because Mother was so sick and had suffered so much.

Dear ones, your deaths will remain on my conscience, and never, ever in my life (assuming I will live, the chances of which are not great) will I know peace. I am to blame for all your terrible, tragic suffering. I only hope that you forgave me, especially since I managed to save your beloved little doll. I was unable to fulfill Mother's last request to be buried properly. To my chagrin, she was not the only one. Tens and hundreds of thousands were lost that way, murdered in Treblinka and in other, similar Treblinkas.

Only about Jacob I do not write. My hands are trembling, and my heart is threatening to burst when I think about him. I'm lucky not to know the circumstances of his murder, nor do I wish to know. A guy by the name of Solomon, who was saved after he managed to escape from one of the trains to Treblinka, is saying that the fate of the Jewish policemen was the cruelest of all. I can't listen to those stories, I'm better off never knowing.

If I want to live for something, it's to arrive at the moment of revenge, the moment when I could avenge the death of my husband, my parents, uncles, aunts, cousins and all the rest of my family.

But it's for naught. There's no chance.

Chapter 17
IRENA

A short while after Rachel had come to us, I found work in a small grocery store not far from our house. Rachel's presence in the house helped me come out of my depression and my crisis, and slowly but surely I returned to functioning almost fully. Even the nightmares were decreasing. During the day, my mother took care of Rachel and my nephew Stephan, who had become like brother and sister. Of all the family members, it was my brother Kazimir's toddler son who related most naturally to Rachel's presence. He was almost a year older than her, and the two of them spent most of the daytime together. Stephan loved making her laugh and teaching her to do things he himself had only recently learned to do.

I was usually quite late coming home from work, and Rachel, even though she was very tired at that hour, would sit up and wait for me on the big armchair in the living room, fighting the sleep that threatened to overcome her any minute. Tiny as she was, she was already stubborn beyond belief and usually managed to stay awake until I came home. As soon as she'd see me walking into the living room, she'd start screaming. When this first happened I got very scared, not knowing what made the little one cry so hard, but my mother immediately calmed me down. "She just wants you to pick her up," she told me as if reading Rachel's mind. I lifted her in my arms, hugged her strongly, and she put her little head on my shoulder and slowly calmed down from the crying. I rocked her gently and sang her calming lullabies in Polish and French until she fell asleep. I continued to hold her a very long time afterward. Each day I would wonder anew how long we would still be able to care for her. The situation at home didn't improve much even after my brother read Zippa's letter. Almost every day he asked me and my mother what we intended to do with the girl, and each time we had to come up with a different answer to satisfy him for the time being.

Many elements in our environment presented a substantial threat to Rachel's life, most prominently our neighbors. One heard many stories in town about Poles who hid Jews in their homes, were caught and promptly sentenced to death alongside the Jews they were hiding. It was also known in town that many Poles "specialized" in discovering hidden Jews and informing on them to the authorities. If they found Rachel with us, we'd all be executed together with her. In addition, the Gestapo headquarters was not far from our house, and the risk of a search and questioning constantly hovered over our heads.

Since we didn't know how much time we'd still have to shelter Rachel, we decided to offer her a normal life under a fake identity. Many Polish families had broken down as a result of the war: conscription to the military, men and women abducted into forced labor, the bombing of civilian populations. We figured, therefore, that Rachel could be a distant relative who came to stay with us for a while. Slowly, and not without great apprehension, my mother started taking her on short trips to the back yard.

"Who is the little one who joined your family?" our neighbor from another apartment facing the courtyard asked my mother one day. She was known on our block as a busybody.

"She's my cousin's daughter," my mother answered naturally. "He enlisted and his wife got pneumonia. She asked us to watch over her for a while."

"And how old is this little swarthy beauty?"

"She's one year old, look how well she's walking," said my mother with pride, elegantly ignoring the comment about Rachel's skin color.

"And what's the sweet one's name?" the curious woman pushed on.

My mother later told me that her heart skipped a beat as soon as the neighbor asked about Rachel's name. "What's her name?" such an innocent question, pregnant with so much danger. We hardly noticed the fact that we hardly ever called Rachel by her name. To us, she was always Lalechka, Dolly, just as her parents used to call her. We made up a cover story, tied all the ends together, and never gave a thought to this little item. "What's her name?" The question remained hanging in the air another millisecond until my mother uttered the first name that came to her: "Mariana."

"Good luck," said the neighbor.

The name we gave Rachel and her cover story didn't solve the main problem in our house. Six of us shared an apartment that included a small living room, a kitchen, two small bedrooms and an attic. Bathing was done in a tub in the kitchen, with a set schedule. And if that weren't enough, a few months after Rachel came to us, another family arrived, my mother's relatives, an older couple who used to live in a luxury home in a wealthy neighborhood in town. Because of the size of their house, and because it was modern and comfortable, the Gestapo confiscated it and the couple found themselves without a roof over their heads. My mother was her cousin and closest friend and just couldn't refuse her request to come live with us. We gave them the attic. Now the congestion at home had become intolerable, and the danger of Rachel's exposure was constantly hanging over our heads, to the point where keeping her at home with us was becoming impossible.

After weighing all the alternatives, my mother and I decided that the best thing for Rachel would be to enter her in an orphanage for at least some period of time. I telegraphed Sophia, asking her to come to Shedlitz. Zosha managed to take time off from her work and came to town for one day. We went together to meet Father Jan Szesevski, an acquaintance of Sophia's parents, to ask for his help. We knew that on Cmentarna Street there was an orphanage belonging to the convent near the great cathedral of Shedlitz. Szesevski was a well-known figure in the Shedlitz Christian community. After Zosha had told him Rachel's story without concealing any detail, the priest promised to speak to the orphanage headmistress that same day. Sophia asked him not to reveal to the headmistress Rachel's origins, and when we left the meeting she told me that, should we want to take her out of the orphanage later, it would be easier to do it if it weren't possible to prove her origins.

We arrived with Rachel at the orphanage on a cold and gray morning in early November 1942. It was a two-story stone building, long and rectangular, at the intersection of Sokolowska and Cmentarna. I thought to myself how fitting the name "Little Cemetery" is for this place. On one side of the orphanage stood the Jewish ghetto, which was now silent just like a cemetery, and on its other side, at the end of Cmentarna Street, stood the town's Jewish cemetery, the street's namesake, from which the occasional sounds of shooting and screaming still emanated. Not far from the orphanage stood the gothic cathedral of Shedlitz, with its tall steeples, miraculously spared from the German air raids.

In front of the orphanage stood a single, naked acacia tree, with a giant iron cross leaning on it in a way that made it look as if they were keeping each other from collapsing. The gray and gloomy building was surrounded by a tall, stone wall, and a rusty iron gate that creaked the moment I touched it, and led me into a dilapidated courtyard with only a few plain trees. An old seesaw hung on one of those trees.

I was received at the entrance by the headmistress, a nun with a delicate face and colorless eyes.

"Father Szesevski told us you were coming," she said, examining Rachel with her eyes.

"I beg you to take good care of this child. You are her last hope."

She didn't ask where Rachel had come from and who her parents were, but I guessed that she knew. Maybe she preferred not to be told, so she wouldn't have to lie in an interrogation. She led me into a structure that was buzzing with the crying of babies, some only a few weeks old and others toddlers of two and three years. Young nuns were running from one to the other, feeding them and treating them patiently.

"You must understand, Miss Zawadzka," the headmistress told me in a quiet voice, "the situation right now is not easy. Dozens of children have come to us since the beginning of the war, and we're trying to provide all of them with minimal conditions, but I want you to know we greatly lack food, medicine, and clothes, and we can't always give the children everything they need."

"Do whatever you can," I told her, "and may the good Lord be with you."

The headmistress called over one of the young nuns, who came and picked up Rachel in her arms. As the little one was being carried away, she gave me a questioning look from behind the nun's shoulder, but her attention was quickly diverted to the meager toys the nun showed her. Rachel immediately sat down to play. I stood and looked at her until the headmistress signaled for me to follow her. She accompanied me to the exit gate.

"Her name is Maiana," I told her before leaving.

She smiled and said nothing.

When I brought Rachel to the orphanage, she was thirteen months old, a happy and giggling baby with pink, chubby cheeks. A short while earlier she had begun to walk on her own and would reach anywhere around the house. Two weeks later, when I went to visit her at the orphanage she was very thin, her cheeks pale and sunken. There was no trace of the vivacious girl who had arrived here two weeks before. I found her sitting on a mattress on the floor, playing with cubes. When she saw me she stared at me with indifference and continued to play. I came closer and gave her a few cookies I brought with me. Rachel ate them with gusto, but she wouldn't smile, and she barely acknowledged my presence. I left there with apprehension, even though I knew the nuns were doing whatever they could for her.

In early December, I returned once more. Heavy snow was coming down outside, and when I entered the building, I was shocked to discover it wasn't heated. Rachel was lying down on a mat that was spread on the floor, her whole body trembling. She was under a thin blanket that barely covered her. When I took her in my arms, she was as light as a doll. "She's a little sick," one of the nuns told me, as Rachel started to cough heavily

"I'm taking her back," I told the headmistress, and she expressed no objection.

After I had taken Rachel out of the orphanage she had to be taken to a doctor urgently. The little one was coughing so hard that every time she coughed her entire tiny body was rattled and looked like it would come apart. Since we couldn't take her to a hospital, I passed a message to Dr. Grebski, Sophia's friend, who came to my house to check on Rachel. He diagnosed a serious case of pneumonia and prescribed medicine.

Rachel returned to live in my house, but our situation had not improved in the least. The congestion was still terrible, my brother was tense and volatile, the neighbors started asking questions again, and the Gestapo soldiers were forever out there, loitering on our block.

Chapter 18
ZIPPA

November 1942. The Cabalists' fears regarding the year 1942 have been fully realized. Most of the Jews of Shedlitz have been eliminated over the past few months. Every day we hear about the Aktion being conducted a second time here and a third there. Why haven't they touched us yet? This time we do not delude ourselves. We know we will not be spared.

For the time being, the situation is too tragic to comprehend or even describe. Every day representatives of the labor ministry and other authorities show up in the neighborhood, passing through the ghetto streets yelling: "People are needed for work!" For coal —25 men, for bricks—100 women, for Rekman—70 women, for Palgar—100 women, and so on. "People to work!"

The good ones, the pretty ones, the healthy ones, have all been shipped to Treblinka, and here, the rear guard made up of the sick and the weary—here they need people for work. Why don't we go to Treblinka? Why not stop the new train cars traveling to Treblinka? The reason is that they don't really need people—they need Jews to torture till the end, to squeeze the last bit of strength out of them before they die. It's no big wonder, then, that no one wants to show up for work, and every day begins with the sight of people in the neighborhood being captured for forced labor. Every guard or employee at the Rekman firm, for example, is allowed to beat you, curse you out. You're not a human being; you are a work ox for the Germans. Our life is concentrated on one thing: news! What have we heard at the train station? Are they transporting people in cars? Do the Aktions continue? Has anyone come back? What do they have to say?

I'm constantly reenacting the stories told by those people who had been at the square and managed somehow to be spared from deportation to Treblinka: there's a cart full of corpses, piles of human beings who until two days ago were living normally and hoping to live through the war. A body falls off—they pick it up and throw it back on, like a slaughtered animal! And why not? An animal today has more of a right to life than did those who were assembled in the square. Those were not so much people as flies on the wall. "Water," "Give us water," "Must drink," "I'm getting nauseous," "I'm hot"—those screams merged into one great cry of despair by innocent murder victims. The Jewish policeman who handed his mother an apple and some water was ordered to go sit in the crowd and his papers were taken away. Another escaped the bullet at the last minute, having attempted to get near his wife and children. Cries of "Sh'ma Israel" and "God of Israel" are heard from all over. People, what's the point of calling God? Rise up; you're sentenced to die either way! You all know what the meaning of Treblinka is! But that doesn't happen; instead the desire to live overcomes them. Only one man mutinied, knowing he has nothing left to lose and deciding to die without giving up his last shred of dignity. It was the History teacher, Mr. Taub, who walked among the Jews sitting in the square and asked them to guard their honor in their last hour. A Ukrainian who spotted him was quick to extract him from the crowd. A moment before he was shot, Mr. Traub managed to yell out, "Your time will come, vermin!"

At noontime, a special liquidation unit made up of Ukrainians and Gestapo soldiers arrived at the square. According to what I've been told, they exchanged words with the man in charge of the place. They wanted to send everyone at the square to immediate elimination while the supervisor wanted to keep in the ghetto a small number of young people for work. A few hours later an order came down for all the men ages 15 to 40 to form a line, as they were going to pick who among them would be kept for labor. All the men got up and started to run toward the line, stepping over one another. Each one of those poor wretches was hoping he might be chosen for work and be spared. I can understand it, but at the same time I can't begin to comprehend.

The Gestapo soldiers were finally able to set up the line with relentless blows. The chief Gestapo officer walked among the men, pointing out with his baton who would live and who would die. Those he was picking he would first question about their trade and then examine their hands to make sure he made the right choice.

Whoever had in his possession a document certifying him as a member of the Judenrat was immediately sent to the left, to die. Those picked to die were beaten ceaselessly on their way to the cemetery.

That evening the men of the Shedlitz fire department arrived at the square and sprinkled water on the exhausted and dehydrated crowd while the Gestapo soldiers were sitting on the ruins of the nearby synagogue, drinking beer. Now and then the soldiers would shoot into the crowd while eating and drinking. The Jewish policemen passed through, picking up the bodies of the murdered and bringing them to the cemetery, where they themselves were made to stand before open graves and were shot by German soldiers. One of them managed to survive and reached the Smaller Ghetto. He said that while they were being shot, the women were yelling, crying, and some even tried to resist their death sentence, although they knew full well they didn't stand a chance of leaving there alive. The men stood quietly and awaited their death.

November 6, 1942. An official announcement appears in the newspaper, regarding the creation of new residential neighborhoods for Jews in a few towns in the Warsaw and Lublin regions. Shedlitz is counted among them. The mood is improving, we don't believe they'll let us live, but maybe our sentence would be delayed. A day or two passes by in relative tranquility, but that, too, is only temporary. On Sunday, rumors have spread that all the Jews of Lukow, which was also on the list at the time, were taken to the squares. First we didn't believe it, but later we understood the rumors were right. What, then, was the meaning of the announcement in the paper? We know nothing, understand nothing, except for this: we've been sentenced to a terrible, tragic death, for no rhyme or reason, and all that's left is to await our execution.

Chapter 19
SOPHIA

I was busy creating a new school when the telegram from my father arrived, asking me to come to Shedlitz urgently to meet him.

Based on the information that reached us from underground activists in the field, Katja and I decided this time to wander off a bit further north, because the area where we were staying, including the village of Zakrzówek, was included in the German plan to establish a German state inside Poland. They began evacuating entire villages, planning to replace them with German citizens who would settle down and work the lands of the displaced farmers. The Jews of the area had been taken to the Belzec camp, and the Poles were sent to transition camps or to labor camps in Germany. There were also many Ukrainians living in the area who were collaborating with the Germans and the situation was turning very dangerous for us. We succeeded in finding a suitable place in a small village not far from Zambrów, north of Shedlitz, where we began to establish the new school.

Over the past few years I've been seeing my parents only infrequently, I was busy with the schools issues and only once or twice a year did I arrive in Shedlitz to visit them and my older sister who was working in a factory out of town. The last time I had seen my family was in August when the Nazis began the liquidation of the Jewish ghetto, and Zippa managed to escape along with her Rachel. When Zippa decided to go back into the ghetto, I knew she was writing her own death sentence, but I also knew that her fate outside the ghetto was also murky. What finally decided it was her endless worry about her parents and her great love for Jacob. Rachel-Mariana already was in good hands, with Irena and Sabina Zawadzka, and Zippa, tormented by guilty feelings for having survived, knew she could never forgive herself if she didn't return to try and find her parents and husband. I didn't know what happened to her since her return to the Smaller Ghetto. The underground people had a hard time getting information about it at that time.

I arrived in Shedlitz shortly before Christmas. The town was under a heavy blanket of snow, and I recalled with an ache my childhood when I would wait each year for the holiday season. How I loved walking through the streets wrapped in a warm overcoat, my feet tucked in new, fur lined boots, and my hands inside caressing leather gloves. Bright lights sparkled in the windows and the people in the streets were rushing to stores that were laden with goods, to buy gifts for their loved ones. The Shedlitz I entered on December of 1942 was a beaten and bruised town, the residents who remained there after the Nazi deportations and murders were hungry and exhausted, no one was thinking about decorations for the holiday tree. The stores offered only meager goods, and most of the homes were dark and abandoned.

When I passed by what once had been a vivacious Jewish quarter, and until recently the Jewish ghetto, I began to better comprehend what had taken place in town over the last few months. Entire streets lay in ruins; stone houses became piles of rubble, wood houses were charred and smoking, there wasn't a living soul around. The snow that covered the entire ghetto area made it appear even more devastated and desolate than it had been when I surveyed it with Hanka in August, but at least now you couldn't smell the ghastly odor that emanated from the place in August.

I found my father in his little pharmacy, two blocks away from our house. When he saw me at the entrance, his gray eyes lit up, and he extended both his hands to embrace me. My father was not the kind of man who normally expressed his affection with such gestures, not even to his daughters or his wife, which is why I was taken aback by his behavior. My father was a very educated man who achieved all he had with his own two hands. In addition to being a Doctor of Pharmacy with a PharmD degree from the school of medicine in Poznan, he also earned titles in Philosophy and History. Most of his time was devoted to his work, which he viewed as almost a religious vocation.

He turned over the sign hanging on the inside of the front door, a rare occurrence, then led me into his small lab in the back room, where he conducted chemical experiments and developed medicines he was never able to mass market. We sat down by a table with test tubes and glass jars full of various substances.

"How are you?" he inquired as if we had only seen each other a week ago.

"Father you told me to come urgently, what's going on?"

"You were always straight and to the point," he said and smiled, but the smile vanished quickly, and his face darkened. He removed his small, metal-framed spectacles and rubbed his eyes. He hesitated another few, long seconds as if looking for lost words.

"It's ok, Father, I'll wait until you're ready to tell me." I felt he needed my encouragement.

He returned his spectacles to the bridge of his nose and trained his gaze on me.

"In late November the Nazis conducted several more Aktions in the Smaller Ghetto," he told me, almost in a whisper.

I felt my heart sinking. When Zippa returned to the ghetto, it was after the mass deportation to Treblinka. I had been hoping that perhaps the worst was already behind us, and the remaining

Jews might be transported elsewhere. I tried to read in my father's face what he was about to tell me.

"One morning, a Polish guy with a special entry permit for the ghetto shows up here. He used to get into the Smaller Ghetto every day, to clean up and spread pesticides for the Germans. He worked for the town Health Department, Hanka knew him and asked him to look for Zippa. He came to me a few days before they began to eliminate the smaller ghetto and to move all the surviving Jews to 'Gansza Barki.'"

"Where?" I asked.

"To 'Gansza Barki,' it's a camp outside Shedlitz, where they assembled all the Jews who survived the Smaller Ghetto."

"And what did they do with them?" I asked.

"They sent them by train to Treblinka."

"Dad, Zippa could have hidden someplace, she could have escaped, there are bands of partisans in the woods…" I had the feeling that I already knew what my dad was about to tell me, since I couldn't imagine a scenario with Zippa escaping from the Smaller Ghetto and surviving, but I still was not willing to believe it. He nodded his head slowly and wiped his foggy lenses.

"What did that Polish guy who came to you want?"

"He brought me a letter from Zippa," said my dad. He got up slowly from his chair, opened a desk drawer, took out a wrinkled piece of paper torn out of a notebook and handed it to me with trembling hands.

Dear Mr. O,

For the past few months I've been staying in the Smaller Ghetto along with a few hundred miserable and hopeless Jews like myself. We're subject to daily persecution, abuse and torture by the Nazis and their collaborators. Every morning representatives of different businesses in and out of town arrive here to kidnap people for forced labor. Only a few remain alive in those "work" places, due to the horrible conditions. The

Ukrainians, the Polish cops, the gendarmes, and, above all, the Nazis—combine their efforts to drive the few wretched Jews who still remain here through the seven sections of hell. It is my feeling that we've now arrived beyond the final section.

All of the above is added to the shocking filth, the famine (food smuggling has been out of the question for a long time), the approaching winter frost and the many diseases which are felling their victims daily.

The only reason I've struggled so long to stay alive through this hellfire was the notion that my daughter made her way out of hell, and if I survive I would see her again. The knowledge that my beautiful little girl is in good hands and there was still a spark of hope that I could hug her once more, has kept me among the living even as I was praying for an end. In recent days we've found out that the Aktions are back in many towns around Shedlitz, and there is solid information that even if it is delayed for some reason, sooner or later the death sentence will reach us here as well.

Dear Sir, I beg of you to help me avoid the humiliation and suffering of abandoning my life in the hands of the murderers. I know that it is in your power to enable me to end my own life with a last shred of dignity. Please do me this final favor by handing Mr. P. the necessary substance for me.

Gratefully.

I breathed deeply and then heard myself asking my father: "Did you give it to him?" I wasn't sure at that moment which response I wanted to hear. My father didn't answer, but his eyes welled up with tears and his hands, still holding the wrinkled note, were trembling.

After I left the pharmacy, I was strolling restlessly through the deserted streets. I knew where I had to go, but I had no idea how I could relate to Irena what my father had just told me, I wasn't sure that delicate, fragile Irena would be able to deal with the news. I decided to see Hanka and Jadzia first, expecting them to be better able to take the news. Both of them reacted with tears, although they were not surprised. Hanka told me that in her department in City Hall people knew precisely what went on during the liquidation of the ghetto, and anyone with the slightest interest could have guessed the fate of the Jewish residents. Poor Jadzia, who had become very attached to Zippa, especially since she had returned from Lvov, couldn't hide her pain and comforting her was difficult. We decided to spare Irena the harsh news for now.

When I reached the Zawadzky home that evening, even before setting foot past the front door, I was determined to take Rachel with me. When I saw the conditions in Irena's home, my resolve became even stronger. The congestion inside the Zawadzky home was intolerable. Sabina, Irena and Rachel slept together in the small bedroom, Kazimir, his wife and his son slept in the other room, and a couple of Sabina's friends cohabitated up in the attic. The living room doubled as a dining room and the kitchen as a washroom, and everywhere there were crates and packages. Nevertheless, the place was clean and well organized. Sabina Zawadzka was not about to let the war change her well-established routines.

Irena practically fell into my arms when I came inside, as if she'd been waiting for me by the door. Her pale cheeks at once became awash in tears, and after she had calmed down a bit she called Rachel over and started to tell me about her in endless bursts of details one expects from a mother talking about her daughter. Besides reports about the things Rachel can do and what she likes to eat, she sneaked in a few harsh notes regarding her brother Kazimir whose objection to Rachel's presence was growing stronger with every passing day, complete with notes on their life in the crammed house, and above all, the threat of death which hovered over their home day and night. Irena was so agitated and excited, she didn't even think to ask about Zippa. Finally, I expressed my wish to take Rachel with me, explaining that in the village where I lived now no one knew me, and I could provide a better life for Rachel.

Katja almost passed out when she saw me arriving in school with a girl in my arms. "Don't worry," I told her with exaggerated confidence, "it'll be fine." But I wasn't all that certain. We did give Rachel a new name and cover story and made sure to destroy all the telltale ghetto insignia, but there was still one thing I had to get for her so she could pass through the numerous police and Gestapo checkpoints. The cover story was not enough; I had to procure for her a certificate of baptism. Without such a document, I knew, her chances of survival were dim.

The next morning I drove to the Zambrów church and asked to see the priest. "He'll only be in tomorrow," I was told by a young apprenticing priest who was cleaning the place. "Come back at noon." I got the feeling that someone was testing my patience, but I wasn't about to let it sway me.

The Zambrów priest was affectionate and sweet when I approached him the next day and asked to have a word. Despite his snow white hair, I guessed he was only about fifty. His facial skin was light, almost translucent. He reminded me of my uncle from Krakow, whom I hadn't seen since the beginning of the war. We sat down on a wooden bench in the front pews. I was hoping he wouldn't ask me when was my last visit to Church, since I hadn't had the time in the last few years and I didn't want to lie to him.

"Father," I addressed him, "a couple of friends of mine baptized their daughter about a year ago and I wish to send them a greeting card for her birthday, but I can't recall the child's name, and I want the card to be a surprise. Since I have no one to ask, I was hoping to look into your baptismal records and find the child's name by her date of birth and her parents' information." I was speaking fast, hardly pausing to breathe between sentences so as not to permit the kind priest to ask questions and poke holes in my story. I was hoping that I wasn't revealing anything with my rapid speech and that there were no other exterior indications of the storm raging inside me. Everything rested on my getting that priest to trust me.

"I'll go get the baptismal book," he said and walked over to his office, in the rear of the church. He came back a minute later carrying a large book in a brown leather jacket. He sat down next to me and started to leaf through the book.

"What date was the little one baptized?" he asked, and for an instant I wished he were a little less kind.

"You must be very busy," I said carefully, "I can look by myself, who knows how long this will take…"

"As you wish. I'll be in my office if you need me."

I opened the book and started going through the names registered in September and October of 1941. Rachel was born on October 1, and I needed the name of a girl who was born around the same day. When I visited Irena they were calling the child Mariana, and I didn't want to confuse her with yet another name, so I was looking for a girl with the same exact name. The names ran past my eyes: Czeslawa, Martina, Zuzana, Katarina. I had reached the end of October when I suddenly saw the name I needed: Mariana Timinska, daughter of Nadja and Radoslaw Timinska, born in the village of Galbucz on October 30, 1941. I memorized the child's details again and again; I couldn't skip any bit.

I closed the book and went over to the priest's office.

"Unfortunately I didn't find what I was looking for," I said, hoping not to sound too cheerful.

"I'm so sorry, my child. Is there anything else I can help you with?"

"It's all right; I'll manage. Thank you."

I waited a few days. Meanwhile we arranged for Rachel a place to sleep, and I told the teachers at school that she was the illegitimate daughter of my friend from university who had been sent to forced labor in Germany. I only told Katja the truth. At first she was very worried and said I was taking too big a risk, but I managed to persuade her to agree, after promising to arrange an authentic baptismal certificate for the girl. I was hoping with all my heart that Katja wasn't sensing just how uncertain I was about my prospects.

A few days after my visit to the church of Zambrów, I called in one of the older boys who attended our school. He was a kind and quiet lad, not the type that's too curious about life around him, and most important, not the type who asks too many needless questions. I told him that my good friend Nadja Timinska lived in a remote village with her daughter. Nadja's husband was sent to the war, and she couldn't leave the house to travel all the way to Zambrów. She asked me to get for her a copy of her daughter's certificate of baptism after a fire destroyed all her documents. I sent the boy to the priest with all the necessary information, but not before I made sure that he memorized very well all the details regarding the child and her parents.

That whole day I was extremely tense and had a hard time concentrating on the lessons I was giving. Every minute I would stare at the window to see if the boy had returned with the certificate, but the hours went by, and he was not back. Late in the evening, after putting Rachel to bed, I walked exhausted into the small room that served as my office. On the desk, I found a brown envelope that contained Mariana Timinska's certificate of baptism.

With the certificate in hand, I had no problem issuing for Rachel a "kosher" Polish birth certificate. In honor of Mariana's "baptism," I bought her a medallion with an icon of the holy mother and hung it around her neck. I asked myself what Zippa would have said had she seen her like that, but I found comfort in the fact that we succeeded in making Rachel Polish even without an actual church baptism.

Rachel was fifteen months old at the time and had only just recovered from the serious pneumonia she incurred at the Shedlitz orphanage. Over the previous four months she had been transplanted too many times, and it was starting to show. It was late at night when I took her from Irena's house, and she was deep in sleep, but when she woke up in the new place she started to scream so hard it took her breath away. Her face turned blue from crying so loudly, and she finally calmed down only after I picked her up in my arms and started to sing to her a Polish lullaby I remembered from my childhood.

One of the school girls asked to take care of Rachel and of Janek, Katja's boy, who just turned three. The girl was eighteen and had just finished her studies, but since she didn't have anything else to do anyway, she asked to stay and help around the school. She helped with the cooking and cleaning and occasionally would go into a classroom to help the younger students with their work. Her parents had five other children so that in addition to her high motivation she also had a great deal of experience caring for children.

Janek and Rachel played together the whole day, ate together, and at night slept next to each other on the mattresses we spread out for them in the guest room. The flat Katja and I were sharing at the time had only one small bedroom and a tiny guest room. It didn't have a kitchen, and we ate in the school dining area, together with our students.

As with all siblings, Rachel and Janek experienced jealousy and anger along with their great love for each other. Janek was used to being an only child; he grew up in a home in Warsaw with his mother and his father's parents who treated him like a little prince. Until Rachel showed up, he was our only child as well, and all the teachers and students used to play with him and spoil him. When Rachel arrived, he was very angry that she was stealing his exclusive position, and would hit and bother her quite often. But the little one was not about to give in, and when he came to sit in my lap, she would push him off and wouldn't let him climb on me.

Rachel-Mariana, or Marisha as most of us called her, was turning into a healthy girl with a great appetite. She ate almost everything I prepared for her, but most of all she loved sweets. Except sweet couldn't be gotten back then, and sugar was rationed. What we did have in the village were fresh eggs, and one day I decided to make her a delicacy that I loved eating when I was little. I broke the egg white into a bowl and beat it to a froth with a bit of sugar. In a separate bowl, I placed the egg yolk, which I also mixed with a little sugar and added to the foamy white. I let her taste it. I was sure she would refuse to eat the frothy egg, but to my surprise she devoured it and when she was finished asked for more. "It's called Gogle-mogle," I told her. The name made her laugh, and each time I would tell her, "Marisha, your Gogle-mogle is ready," she'd laugh and come running to eat.

Mariana was, for the most part, a strong and healthy girl, but, nevertheless, near the end of 1943 she became very sick and complained of an aching throat. Since she had a birth certificate, I took a chance and brought her to a doctor in Zambrów. I figured, even if they ask me questions, I had a cover story and the child had legal papers. I drove her to a female doctor that one of the teachers at school recommended. The doctor, a sweet woman in her early fifties, checked Mariana and prescribed her some medicine. She didn't ask me any questions about her, except how old she was and what was her name. Near the end of the visit, when I was about to leave, she looked at the girl and told me, "These children are very strong, you'll have an easy time raising her." I didn't answer. What could I say?

At the beginning of 1944, a young woman came looking for work in our school. Even before I had a chance to ask, she produced papers testifying to her being a Christian Pole. By her looks and accent, it was hard to tell if she was, indeed, Christian, or a Jew. I hired her.

She worked diligently, cleaned, organized, and now and then helped with the cooking. But she didn't speak much with the rest of the workers and spent what little free time she had sitting quietly in the school yard. I arranged lodgings for her in the school kitchen, the only area where one could sleep. Very early on I observed that she was most intrigued by Mariana, smiling at her and speaking softly whenever the child would approach her. One day I saw her standing at the corner of the yard, staring at Mariana who was playing with Janek. Her eyes didn't budge from the girl.

The woman doctor who recognized Rachel's origins, the new employee who probably also guessed that Rachel was Jewish—those two incidents, in addition to the fact that we had been in that one place for over a year, led me to realize that it was time once more to move to a new place.

Chapter 20
IRENA

At the end of July 1944, the Red Army was beginning to liberate the eastern part of Poland, between the Bug and Wisla Rivers, and by the beginning of August its forces reached Shedlitz as well. The arrival of the Soviet soldiers in town was received with joy and great relief, the town dwellers breathed easy again at the sight of Nazi soldiers evacuating from the town they had occupied five years ago—but not before those soldiers burned and destroyed numerous buildings, particularly factories in and out of town. We waited impatiently the start of a new era and meanwhile residents began to clean, rehabilitate and build anew everything that had been ruined during the war years.

But the happiness at the German defeat did not last long, since a short while after their arrival the Soviet soldiers also began to terrorize the town residents. Most of the houses in our neighborhood, our own among them, were confiscated by the Soviets shortly after their arrival. Because the former Gestapo headquarters, which the Soviets overtook immediately, was in our neighborhood, and because most of the neighborhood homes remained in relatively good shape, the Novo-Shedlitze quarter became a Soviet enclave and we, too, were forced to clear out of our home and move in with my aunt in her house in the country.

In the two years since I had taken Mariana out of the orphanage, she stayed most of the time with Sophia. She would come to us for the summer, when Sophia was on vacation from school, or when Sophia was forced to leave the school where she was staying at the time and go look for a new place. During one of her visits near the end of the war, when we were already living in my aunt and uncle's village house, Sophia requested that I follow her to a quiet place because she wanted to tell me something. We went to my uncle's barn and there, sitting on a bale of hay, she suddenly burst into tears. I didn't know how to respond, I was so taken aback. I couldn't recall when, if ever, I had seen her cry like that before. I never saw her cry when we were children in school together, nor when the war had broken, nor when we were sitting with Zippa in the attic in August of 1942, knowing that we might never see her again. Usually, it was I who cried on every occasion, and the sight of the stalwart Zosha weeping bitterly was hard to take, precisely because it was so rare. I hugged her trembling shoulders, the same way she used to do mine when I cried, and she grasped my hand firmly as if to thank me for the gesture, and then took out of her bag a letter and asked me to read it. Even before I was done reading, she said in a broken voice, "We didn't save Zippa."

"We saved Mariana," I told her almost in a whisper. My eyes continued to scan the final words Zippa wrote Mr. Olszakowsky. "I'm sure this would have made Zippa happy." Still, after Zosha showed me the letter from Zippa to Zosha's father, sent days or hours before her death, I began to experience once more the nightmares, which were almost gone lately. The thoughts about Zippa's last days in the ghetto were so inconceivable, and still I found myself imagining time and again what happened there. True, there were rumors circulating in town about the annihilation of most of the Jewish residents, and we also witnessed the cries that came out of the ghetto in August of 1942, but I had never before run into such tangible testimony to those events like Zippa's letter. I tried to imagine how Zippa felt after discovering the loss of her family, her parents, her husband, and when she realized she would never see her little daughter again. But those fantasies were threatening to drive me insane, so much so that Mr. Olszakowsky was called immediately to help me.

Following the end of German occupation, Sophia returned to work for the organization that employed her before the war, which meant she had to travel frequently across the country. Since Mariana's life was no longer in immediate danger, we decided that she come live with us, in my aunt and uncle's house in the country.

The skinny and sickly baby I removed from the orphanage in the winter of 1942 had turned into an active and mentally sharp toddler, but also exceptionally stubborn and opinionated. When she didn't get what she wanted she would go to the corner where she slept, sit down on the mattress and frown. She didn't cry, didn't yell, only sat and waited until we gave in. Her dark and clever eyes always appeared to be concealing some secret, and much of the time her mouth was twisted in a kind of bitter smile. She hardly laughed or horsed around. But despite her almost rebellious stubbornness, Mariana managed to mesh with my family and especially captured the heart of my aunt Felicia, who treated her like her own granddaughter. Even my brother slowly abandoned his resistance to her presence.

The three-year-old Mariana loved life in the village, the fields and the open spaces, the animals strolling everywhere and the freedom she was given to play outside. Wherever she went, she took along Stephan, my nephew, an unrivaled rascal. Their deep love-hate relationship stretched over long hours of games and walks together, but also fights that often ended in tears, usually Stephan's. When we lived in the village, I worked for a local miller who was on friendly terms with my aunt and uncle. My mother and my aunt Felicia looked after Mariana and Stephan, who became completely independent and often disappeared for long hours. When they wouldn't come home in the evening, my mother and I were forced to go looking for them throughout the village. Usually, we'd find them playing with the cows or sheep out in the fields.

Every once in a while Sophia would visit or take Mariana with her for a few days. When Mariana would notice Sophia, she dropped everything and ran at her crying, "Mama, Mama." The child would attach herself to Sophia for the longest time, refusing to let her move unless Sophia picked her up in her arms. Their separation was turning more and more difficult until Sophia was forced to leave only after Mariana had fallen asleep. Of all the different women who took care of Mariana during her first years, it was Sophia who merited the title of Mother. I remained forever "auntie," which didn't stop me from treating the child as my own. I loved her with all my heart, and every time I'd stare into her big, black eyes, I remembered the black-eyed girl who arrived at elementary school on May 1 Street 23 years ago, and whose suffering later in life was too great for me to even ponder.

By the beginning of 1945, the Red Army had liberated all of occupied Poland, and in early May we heard on the radio about Hitler's death and the surrender of Germany. Since the Red Army units remained in Shedlitz and continued to occupy many homes, including our own, we stayed with our aunt and uncle well after the war had really ended.

One bright morning in the beginning of July 1945, I suddenly noticed a figure approaching our courtyard gate. The children were busy playing cheerfully with Poppy, our dog while I was hanging the clean laundry on a long line stretched between two birches. My mother and aunt were inside the house, and my brother and his wife were at work. The figure came closer to the house, with heavy, hesitating steps. It turned out to be an elderly man, his back stooped, his long hair thin and gray, and his clothes hanging loosely on his thin and bent body. On his back, he carried a tattered duffel bag, and on his head he wore an officer's hat. He was walking slowly, leaning on a wooden cane. Only when he came really close and entered through the gate did I recognize Uncle Valente.

When he went to war, six years ago, Uncle Valente was a tall and handsome sixty-year-old man. His face was round, and he had a brave and determined look in his eyes. His well-cropped haircut and broad, dark mustache made him look like a general. A retired physician, he was recalled to the Army following the start of the war. But the man who walked through the gate to our courtyard in July 1945, looked nothing like my uncle who re-enlisted in 1939. I ran toward him and hugged his neck, and he almost collapsed under my weight. The first thing I noticed were his dull and tired eyes, so different from his vivacious eyes before the war. Then I saw the deep wrinkles carved in his face. When the children arrived squealing in joy they hugged his legs, even though they had no idea who was this stranger and what he was doing in our yard. When they heard the noise, my aunt and my mother came out of the house, and when my aunt recognized the man who was surrounded by the members of her family, her legs gave in and she passed out on the gravel in front of the house.

My uncle returned from captivity with a broken body and soul, a victim of sclerosis. My aunt took care of him day and night until he recovered. He quickly became the children's favorite. He spoke to them like grownups and knew how to calm and cajole them, as if he raised them from infancy. He accepted Mariana like his own grandchild and gave her love gently and calmly. When Stephan was not around, the girl would sit on his knees, and he would tell her long stories made up on the spur of the moment.

One day, a few weeks after his return from captivity, he told me, "Irena, I admire very much what you've done for the child and the risks that you took."

"I would do it again if I had to," I told him with complete conviction. I couldn't imagine my life without that mischievous girl.

When the war was over, I was thirty and yet to taste the love of a man. Having gone all my life to girls' schools, I hardly dared staring straight into the eyes of the boys I would usually meet in dances or at the Church youth movement. I felt homely and ugly compared to all the other girls who looked so beautiful to me, and so self-assured.

Zippa used to always tell me I had the most beautiful nose she'd ever seen, but I never actually considered my nose or any other part of my body to be pretty. I was shy and frightened, and when I grew up, I realized that those feelings were only becoming stronger. When I was in university my fellow students tried to talk me into going out dancing with them, but on those few occasions when I succumbed to their pressure I found myself standing on the sideline, scared as a trapped rabbit, waiting impatiently for the party to be over. When one of the guys would approach me and ask for a dance, I would mumble something and flee to a different corner.

When I arrived in Paris and met new friends, I was hoping that maybe there, far away from familiar people and places, I would be able to become friends with a guy and maybe even fall in love. That's when I met Rafael Alfonso Morales, a Spanish lector who fled from the Spanish war and settled down in Paris. He was so handsome and smart that I didn't delude myself even for a minute that he would pay any attention to me. And, indeed, he hardly knew I existed, but I continued to admire him secretly, gulping down every word he uttered in class, and dreaming about him day and night. The Spanish female students in my class were gossiping that his lover, a famous flamenco dancer, was executed during the civil war. After her death, he vowed never to fall in love again. When I heard Rafael's story, I, too, vowed never to fall for another man. I knew I would never meet anyone as handsome and as smart as he, and no one else could ever be the subject of those addictive feelings I harbored for him.

Now I felt as though Mariana was the child I could never have had. I spent long hours with her every day, playing games, reading her stories, teaching her new words, and brushing her black, full hair. She loved to show off her intelligence and quick grasp, and most of all she loved finishing the words in the stories I read her. Sometimes she only had to hear a story once or twice to complete many of the words in it. Before bedtime, she loved listening to fairy tales, and each night she asked for a different tale, but of all of them she loved the most the story of Jahsz and Maugusza, Hansel and Gretel.

"Once upon a time there were two children. The boy was named…"

"Jahsz," she would call out in glee.

"And the girl was called…"

"Maugussa," she would sweetly mispronounce the name.

"Jahsz and Maugusza lived with their parents in a wood cabin…"

Most of the time she would be asleep before I reached the end of the story. She was too young to understand the deeper meanings of that particular fairy tale, and I wondered if in the future she might start asking me about her own parents. At those moments, I would remember Zippa with such longing, the beautiful, innocent girl who married her dream knight, and both of them died so tragically. Sometimes those nightmares became so frequent, I had to get additional pills from Mr. Olszakowsky.

Mariana was not interested and didn't ask questions about her family. She was satisfied with the knowledge that she had Mamma Sophia, Grandma Sabina, Aunt Irena, and Aunts Christina and Felicia, who, since the return of Uncle Valente, were spending less and less time with the little girl. Sophia and I decided to push off the moment of truth and let Mariana enjoy some peace in her childhood years. She had been through enough agitation in her life, and the miserable truth about her beloved family could wait for quieter days after the war was completely over, and the child grew older and stronger. At least, that's what we decided at the time.

Once Uncle Valente was feeling a little better and was so inclined, he would play with the kids, making them laugh at his impersonations and different voices. They loved to stare at him while he was preparing a new face, clearing his throat before making a new voice. He loved to imitate animals, different village people, and sometimes even the thunder and the rain. But the act Mariana and Stephan loved the most was, without fail, when Uncle Valente picked up his pipe, emptied out the tobacco, inserted the bowl in his mouth and gave out a loud shriek. "Elephant, elephant," the two of them would yell out and roll on the floor laughing.

Since coming back from captivity, I would often find my uncle sitting for long hours on the house porch, bluish smoke rising from his pipe and his eyes stuck on some invisible point on the horizon.

One rainy, winter Sunday, a few months after he had come home, I dared inquire about his imprisonment in Germany. The whole family was in church, but I stayed with him because he wasn't feeling good that day. Since his return, my uncle refused to accompany us to church.

"Irotchka," he answered in his quiet voice, "why do you need to know what and how it was? Why is it so important? The main thing is that I managed to come back."

"Is it true that you were tortured?" I asked him. I had found this unintentionally from my brother. I wish I hadn't.

He remained silent for a few, long seconds, then emptied the tobacco from his pipe, filled the bowl with a fresh load, lit it up with much pumping and inhaled deeply. "It wasn't a church summer camp, that's for sure," he finally answered. His gaze floated in space. "More than that, I beg of you, please don't ask me."

Chapter 21
SOPHIA

The last year of the war was characterized by our adjustment to the annoying sight of Red Army soldiers taking over Poland, in place of the Nazi soldiers. That year I went back to work for the PoEm corporation, which I had left when the war broke out, and now I was traveling all across the country. Based on Irena's reports and my own impressions during my visits to the Zawadzky family, it appeared that Mariana was easily accepting the transition to their household. She was familiar with village life from her years with me in the schools I used to manage, and at any rate she was so used to moving from place to place that it became part of her life.

In the course of my work, I was exposed to the great horrors that took place in Poland in recent years. The Nazi occupation left behind ruin and destruction, and in many cases we were forced to build factories, plants and corporations literally from scratch. Manpower was way down in our organization and work was only increasing. The communist government that took over Poland passed many new laws that only intensified the depressed atmosphere everywhere. It was hard to believe that the Communist Party, which until recently was outside the law, had now become such a routine part of life.

My visits to the Zawadzky home throughout that year were usually short and unsatisfying, and parting with Mariana was getting more and more difficult for both of us. My distance from her was causing me surprisingly severe frustration and longing. Each day not spent with her was a lost day as far as I was concerned, a day when I missed out on new words she pronounced, new tricks she learned, her rolling laughter, and her big, brown eyes. After a whole year during which I visited hundreds, if not thousands, of factories, farms, plants, and offices, all in dire need of rehabilitation, I decided to return to Shedlitz.

When I arrived in Shedlitz in the summer of 1945 and the clouds of war above were slowly dissipating, I finally comprehended the magnitude of the tragedy that befell my town. Shedlitz was still in ruins, and its residents were emotionally broken. In addition to the great destruction wrought on so many houses in town, Shedlitz lost more than half its population. The 15 thousand strong Jewish community had been erased. Its few remnants were mostly residents who fled to Russia at the start of the war and managed to survive there in unimaginable ways, and who were now beginning to come back to town, confronting much hostility and abuse on the part of their Polish neighbors. In a few cases, this abuse ended in murder. And so, Jews returning from Russia, as well as those few who survived the death camps and assumed naively that the worst was behind them, ran into Polish citizens in their homeland, whose hatred and revenge fantasies were still burning as before. Consequently, the great majority of Jewish survivors who returned to Shedlitz after the war left town shortly thereafter and started wandering between relocation camps all across Europe, en route to Palestine or other countries. The few who lingered ended up leaving later, realizing they could no longer live in peace in their hometown.

Hanka was still working for the Shedlitz board of health, as she had been doing throughout the war years. Her husband returned from the battlefield, and a few weeks later she became pregnant. Since she did not plan to continue working full-time after giving birth, she managed to arrange for me to take her place. Now, in the course of my work for the City, I was trying to find out exactly what had been the fate of the Jewish residents of Shedlitz, and especially the circumstances of the deaths of Aaron and Josepha Jablon, and Jacob Zonshein, but I ran into a brick wall. To my great astonishment, no one would talk to me on the subject or help me in any other way, as if they were all trying to return to a routine, as if nothing had transpired here in the last six years. Entire rooms in the town hall building remained sealed and only a few people, all Communist Party officials, had access to them. I was sorry that none of my underground comrades had squeezed their way into the party's higher echelon, but I knew the chances of that were miniscule. My idealistic colleagues went in completely different directions. Still, what limited information I did obtain was incomprehensible.

Shortly after my return, Mariana was once again living with me in my parents' home. In the summer of 1945, the Zawadzky family moved out of their relatives' village home and back to their home in the Novo-Shedlitza neighborhood. Irena's brother and his wife had no intention of leaving that house and finding their own home, and as much as I tried, I was unable to forgive Kazimir for his treatment of Mariana during the war. Even when she was in mortal danger, he refused time and again to accept her into their home.

Things at home were different now, we no longer needed to provide explanations to curious neighbors or worry about visits by the Gestapo. The minute the Germans left town, the residents lost interest in their neighbors' affairs and tried mostly to get back to their own routines. Mariana received her own bedroom and was delighted with the new set of grandparents added to her life. My mother and father were happy with their new "granddaughter" and showed her off as if she really was theirs. I signed up Mariana at a kindergarten that opened up after the war really close to my parents' house, and at noon my mother would pick her up from there and be with her until I came back from work. Every evening Irena would come over to spend time with Mariana. Hanka and Jadzia also tried to visit frequently. Hanka would usually arrive with her two sons, the elder almost eleven and the younger about six. Both boys were not that interested in Mariana, even after being told a new baby would be joining their own family soon, but she was crazy about them, constantly trying to get their attention and doing her best to make them laugh. Jadzia went back to working with her father at the fabric store that had been closed for three years. By the end of 1942 her father was captured by the Gestapo, who accused him of helping Jews. He was jailed in a camp outside Shedlitz and released shortly thereafter, but not before his store was confiscated, and he was forbidden to open another. During the war years, while his store was closed, Mr. Valczek did not keep still, and with Jadzia's assistance continued his business, mainly on the black market and in all kinds of shady deals. After the Germans left Shedlitz, Radek Valczek was able to re-purchase his store but was forced to renovate it almost from top to bottom. Jadzia, her parents' only child, continued to work alongside her dad. When she told me after the war about the different deals she put together while working for her father, I told her it was a shame she hadn't put her skills to use for the underground. My comment angered her, and she refused to speak to me for a long time, and it took Irena's and Hanka's intervention to make us talk to each other again. I knew Jadzia and her father helped many Jews, including Zippa, while it could still be done, but I just couldn't accept the fact that, most likely, some of their dealings were with the Germans, too.

On October 1, 1945, we celebrated Mariana's birthday for the first time. The tension, fears and uncertainty during the war, together with our frequent moves from one place to another, prevented me from keeping her first, second and third birthdays. In honor of her fourth birthday, I decided on a little party and invited all of Zippa's childhood friends. After years of suspense, terror and dread, it looked as though life was returning to its quiet and secure track, and the dear child appeared happy and relaxed.

We assembled in the afternoon in my parents' house; fall was at its peak, and the air was cool and clear. The tall trees in my neighborhood were starting to lose their leaves, which were piled on the broken and maligned sidewalks, those remnants of the past few years. A holiday atmosphere permeated through the house: Irena baked a chocolate cake, which Mariana decorated with five candles, Jadzia and Hanka bought the child new clothes and I brought her a small bicycle I found at one of the neighbors' and managed to fix and paint. I put around her neck a gold necklace with a small cross, a gift from my grandmother for my communion. I stashed in a little box the medallion with the holy mother's picture that I had given her after her "baptism." Maybe when she grew up, she'd want to wear it too. Little Mariana's eyes lit up when she blew out the candles on the cake and made a wish. She giggled as if at a private, secret joke, and immediately asked for a slice of the sweet cake, and then another and another.

The only friend of ours who didn't make it to the birthday party was Chaya Luterman. We tried for many months to find out what had happened to Chaya, the tailor's daughter who used to be one of us for so many years, an equal member of our gay and united group of girls that believed we'd stay together forever. The annihilation of the Jews of Grodno began in November of 1942, but only in January and February of 1943 did the mass transports to extermination camps begin. During that period, some ten thousand Jewish residents of Grodno were sent to Auschwitz, where most of them perished. In mid-February, some five thousand more of the city and its environs were sent to Treblinka. The Luterman family was sent to Auschwitz in the beginning of January 1943. As in Shedlitz, in Grodno, too, the Jewish community was erased, as if it had never existed.

The day after the birthday party, even before I had a chance to open my eyes, I heard a knock on the front door. Judging by the silence in the house, I assumed my parents were still asleep. I opened the door and saw before me a man of about fifty, dressed in a style reminiscent of the Jews of Shedlitz. Seeing a Jew at my front door was a big surprise. It was several years since we had seen any Jews at all in Shedlitz. Only in recent months did a few of them begin to come back to town.

"Are you Madam Sophia Olsakowska?" he asked with a heavy Jewish accent.

"Yes," I answered.

"May I come in?" he asked quietly. "We need to talk."

"What is it?" I asked him. Mariana was still asleep, and I was afraid she'd wake up and be frightened by this strange man. I couldn't imagine what he would want to discuss with me, now that all my Jewish friends have not been among the living for so long.

"I'm a member of the Jewish Committee of Shedlitz," he said, taking out of his pocket a document, as if to support his statement. When he saw I wasn't reacting, he continued: "We're searching for Jewish children who were saved from the war…"

My head started spinning, and a pall fell over me. "I can't talk to you right now," I said, praying that the man won't notice my sudden faintness. "I'll be happy to meet you at a different time and place."

The man wrote down an address on a piece of paper and requested that I visit his office at my earliest convenience.

The following days I tried to put my thoughts in order. I couldn't figure out how the man found out about Mariana, but I knew it wouldn't be long before he or someone else would show up at my front door again, asking about her. For an instance I thought of involving Lucina in finding shelter for Mariana and me, I knew that no one could ever find us in the chaos that reigned in Poland at the time, but, of course, I chased that thought away.

A few weeks later, even before I managed to tell Irena about the visit of the man from the Jewish Committee (and I had great trepidation about her own reaction), a messenger delivered a telegram to my house.

To: Madam Sophia Olsakowska, 3 Alexandrowska Street, Shedlitz, Poland.
From: Shimon Jablon, 60 Sheinkin Street, Tel-Aviv, Palestine

Dear Madam,
I request information regarding members of my family, providing you know any.

Shimon Jablon, Tel-Aviv, Palestine

Shimon Jablon, Zippa's elder brother, has emerged from the abyss to steal my daughter from me, was my first reaction to the telegram. But Shimon doesn't know anything, I was thinking next, he might not even be aware of Mariana's existence. Shortly before she was born, in October of 1941, Jacob and Zippa had moved, together with Zippa's parents, to Aslanowicza Street inside the ghetto. Even if they managed to send him a letter from the ghetto and told him about Mariana, he had no idea of what happened to her. What would I do if he wanted to take her for himself? How could I part with her? This little girl, who had been through so much abandonment in her life, how could she part once more with the only people she knew and had ties to in the world? Those thoughts continued to roam in my head without order, exactly as they did after the Jewish Committee man's visit.

I recalled Zippa's letter: "I ask you that after the end of the war you'll look for my brother who immigrated to Palestine and give him this small child." That was her request in the letter she left Irena's mother when she brought Mariana to the Zawadzky home in August of 1942. Irena and I used to read that letter every time we got together, sitting up in the attic and keeping a vigil for Zippa, sometimes without saying anything. It was our private memorial service, and we both knew that letter by heart. How could I refuse Zippa's last wish?

I went to Mariana's bed and caressed her dark head. The child was deep in sleep, one hand hugging the worn out teddy bear she was given by one of the teachers back in Zakrzówek and never parted with, and the other hand hugging the doll in a blue dress my parents gave her for her birthday.

The next morning I went to the local post office to send a telegram to Shimon.

Chapter 22
SHIMON

After the war, I was hired as warehouseman for the Mashbir Merkazi department store and began to follow obsessively all the newspaper articles about the fate of European Jewry. None of the other warehouse workers were interested in those articles, so each day I would pick up the papers they left behind and read all of it in the evening, in my apartment.

In July of 1945, the Jewish Agency began publishing thin booklets with long lists of the names of death camp survivors. Each time one of those booklets was published, I was quick to lay my hands on it and painstakingly check every name, column after column, page after page, a sea of crammed, tiny letters bunched into names, each telling the tale of a lifetime. In October, the Search Bureau for Missing Relatives put out the Book of Survivors, containing the names of the 58 thousand who survived the death camps. I hurried to purchase that one as well, but couldn't find in the long lists even one name I recognized. Jewish survivors started to arrive in Eretz Israel illegally, and their stories were occasionally published in the papers, although not prominently. The more I read, the harder it became for me to comprehend the magnitude of the horror. I visited several times the Jewish Agency, whose offices were on the brink of collapse from the sheer number of calls they were handling, but not once did I succeed in gleaming even a trace of information about any member of my family.

Throughout that time, I was also waiting with bated breath for Sophia's response to my telegram. I knew that if anyone knew details about my family, it would be Sophia Olsakowska, Zippa's tough, assertive friend. This is why, once her telegram reached me, my hands hesitated for the longest time before I opened it. I was hoping that maybe she, too, knew nothing about my family, or that maybe they managed to flee to Russia in the end, or were somehow saved from the transports and were now roaming across Europe. Maybe…

To: Mr. Shimon Jablon, 60 Sheinkin Street, Tel-Aviv, Palestine
From: Miss Sophia Olsakowska, 3 Alexandrowka Street, Shedlitz, Poland

Dear Sir,
Your parents, sister, and brother-in-law are no longer among the living. Left is a four-year-old girl named Rachel, daughter of Zippa and Jacob Zonshein.

With deep regrets,
Sophia Olsakowska

No longer among the living… Four-year-old girl… The words jumped before my eyes. I failed to comprehend their full meaning.

That same week I drove once again to the offices of the Search Bureau for Missing Relatives, but this time I possessed accurate details regarding whom I was looking for and where. I was searching for a small girl named Rachel Zonshein, who managed to survive the hellfire alone out of all her relatives. I didn't know what she looked like, what she liked to do or what she knew about her family. All I knew was that this girl had to come to Eretz Israel soon. In the Bureau I was told there wasn't yet an official body responsible for the search for the Jewish children who survived the war, but since it was known that many children were hidden with Polish families and in monasteries, various diplomatic efforts were being made to reach an agreement with the Polish government and the Church leadership there. A polite clerk took down Rachel's details and Sophia's address and advised me not to expect miracles. In any event, I was promised, it could take many long months. I returned to Tel Aviv in despair. I didn't have the means to travel to Poland myself, and, anyway, it was an impossible feat in those days.

In the beginning of 1946, my eyes caught an ad in the paper. The Chief Rabbi, R. Herzog, was about to leave for Europe to personally advance the search for Jewish children in Europe. One of my co-workers in the warehouse was a religious fellow who belonged to the Mizrachi movement. His cousin worked for the Chief Rabbinate in Jerusalem and was acquainted with the Chief Rabbi's secretary. The offices of the Rabbinate, like the Jewish Agency, were under a relentless barrage of people looking for every conceivable way to locate their relatives. But my co-worker's cousin's efforts to connect me to the Chief Rabbi failed, and since the date of the Rabbi's trip to Europe was fast approaching, I finally decided to contact him in writing.

To the honorable Chief Rabbi of Palestine/Eretz Israel, Rabbi Yitzchak Halevi Herzog Shlita,

I've resolved to approach the honorable Rabbi with my request as I've been reading in the papers that his honor is about to visit Poland. I plead with his honor to help me find my niece who lives in the town of Shedlitz, Poland. She is four years of age, her name is Rachel Zonshein, she is bereft of all her relatives, since her mother (my sister), father, grandfather and grandmother, and all the members of her extended family, were annihilated by the Nazis. The child is staying with Madam Sophia Olszakowsky at 3 Alexandrowka Street, Shedlitz. I won't presume to explain to his honor the importance of saving this Jewish child and bringing her to Eretz Israel, especially since all the members of her family have been murdered, and I am her only living relative. Having

myself fought on European soil during the war, I implore the honorable Rabbi to do what he can to save my niece.
Respectfully, Shimon Jablon

A month later, I received a short letter from the Chief Rabbinate:

Dear Sir,
We passed your request regarding the girl Rachel Zonshein over to the care of Rabbi David Kahana, Chief Military Rabbi of Poland.
We thank you for contacting us and wish you success.
General Secretary, the Chief Rabbinate

With help from my religious co-worker at the warehouse, I started to dig up details about Rabbi Kahana. I found out that he himself managed to save his family by hiding them in a monastery, then spent the war years in the Lvov Ghetto and at the end of the war enlisted in the Polish army, was appointed Chief Military Rabbi of Poland (in addition to his role as Chairman of the Jewish Communities), and immediately undertook the mission of saving Jewish children who were left in monasteries or with Polish families. Rabbi Kahana appointed his deputy at the Military Rabbinate, Rabbi Isaiah Druker, to manage the task directly. Druker, an officer in the Polish Army, fled to Russia at the beginning of the war, was arrested there by the Soviets, stayed in a labor camp in Siberia until 1943, then joined a Polish unit fighting alongside the Red Army. With that unit, he arrived in Berlin in April of 1945 and witnessed its surrender. Druker, a military rabbi in the Polish Army and an employee of the Board of Jewish Communities, personally executed the search for Jewish children and their extraction from their Polish families and from monasteries statewide.

I wasn't completely happy with my choice to beseech, of all people, the religious, who were acting independently and apart from the other Eretz-Israel Zionist organizations. They were very distant from me in their views and opinions, and I had no real knowledge of their methods in searching for the Jewish children in Poland. In my father's house in Shedlitz, and in the youth movement of which I was a member, I was brought up to love Eretz Israel and the Jewish tradition, but we never saw ourselves as being religious. Nevertheless, I decided not to let those differences interfere with the only goal I saw before my eyes. Rachel was the last remnant from my family, and I couldn't imagine leaving her in Poland even one needless moment.

In June of 1946, I married Penina, whom I had met at the training camp in Poland in the early 1930s. Like myself, Penina made aliyah to Eretz Israel before the war, but since she left before me, our paths parted. Shortly after the war, I met her at the Jewish Agency office. She, too, was there to find out the fate of her family members. I was hoping she wouldn't mind my bringing over my little niece, but I was so busy searching for Rachel that I never bothered to stop and ask Penina's opinion.

My communication through telegrams with Sophia and with Rabbi Druker lasted almost half a year. The rabbi himself visited Sophia's home and sent me an update. It turned out he wasn't the first visitor to reach her, as members of the Jewish Committee of Shedlitz were also conducting visits to homes that kept Jewish children. As soon as Sophia understood that I was interested in the child, and considering that this, according to her, was also Zippa's last wish, she assured Rabbi Druker she would do everything to send the child to me as soon as possible. Despite those assurances, I could not relax. I never trusted those Poles and feared that Sophia would have a change of heart and do something to somehow keep Rachel. She managed to fool the Nazis all those years, what could prevent her from fooling some rabbi?

In September of 1946, a letter arrived from Sophia.

Chapter 23

RACHEL

I was almost five when Mr. Olszakowsky took me by train to the big city. It was my first time riding the train, and I was terribly excited. A few days before the trip, Mamma explained that I was traveling to a new place now, where they will take care of me and I'll be fine. I asked when she would come to this new place, but she didn't answer. I saw that her eyes were red, and when she hugged me strongly, I felt her shoulders quivering.

When we left the house on the day of our trip, I was very hot because Mamma dressed me up in many clothes even though it was summer. She also packed me a suitcase with more clothes and prepared some food for the road. She and Aunt Irena accompanied us to the train station in our town, and before we boarded the train, Aunt Irena was crying so hard she couldn't say a word to me. The last thing I remember is that she hugged me and that her cheeks were warm and moist.

Mamma said to me in a trembling voice, "You're going to a new country now, where you'll meet your Uncle Shimon."

I didn't know I had an Uncle Shimon, but Mamma explained that he was the brother of my real mother. She took out of her bag an envelope with three pictures, which she showed me. The first was of a woman in a white dress, with a big smile, holding up a baby girl in a dress and a sweater. The baby also had a big smile.

"That's you with your mother, Zippa," Mamma told me. "She was my best friend, but she is no longer here, she's with the angels now. Your father, Jacob, is also with the angels." She showed me the second picture, of a good looking man in a soldier's uniform, holding in his arms the baby from the first picture. In the third picture, there was an older woman, also holding the same baby, me, in her arms.

"This is your grandmother, your mother's mother," Mamma told me.

"But Grandma Sabina is my grandmother," I answered her. I couldn't understand why all of a sudden I had so many grandmothers and mothers.

"This is your real grandmother," Mamma said, and her eyes also became very moist. She hugged me strongly and now her entire body was quivering.

"Your mother asked us to send you to your Uncle Shimon; he's her brother, and she asked that you live with him," Mamma told me. "We also think this will be the best place for you."

After we hugged again, Mr. Olszakowsky gave me his hand and we boarded the train together. I had many questions, but I was afraid to ask them. The entire ride I was looking at the pictures Mamma gave me before getting on the train, and only after we'd been going a long time did I notice there was writing on the back of the pictures.

"What does it say here?" I asked Mr. Olszakowsky, glad we finally had something to talk about. Even though I was living in his house, I always called him Mister and not Grandpa.

Mr. Olszakowsky took a pair of glasses out of his bag and looked at the first picture, the one with me and my real mother. His eyes also started to redden, and it looked like he would start crying any minute now. After a long time passed, he said, "It says here: This is your Mamma, my little doll, your Mamma who couldn't raise you and who wishes that never in your life will you feel the absence of your Mamma, and that life will bring you happiness and goodness, and whatever you want out of life.

These are the blessings of your wretched Mamma. Shedlitz, August 1942."

"What's 'wretched?'" I asked Mr. Olszakowsky.

"It's someone who loved her daughter so much, but she had to say goodbye to her and now she's very sad."

"And what does it say here?" I handed him the second picture.

"You are now in your father's arms; you loved playing with that hat of his and the cane. At eleven months, he saved you from certain death and then said goodbye to you. I bless you that you'll have in your life everything that he now wishes for you. Shedlitz, August 1942."

"What's 'death?'" I asked him.

"It's when someone has to leave and never come back."

"Like my real Mamma and Papa?" I asked him.

"Exactly," he said almost in a whisper.

I gave him the last picture. I was hoping that behind that one it wouldn't say Wretched or Death.

"Dear, beloved Dolly! This is your grandmother; remember her well because she loved you very, very much and gave her life to save you from certain death. The whole town knew about her great love for you, and I wish you will have in your life everything that she wishes for you. We can't show you your grandfather, but he, too, loved you very, very much. Shedlitz, August 1942."

"When do we get there?" I asked Mr. Olszakowsky.

"Soon. There's Warsaw, look over there."

When we arrived in the big city, Mr. Olszakowsky took me to a large building with many rooms. All kinds of people were walking around, speaking a language I didn't understand. He brought me to a room where we met a short woman with white hair like Grandma Sabina. Mr. Olszakowsky spoke quietly to her, and I couldn't make out what they were saying. Before he left, he gave me my suitcase, hugged me and told me, "Don't worry, sweetie, everything will be all right." He kissed me on both cheeks and left.

The white-haired woman sat me down next to two other children with suitcases and told me to stay put. Later she called me into her room and asked a lot of questions, not all of which I could answer. She wrote everything I said in a big notebook. Then I sat once more and waited next to the other two children until some tall man came and spoke to the woman. Then they approached us, and the woman said, "Meet Captain Druker. He will take you to Zabrze."

The tall man was wearing a soldier's clothes, and his hat reminded me of my father from the picture. I asked if he knew my father, but the captain didn't know my father, he only asked, "Are you Rachel Zonshein?" I told him my name was Mariana Timinska, but he only nodded his head and whispered something to the woman. Then he turned to the children sitting next to me on the bench: "Are you Chayim and Moshe Liebeck?"

"Yes," said the boy who looked a little older. Both children looked alike, both had on oversized clothes and old shoes, both were thin, and they hardly spoke.

The captain took me and the two boys to a big car. I asked him where we were going, and he said we're going to a lovely place where they'll treat me nice. I told him I came from a lovely place where they also treated me nice, but he didn't answer.

"Mamma told me they'll take me to a new country, where my uncle is waiting," I told him.

"We will, indeed, bring you to Eretz Israel, but not right away. First I'll take you to a place with other children like you, where they'll take care of you until all of you can go together to Eretz Israel. You have nothing to worry about."

Except that, having been told so many times not to worry, I became very worried. When would I see Mamma and Aunt Irena? Who would wait for me in the new place? Why can't I just go to my uncle in the new country? Many questions were running around in my head, which is probably why I became so tired and fell asleep in the captain's car.

Late that evening we arrived in the town the captain called Zabrze. The streets were dark and quiet and at first I couldn't tell that it was a town. I was getting a little cold and was glad that

Mamma dressed me up in so many clothes. The captain stopped the car outside a large, gray building and said, "We've arrived, you can get off." He took our suitcases and led us into the house.

A young woman in a black dress with white collar came toward us and she, too, asked me, "Are you Rachel Zonshein?" I didn't answer, and the captain whispered something in her ear. She looked at me and said, "You'll get used to it, sweetie. Rachel is your real name, the name your father and mother gave you." I wanted to say that I didn't have a father and that Mamma always called me Marisha, or Lalechka, but then I remembered the pictures Mamma gave me before I got on the train and decided not tell her anything.

The two boys who came with me from the big city went with some guy who arrived together with the woman in the black dress. When we were in the car, on our way from the big city, the older of the two told me they were brothers from Lublin, that their entire family was gone, and that in recent years they were hiding with a family in a small village and every morning they had to milk the cows and feed the barnyard animals. I didn't understand why they were so sad, since I also used to live in a village and used to go with Aunt Felicia and Stephan to milk the cows and feed the animals, and it was very lovely. The younger brother was crying almost the whole trip from the big city, and the older brother was always hugging him and caressing his hand.

The woman in the black dress took me into a small room with six wooden beds that looked exactly the same. The beds were arranged in two straight columns and covered with gray, wool blankets. She told me to put my suitcase under the bed nearest the door. I was glad Mamma packed a pillow and a sheet in my suitcase because the gray blanket on the bed was itchy and hard. Then the woman told me to follow her to a big room with showers and a line of sinks. She sat me down on a high chair in front of a mirror, and before I could stop her, she cut all my hair, leaving me with cropped hair, like a boy. Then she shampooed my short hair in the sink with a substance that smelled like

Mr. Olszakowsky's lab. When she was done, she toweled my hair, combed it very forcefully, and took me to a hall with lines of narrow, long tables where many children were sitting and eating. On the walls, there were blue and white flags. I didn't want to enter this dining room with all those children, because I was very ashamed of my short hair, but the woman in the black dress and white collar held my hand tightly and led me to a table with girls about my age. Their hair was as short as mine, but I still felt different and ugly. I couldn't eat anything, even though I was very hungry. The food looked strange, and I felt my stomach shrinking. At the end of the meal, they gave every child a cube of chocolate, which I quickly put in my mouth. Chocolate was the thing I liked most, except for the Gogle-mogle Mamma used to make for me. One girl asked if she could take the food that I left on my plate. Her own plate was completely clean, but she kept her chocolate cube on the side. I gave her my plate and pointed at her chocolate cube. She gave it to me and said, "Take it. I hate brown food."

During the first night, I couldn't fall asleep, even though I was very tired. Before the lights were turned off, some of the girls in my room got off their beds, sat down on their knees and prayed. I remembered how Grandma Sabina and Aunt Irena would also do that before bed and sometimes I would join them, but now I didn't feel like joining those girls. I took out the pictures of my mother and my father and my grandmother and looked at them until the woman in the black dress and white collar came in to turn off the light. After lights out, I could hear the girls in my room sobbing quietly under their blankets. I was very confused by that entire day, and there was no one to explain anything to me.

In the morning, we went for a walk around the children's home, and later all the boys and girls played in the yard. There were bigger kids, too, who frightened me, so I sat on the side and just stared at them. That's what I continued to do every morning at the children's home in Zabrze. It was a dirty and gray town, and I didn't want to stay there at all. Every day I asked the women taking care of us where my Mamma and my aunt were and why they weren't visiting me, but the women didn't know.

One evening a week we'd arrange the tables in the dining room as one, big, long table, which they covered with white tablecloths and nice utensils. We all sat down around the table and the headmistress, whose name was Nechama, lit two candles, and one of the teachers said something I didn't understand, but afterwards he always drank a little wine and we got some, too. The captain who brought me here would arrive every once in a while on those special evenings and participate in the ceremony they called Kabbalat Shabbat. He would always sit at the head of the table and tell many stories, most of which I didn't understand so much, but the rest of the children were listening in perfect silence. Every time he came I wanted to ask him about my mother and my aunt, but I was afraid that he wouldn't remember me. On the Kabbalat Shabbat evenings, they made us strange food that I didn't recognize and didn't want to taste, except for the sweet challah, which reminded me of the challah Aunt Irena would bake sometimes. I wanted Mamma and Aunt Irena to come get me already and make for me the food that I liked, but they didn't come and I just kept waiting for them.

Chapter 24
SHIMON

Shedlitz, September 1946
Dear Mr. Shimon,

I've acted in accordance with your wishes, meaning, I handed the little girl to the rabbinate, where there will apparently be a visa waiting for her. The child was supposed to wait about six weeks for the trip abroad, in the town of Żabrze, in Silesia. I've visited the place several times but was unable to see her on any of those occasions, since contact with Poles is forbidden in the children's home. I was very troubled by this, but at the rabbinate they assured me that the little girl was there or had already left.

We must hope that by the time this letter reaches you, dear Sir, the little girl will already be with you. I ask that you write me at once because I'm extremely worried. I handed over the girl with great heartache since I've grown so accustomed to her. Children are much too forgetful, although I hope that this is for the better, as she will thus enjoy a calmer future.

For the sake of good order I wish to record that Mariana (that's how we've been calling her) took with her a blanket, a pillow, bedding, a teddy bear, a doll and a suitcase containing both winter and summer attire. I wish to know if all of the above has arrived with her.

Sir has written that he does not have his own children, has he been married in the past? Who takes care of the household? Won't Sir be burdened by his attempt to manage with a small girl? Although she is quite big already, as well as smart and independent, she's still just a child. In the town of Shedlitz, she attended kindergarten. Will Sir be able to enroll her for a few hours a day in his home town? I'm curious to know how she will get by with the foreign language (which language are you using over there, English or Yiddish?). I wish to remind him that she must consume a lot of fruits, and I assume that in Palestine they shouldn't be difficult to procure.

I should inform you that Mariana was not baptized. Her CV reads roughly as follows: She was born on October 1, 1941, inside the ghetto. Conditions at the time were still bearable since entering and leaving the ghetto was not yet restricted. The situation changed a few months later. By the end of August 1942, they began to liquidate the ghetto. Your parents were killed during the train transports to the Treblinka camp. Zippa hid with the child in an attic for two days, then managed to flee and brought her to Mrs. Sabina Zawadzka.

The persecution of Jews in hiding and the Poles who hid them was terrible. Zippa hid for two weeks in an abandoned house outside Shedlitz but she couldn't tolerate the isolation and the uncertainty regarding the fate of her family members, so she returned to the ghetto, which at the time had shrunk significantly. By the end of November, the ghetto was barred completely, and the Germans were beginning to remove groups of people and transport them to Treblinka for termination. Zippa was aware of the situation and acquired poison. Once the order to prepare for deportation had been given, she swallowed the poison. Her death came very quickly.

According to rumors, Jacob was on the transport to the termination site. I was told that he was deeply depressed, and while others attempted an escape, he gave up on it (chances for success were miniscule). All the information I possess concerning the Treblinka camp is based mostly on rumors.

Without her obvious Semitic appearance, we might have been able to save Zippa. She died heroically, refusing to hand her life over to the enemy. She was strong enough not to let them kill her physically in the gas chambers, together with thousands of others. In effect, hers was a lengthy and agonizing death: the ghetto executions, the murder of her parents and of Jacob, the separation from the girl and the awareness of her own impending death. One thing, I hope, served to calm her spirit: Irena and I promised her we would look after the child as if she were our own, and after the war contact you, honorable Sir.

At first, Mariana spent some weeks in a home for infants, and then Irena Zawadzka took her to her mother's home because Mariana had become very sick. Irena and her mother, Madam Sabina Zawadzka, took care of her with great self-sacrifice. A few months later I took her with me, and she attended the schools that I managed. That's how we spent all the war years.

Dear Mr. Shimon, I conclude my letter with a request that you provide me with details regarding the girl as well as yourself.

Kisses to the girl,
Sophia Olsakowska

When I received the letter from Sophia, I already knew everything that could be known at the time about the annihilation of European Jewry. I read every word ever published, listened to every radio program about the Holocaust, and spoke to everyone I knew who had any connection whatsoever to someone who was saved from the hellfire. Still, Sophia's words landed on me heavy as led, and frighteningly painful. It was the first time I received real, authentic testimony about the fate of my family members. I tried to reconstruct where I had been when all this was taking place, to imagine what would have happened had I not made aliyah to Eretz Israel, and tormented myself with the question of whether I would have been able to help them.

***

In September 1939, the news about the war in Europe and the German invasion of Poland shook me like thunder from the sky. I hadn't received any news from my family for a very long time, and what few letters I did receive since leaving Shedlitz have now stopped coming. I felt distant and powerless.

At that time, I had been living in Eretz Israel for four years. I arrived riding my bicycle in the summer of 1935, a three-month trip of a thousand-kilometer course, along with five other friends of the Hapoel Shedlitz bicycle team. We rode from Shedlitz to the Rumanian port city of Constantza, where we set sail to Jaffa harbor, arriving on a muggy and warm September evening. A few days later I found work as a harbor porter and rented a small flat on Sheinkin Street in Tel Aviv.

A few months after my arrival in Eretz Israel, riots broke out in Jaffa, and dozens of Jews were killed, hundreds injured and thousands evicted from their homes. The day after the riots began, the local Arabs declared a general strike. It was the start of a bloody period in the history of the Jewish settlement, later named the Great Arab Rebellion, or the Events of 1936-39. For me, this was the time I became acquainted, for the first time in my life, with the British.

Arab attacks on Jewish settlements were becoming violent and included setting fires to farm fields and assaults against buses and transportation routes. The British Mandate police, unable to provide the needed protection to the settlements, gave their approval for community leaders to hire youths to aid in maintaining security. For me it was a golden opportunity to apply what I had learned in the Polish army and at the same time to defend the land that, although I hadn't been born here, I was already considering my birthplace. I reported for duty at the recruitment office at the Saraphend base, armed with my certificate of discharge from the Polish army, and after I had sworn allegiance to the King of England, before a British officer, I was enlisted as a ghaffir (Arabic for guard). The British supplied me with a khaki uniform, a Turkish kulpak hat, an ancient Greener hunting rifle, a belt with fifty bullets, and the day following my enlistment they sent me to Jezreel Valley, where I remained for three years, engaging in security tasks, protecting farmers, and setting ambushes. Over the years, the kulpak mutated into a broad rimmed Australian hat, the antiquated Greener became an accurate, English Enfield rifle (intended to kill, not just wound), and I evolved from a shy, lonely, Polish youth in a foreign land into a tested and proud Eretz-Israeli ghaffir. I often asked myself what my parents would have said had they seen me going out into the valley fields in chase of Arab pogromists. Is that what they expected when I told them I was making aliyah to Eretz Israel? Is that how they imagined my life here? Were they worried about me? My life at the time was so full of interest, of adventure, of journeys and new acquaintances. Shedlitz was slowly becoming a distant memory from my past.

In the summer of 1940, the Arab rebellion began to die down, and my job as ghaffir was becoming less and less critical. We continued to execute security operations in border settlements, but those were no longer as needed and lacked that seductive aroma of heroism and the pioneer spirit. Many of my pals were starting to weigh the possibility of enlisting in the British Army and fighting on the side of the allies in Europe. The Haganah also encouraged enlistment in the British Army and promoted the idea with extensive propaganda; posters of smiling male and female soldiers in shiny British uniforms were hung everywhere, with the slogans: You Can Make Things Go Faster, or Put On Your Clothes of Glory. Enlisting in the British army, I thought, would be my only option of helping in the struggle against the Germans.

When Italy entered the war and the Axis powers began to advance in the Middle East, the British began to apply even more pressure on potential Eretz-Israeli volunteers. On August 19, 1940, two months after Italy's entry into the war, I joined the British Army. Alas, my experience as a first rate sharpshooter in the Polish army (just to be safe, I brought with me to the recruitment office documentation of my range scores), as well as my recent years as ghaffir, did not persuade the British to enroll me as a combat soldier, and I was assigned instead to the Auxiliary Military Pioneer Corps (AMPC). I underwent one month of basic training at the Saraphend base, comprised of shooting, running, conditioning and most of all—endless hours of marching in three columns up and down the humongous base. At the end of the training, in October of 1940, my company was sent to the Egyptian-Libyan border, where we were attached to the British forces fighting the Italian army, which was advancing from Libya toward Egypt.

We were a company of veteran immigrants as well as fresh newcomers, most of them recent escapees from Europe without any Hebrew at all. We also had natives among us, including Sephardim, Yemenites, and some whose families had been living in Eretz Israel for generations. To my surprise, we even had a few Arab volunteers. We came from different backgrounds, spoke a mix of languages, and the short training period we had undergone was not enough to turn us into a cohesive unit. The only weapon we received after boot camp were garden spades and picks, and armed with those we went out to fight the Axis powers.

***

After reading Sophia's letter, I was waiting each day for a telegram announcing Rachel's arrival. I didn't know when and how she was supposed to appear, but Sophia wrote that she probably had already left Zabrze, so I assumed she was on her way to Eretz Israel. I knew the country's gates had not yet opened to receive Jewish immigrants from Europe, but I was hoping the Rabbinate staff would find ways to bring over at least the surviving children.

A few months had passed and I still received no news about Rachel. I was impatient and started running endlessly to the

Jewish Agency, the Chief Rabbinate, the Youth Aliyah, and to anyone else I hoped could help me. My wife Penina—whose entire family had perished in the war—was already pregnant at the time, and I felt that my great concern for my niece was disturbing her.

Chapter 25

RACHEL

One day, when it was getting a little cool outside, they told us to pack our suitcases and to put on our warmest clothes, because that evening we were traveling to a new place. I didn't want to go because I was afraid that Mamma and Aunt Irena would come to visit me, and I wouldn't be here and they'd look for me and not find me. I couldn't understand why we weren't going to the new country, like Mamma promised me, to the place where my uncle was waiting for me. After supper, when we were supposed to get ready for the trip to the new place, I refused to get dressed, and two counselors came and dressed me up by force. I wanted to tell them I was waiting for my mamma and my aunt, but no sound came out of my mouth. I was afraid I would never see them again and started to cry. The headmistress Nechama arrived and hugged me and told me not to worry, that everything was going to be fine, but I didn't believe her.

They put us on trucks with our suitcases, and we rode to a train station in another town. The whole trip we sat on the floor, and it was dark and cold and I was tired but couldn't fall asleep because my whole body was aching from the bouncing truck. At the station, they gave each child a blanket and we covered ourselves while standing and waiting for the train to come. Some of the children couldn't remain standing for that long, so they lied down on the platform and fell asleep. Finally, our train arrived. It had many bunk beds, and every child got a bed and they told us to put our suitcases on it. We traveled this way many days and wherever we stopped I looked for Mamma and Aunt Irena, but they weren't there.

After all those days traveling on the bunk bed train, we arrived in another country, according to what our counselors were telling us, but it wasn't the new country Mamma promised me. In the new country, Mamma said, the sun is shining all year long, and the sky is blue and you get oranges. In the country we came to now, the sky was gray and it rained. They told us we were staying in that country until we could all come to Eretz Israel.

We arrived at a very large hall with all the children who came with me on the train from Zabrze, and many other children I didn't know, and then they started dividing us into groups. I didn't have a single friend in Zabrze, so it didn't bother me, being divided into groups.

After a few days in the large hall, divided into groups, they told us once again to prepare for a trip and once again I had to arrange everything nicely in my suitcase like the time before. But now I didn't care, I knew I was far away from Mamma and Aunt Irena, and I no longer even had anyone to ask when I would see them because we had new counselors I didn't know.

I rode with all the children from my group on another train, the kind with benches instead of beds, until we reached a station from which we went on foot to a small village, but it looked nothing like the village where Uncle Valente and Aunt Felicia lived, where the cows and chickens roamed freely outdoors. In this new village there were hardly any animals at all, only big houses hidden behind walls or tall trees. We reached a house that was bigger and grayer than the one in Zabrze, and again they told me to put my suitcase under my bed. The new place also had counselors that told all the children what to do, and I wanted to ask them, too, about Mamma and Aunt Irena, but they spoke a language I didn't understand, so I knew they wouldn't get what I was saying.

In the new place they began to teach us Hebrew, "the language of Eretz Israel," as they put it, and French, the language of the country where we were supposed to stay until we could make aliyah to Eretz Israel. Even though I wasn't yet of school age like the rest of the children, I sat with them when a counselor arrived once a day to teach all of us new Hebrew words and Hebrew songs. I liked the songs he was teaching because the tunes were always happy. One of the girl counselors taught us French, but I didn't like those lessons because that language sounded terribly strange. In the mornings, they made us porridge, which I hated but they made me eat it all, and for lunch we got noodle chicken soup every day, some goose fat, potatoes, and a pickled cucumber. For dinner we ate the chicken from the lunch soup, with noodles, and compote or pudding for dessert. The food in the new place was better than back in Zabrze, even though they never gave chocolate, which I missed a lot.

A short while after I came to France, the headmistress took me aside one morning to tell me everything she knew about my real family. After she told me that my entire family was gone, she said I had an uncle in Eretz Israel by the name of Shimon, my mother's brother, the real mother, the one from the picture, and that he would be waiting for me in Eretz Israel when I arrived there. Sophia had already told me a similar story, which is why I believed the headmistress, but I hadn't heard anything from Shimon.

"Maybe you'd like us to write him a letter together?" the headmistress suggested.

"What will I tell him?" I asked her, and I honestly had no idea what to write this uncle I didn't know. Could I tell him how sad I was since leaving Sophia and Irena? Or the long, dark nights when I lay in bed with my tears wetting the pillow? Should I tell him about the annoying children, not one of them my friend? Or how much I would want the people who love me not to ever leave me?

"Maybe I'll write him in your name, and you'll add a drawing?" she asked, handing me paper and pencil.

Even after we sent the letter, we received no response from my uncle in Eretz Israel. The headmistress told me there were people in Eretz Israel whose job it was to help kids like me find their relatives there, and that I must wait patiently until they find my uncle, too. I didn't know what the word "patient" meant, but I understood it meant waiting some more.

When winter came in France, we celebrated a holiday that reminded me a little of Sophia's house. During my last winter with them, Mr. Olszakowsky brought home a tall tree and positioned it at the center of the house. Sophia and I decorated it with whatever we were able to find, including a few small candles, and in the evening we lit them, and I sat and watched, thinking how good it was to be living at home with my family. The next day they told me to look inside the stockings hanging next to my bed and I found a candy wrapped in shiny paper, a doll that Mrs. Olsakowska sewed especially for me, and half a bar of chocolate, the thing I loved the most.

The holiday we celebrated in the new place had no tree or decorations, but every evening they lit one additional candle in this silver object the counselor called a Menorah, which stood in the dining room. I didn't understand why you had to add a candle each day, why not light all of them at once, like we did at Sophia's home during the holiday, but the headmistress explained this was how we do it according to Jewish tradition.

It was very cold during the first winter in the new place; it snowed almost every day, and we hardly ever left the building. Big trucks came and delivered sacks full of old clothes, some of them a little torn, but they were warm and the counselors mended them. Most of the time we kept our coats on indoors, it was so cold. We had already celebrated all the Israeli holidays and the Hebrew I spoke was becoming what the headmistress called "proper and beautiful." I didn't know what "proper" meant, but I guessed it was a good thing, the way she looked at me when she said it.

One winter day, right after my two front teeth came out and I was feeling ugly as a rat, the headmistress approached me with a wide smile and told me they found my Uncle Shimon. "He lives in Tel-Aviv, it's a beautiful city, and you will enjoy living there. There's a big sea there, and the sun is shining all year long, and he's already waiting for you." In France, the second winter was also snowy and cold, so I couldn't comprehend the idea of the sun shining year-round, but at night I began to have dreams about the big sea and the shining sun and the uncle who would take me on walks on the beach. I had never seen the sea before, and I wanted so badly to get to Eretz Israel and meet my uncle. Twice already we celebrated the holiday with the candles in the menorah in the new place, but we still didn't make it to Eretz Israel.

Chapter 26
IRENA

Two years after the war was over, I received a scholarship from the Sorbonne in Paris, to study teaching French as a foreign language. It had been nearly a decade since I left the bubbly and gay Paris of the late 1930s, and now I came back to a city that was still licking its wounds from the German occupation. Even though the city was not as ruined and bruised as the Polish towns, it still suffered from shortages of essential goods and a general paralysis that damaged many key institutions. Governments rose and fell one after the other, and almost every day saw a new strike of this kind or another. During the fall of 1947, city residents were still barely subsisting on food rations, grocery store shelves were almost always empty, and items like meat, bread, dairy products, or sugar could only be procured on the black market, which, unlike state institutions, was thriving. On the first of each month I received food coupons from the university and I ate all my meals together with the other foreign students in a small dining room in the dorms, where I was also sharing a bedroom with an Italian student. For breakfast, we were served dry cornbread with margarine and tea with sugar substitute; for lunch, we received a tiny piece of meat and side dishes, which I never quite made out what they were made of. Once a month, on a Saturday or a Sunday, we, the foreign students, would splurge on a hot espresso and a baguette with cheese substitute in a café at the Latin Quarter. Those were moments of grace, which made us poor students supremely happy.

Cars could hardly be seen citywide, and the most popular vehicle of the day was the bicycle. Young and old, women and children rode them everywhere and every time, filling up the streets with packages tied to their bikes, possibly food purchased on the black market, or an item of clothing they acquired, and on occasion a fresh baguette would stick out of a basket or was tied to the rear rack. Parisian women didn't permit shortages and poverty to diminish their famous love for fashion. In place of silk stockings, whose prices skyrocketed in those days, they smeared their legs with brown makeup cream, they sewed dresses out of curtains and fabric remnants, and makeup was concocted from substances known only to a few. Young French women abandoned the blown up hairdos and elegant dresses characteristic of the 1920s and '30s, adopting instead loose hair with bangs, and opting for black sweaters and short black skirts with pumps. The modest, boyish look was in with most young Parisian women.

When winter came, it was hard to ignore the heat shortages and the frost in the student dorms, and I was often forced to sleep in my day clothes. Blackouts were routine, and I did most of my studying that year by candlelight. Despite the lack of food, clothing, and heat, culture blossomed in the city after years of repression and underground activity. Museums opened their doors to allow residents free access, new theatrical productions went on stage almost every week, jazz and chanson clubs popped up around the city like mushrooms after the rain. In the beginning of 1948, I went with two girlfriends to the Marigny Theater, where they staged, for the first time, a production based on The Trial by Franz Kafka. The show was directed by Jean Louis Barrault, until then a shining movie star. Fellow Literature students protested the show, arguing that Kafka was meant to be read, not acted on stage, but the stage adaptation, by that year's Nobel Prize winner André Gide, as well as the blood curdling proximity to the mysterious death of Czech leader Jan Masaryk, caused me to come out of the show feeling confused and excited.

My university professors would often pride themselves on another cultural activity taking place back then which they witnessed personally. It was happening right under my nose, in the cafés of Saint Germain, a few minutes' walk from the university, where every day the likes of Sartre, de Beauvoir, Juliette Greco, Picasso and their artistic and intellectual friends would assemble. These people, who made the cafés their home, were the most influential cultural and spiritual figures in Paris of those years. They were setting the bon ton, so we were told by our professors; they determined which artists would get an exhibition in this museum or another, which singers were featured by the in—clubs and which authors would be signed by the publishing houses that counted. Sometimes I would look curiously for those artists in the cafés where we sat, but I never saw any of them.

In early February 1948, I received a letter from Sophia. She didn't usually write me in Paris, and since my arrival here, I only got a new year's greeting card from her. The sealed envelope evoked excitement and delight in me, I waited to hear news from home, beyond what my mother was telling me. When I started reading the letter, in which Sophia was telling me she'd found out that Mariana was now in France, I was swept by a wave of joy mixed with sadness and a deep longing. After she had left the children's home in Zabrze, Mariana was supposed to leave for Palestine, but the British were still refusing to provide Jews with certificates of entry, and so, along with thousands of children like her, she was sent to an orphanage in France. According to the information Sophia received from Shimon Jablon, Zippa's brother, it appeared that Mariana certainly was in France, but Zosha didn't know where exactly.

The fact that Mariana was in France took me back to the war years, to the terrifying days when we were taking care of that small and lonely girl—until that miserable day when we were forced to give her over to the men from the Rabbinate. Zosha and I didn't have the strength to accompany Mariana to Warsaw. We decided it would be better, for Mariana's sake, if Mr. Olszakowsky went with her to Warsaw. We were hoping to save her, and maybe us, too, the difficult goodbye scene.

I started running around the Jewish organizations in town until I reached OSE (Save the Children), where I was able to get a list of all 100 orphanages in France, most of which had been established after the war, where they kept surviving Jewish children. I sent letters to all the places on the list, but not one of them was answered. I realized that the only way to find out where Mariana was staying would be to go looking for her in person.

I reached the children's home in Fublaines in early spring, 1948. The school year was almost over at the university, and I wanted to find Mariana before I left for Poland. I had already visited dozens of institutions and orphanages in Paris and its environs, and according to the list in my hand that was the very last of them. I realized that if I failed to find her here I would have to start traveling to the children's homes outside the Paris region.

Fublaines was a small village, east of Paris, some four kilometers from the nearest train station. I arrived there in early noon on a Sunday; the pleasant weather made walking from the train easy. I could hear the loud twitter of the birds from the blooming trees, white butterflies crossed my path as I was walking alongside unplowed fields, and all along the road I could smell the light aroma of a new blossom. Two cherry trees in full bloom stood at the village entrance, one on each side of the access road, and their intoxicating fragrance instantaneously reminded me of Shedlitz, which I left a year ago.

Two girls in light—colored dresses led me to the place where they had, so they said, "many children without parents." The sight of the girls in spotless, bright dresses, their braids circling their heads, like Polish children on Sundays, together with the ringing church bells I could hear whenever I passed by a settlement, reminded me that I hadn't been going to church much since coming to France. On weekends in Paris, I preferred to catch up on my enormous study material, visit museums, and public libraries, and drink in the sights I so admired. I felt I had to complete what I hadn't been able to do on my first visit here, ten years ago. Now and then, during my stroll through the city, my feet would lead me to one of the numerous churches spread across Paris. I would enter the unfamiliar church with great reverence, sit down on one of the long, wooden benches, and listen to the preaching priest. Despite my feelings of closeness and my excitement at the familiar words and images in church, those visits were more touristy than religious in nature, perhaps because the Parisian churches were touristy and ornate, so that, ever so slowly, I began to enjoy my absence of commitment to regular church visits, which I held on to all my life. Of all the churches of Paris, I loved the Sacred Heart the most, overlooking the entire city and seen from everywhere. Despite the great differences, this was the only church here that reminded me of the Shedlitz cathedral, and every time I opened its heavy, wooden doors, I was swept in a feeling of divine holiness. After my visit to church, I used to stroll through the colorful artists' quarter, listening to street performers sing Édith Piaf and Charles Trenet songs, accompanied by the grating sounds of an organ. On such Sundays, I would return to the dorms by early evening, exhausted but filled with satisfaction.

Like the rest of the children's homes I had visited in recent weeks, the one in Fublaines was surrounded by a tall, brick wall completely covered with vegetation. The joyful voices of boys and girls of different ages emanated from the courtyard within. Here, too, I was struck by the notion that children's voices in orphanages sounded just like children's voices any other place where children were playing. The same cries of glee, the same hollering of encouragement, and even the same fights. The children spoke in different languages: French, Polish, Russian, Yiddish, and even German, and it seemed as if they understood one another without difficulty. I stood by the gate, trying to locate Mariana among the playing children, exactly as I had done before in all the other children's homes I visited, but didn't find her. I looked intently, again and again, trying to catch a glimpse of her in the crowd of children, as it had been two years since I saw her off at the Shedlitz train station, and she must have grown and changed, but I found no girl in the courtyard who resembled her.

I pulled the bell rope that hung by the front gate. A few children came running to the gate as soon as the bell sounded and showered me with questions: "Who are you looking for?" "What's your name?" "My name is Loleck," "What did you bring us?" and so on, in different languages.

An elderly woman approached the gate, walking slowly and with great difficulty. She gestured the children back to their games and gave me an inquisitive look.

"I'm looking for a girl named Rachel Zonshein," I told her. Every time I came to one of those children's home I'd feel strange using the girl's real name, Rachel, after all the years in which I thought of her as Mariana, Marisha, or, especially, Lalechka. I was concerned that even if Mariana was inside, they wouldn't let me see her. When she was still at the children's home in Zabrze, Sophia went several times to meet the girl, but they wouldn't let her in. The Rabbinate people who took custody of the Jewish children were concerned about letting them meet their Polish rescuers. We handed Mariana over to the Rabbinate people of our own volition, but there were rumors about Jewish children who were taken by trickery and even by force from the Polish families that saved them. The Rabbinate knew that any meeting between the children and their rescuers could end up in disaster for both.

"Wait here, please," the woman told me in a provincial French accent. Her white hair was collected loosely on her neck, her clothes were a bit ragged, and judging by the large key chain she tied with a rope around her wide waist, I assumed she was the gate keeper. She returned a few minutes later, accompanied by a tall and thin woman in a simple, dark blue, cotton dress. This woman's facial lines were delicate and exact and her skin sheer and taut, almost transparent. Her brown eyes were sunken but full of life and curiosity. If not for her gray hair, I would have guessed she was 30 years old at most.

"I'm looking for a girl named Rachel Zonshein; is she here?" I asked the tall woman, hoping she wouldn't notice the tremble in my voice.

"And who are you?" she inquired.

"My name is Irena Zawadzka; she was with me during the war. Her mother was my best friend. I'm a student in Paris, and I'd like to visit her."

"I manage this place," she told me. "Please, come with me." She gestured for the older woman to open the gate for me.

The children continued to play in the yard, but I still couldn't spot Rachel among them. The headmistress turned toward the main entrance to the home—a large, gray building with chunks of plaster crumbling off its tall walls—and led me up a staircase to the second floor. The inside of the building didn't look much better: the stairs leading up to the second floor were crooked, and the railing creaked when I leaned on it; I hoped no child would fall when running down those rickety stairs. The walls were painted a faded gray, which was peeling to reveal another coat of faded gray. Even though it was supposed to be a children's home, there were no pictures or children's drawings on the walls. This emptiness and shabbiness imposed a sad atmosphere on the place.

"Before the war this building used to be a regional home for the aged," the headmistress told me while we were climbing the stairs. She spoke in fluent French, with a slight accent I couldn't identify. "A Jewish family, among the only ones in the entire area, ran the place. When the war began, the family adopted a forged identity, but somebody pointed them out to the Gestapo, which came down and sent the family and all the building's residents to Auschwitz, turning the building into their local headquarters."

She was telling me all this as if she were guiding a museum tour, absent any accusation or judgment. "After the war, the villagers felt so guilty about the entire affair that when representatives of the Joint came here, they immediately handed them the keys to the building."

We went past a long and narrow room whose doors were wide open. I noticed two straight rows of small, perfectly made, iron beds. Even the beds in this place looked sad. The headmistress stopped at the opening to the next room and pointed to the far corner. Near the tall window, on a small wooden chair, sat a girl in a dark blue dress, her black hair cut short. Her gaze was turned to the open window, and even when I came close to her, she didn't turn her head to face me. The headmistress remained standing another short moment by the door, then I heard her turning and walking away.

"Mariana," I whispered to the girl.

She wouldn't look at me.

"Marisha, it's me, your aunt." I kneeled next to her, trying to catch her gaze, which was trained on a point somewhere in the distance. I sat down on the bed nearest her, took out of my briefcase the chocolate bar I was able to purchase in Paris for a lot of money, a little before I started visiting the children's homes. The bar was a little bent out of shape after my many trips with it, but it remained whole nonetheless. I handed it to her. As a small child, Mariana was crazy for sweets, most of all chocolate, which was unobtainable during the war. Now she didn't even turn to look at the chocolate I was giving her, and her eyes remained focused on some invisible point outside the window.

"Rachel," I called her by her new name.

She continued to ignore me.

I extended my hand to caress her hair; she didn't budge, only remained seated, gazing at the horizon.

"Lalechka," I whispered, caressing her hair. When she left Shedlitz, Rachel was a happy and cheerful girl, who loved doing pranks and carrying on with Stephan and Janek. In Fublaines, I discovered a sad and lonely girl, sitting quietly before a big window, isolated from the world. The tears choked my throat.

After a few minutes of silence, I asked her, "Would you like to go on a walk?"

She shrugged her shoulders. That was the first reaction she showed to my presence, and when I got up, to my surprise, she, too, got up. She had grown taller and even more beautiful in two years, but her face became serious and sad. Her cropped hair made her look older than her six and a half years. I wanted to take her in my arms, hug her and promise that everything would be all right, but I knew I couldn't keep such a promise. We started walking toward the door, climbed down the stairs to the ground floor and went outside. A number of children were still playing in the big courtyard. For a moment, we both stood and gazed at them, and then she went behind the building, where there was a small garden.

"Zosha says hi," I told her. I thought that mentioning Sophia, Mariana's mamma during the war would soften her, but she persisted in her silence. I told her about Janek and Stephan, about my mother Sabina who was like her grandmother, about Uncle Valente who loved to hold his pipe backwards in his mouth while making elephant sounds, and all the other people she loved and all the places in Shedlitz she was happy to visit. And throughout all that, she kept her silence.

We reached the edge of the garden and sat down on a peeling, green, wooden bench. "Would you like me to tell you a story?" I remembered how much she loved it when I read her stories at bedtime, and how every evening when she was staying with me, she would ask me to tell her a different story. I was hoping a story would remind her of our time together. I was afraid maybe she had forgotten everything.

"Once upon a time there were two children. The boy was named…" I stopped and waited. When Mariana was little, she loved to complete the story and was proud every time for knowing the missing words. This time she wouldn't complete the sentence.

"The boy's name was Jahsz," I finished it for her, "and the girl was called…"

Rachel remained silent.

"Jahsz and Maugusza lived with their parents in a wood cabin…" and so I continued to recite the story continuously, to the point when the children found the pebbles Jahsz had left behind and traced their way back to their parents' home. I was in mid-sentence when Mariana stood up suddenly, stared at me with her big, black eyes, and said quietly, "They didn't want to go back at all, because they didn't have parents." Her voice was clear and sharp; she blazed those words as if pointing out to me a terrible blunder I had caused, then turned around and left.

Her words continued to reverberate in my ears for a very long time. I wanted to get up and run after her, hold her in my arms, but I remained seated, allowing her to walk away. The thought of this little girl carrying such a heavy load on her shoulders devastated me with feelings of sadness and regret. Instead of wasting all this time waiting in France, she could have stayed with us and live happily for two more years.

Finally, I got up to leave. When I approached the front of the building, the headmistress came toward me, accompanied by the pudgy concierge. "I think it was enough for now," she said in a clear voice and led me gently but firmly to the front gate.

The following weekend I rode once again to Fublaines, as I did the weekend after as well. Each time the headmistress received me coolly but permitted me to enter. Mariana persisted in her silence and would not acknowledge my presence. On those other visits, she would no longer leave the building with me, nor relate to the stories I tried to tell her. Her face remained sealed, and her eyes continued to gaze out the window, next to which she sat on those two additional visits. After my third visit, the headmistress informed me in her dry and cool voice: "I believe it would be better for the child if you don't come again."

At the end of June I completed my studies and was about to return to Poland. In recent weeks the streets of Paris were filling up with many American diplomats, in town to carry out the Marshall Plan. Shiny, black, American cars were speeding along the city streets, store shelves began to fill up with products, which until now could only be gotten on the black market, and the cafés filled up with tourists. Unlike France, Poland was under Soviet rule, and the letters reaching me from home reported economic distress and political uncertainty. In Paris they talked ceaselessly about the severe tension between Western European states and the states of the East, and I was wondering how it could be that my country was once again permitting others to step on it and whether what the Americans were doing in Paris was so much better.

Before my return to Poland, I decided to travel one more time to Fublaines. I felt that I couldn't leave France without seeing Mariana again. The sight of the girl sitting silently by the big window didn't leave me all those weeks, and the few words she hurled at me on my first visit, when I told her about "Jahsz and Maugusza," were still reverberating in my memory, sharp and painful.

This time, when I approached the gate of the children's home, I was surprised to discover the place was empty and quiet. I attempted to open the gate, but it was locked with chains. I rang the bell and after a few minutes, the short concierge appeared.

"Where are the children?" I asked her.

"They all left. Went to Palestine," she answered indifferently.

My throat was choking, and tears flooded my eyes.

* * *

A few months after returning from Paris to Shedlitz, an unfamiliar young man showed up at my house. "Are you Irena Zawadzka?" He asked. Even though the war was finished three years ago, he looked like a refugee who just came out of the hellfire. He was very thin and his clothes were several sizes too big. At first I thought he was looking for Mariana. Over the past few years, she had been sought by Yechiel, Aaron Jablon's brother, and Moshe, his cousin, both of whom returned from Russia after the war. But this man wasn't looking for the girl, he only stuck his hand inside his backpack, took out a small, wrinkled notebook, and handed it to me. The notebook was covered in tight, round and precise handwriting. Even all those years later I identified it without hesitation: it was Zippa's handwriting.

Chapter 27
RACHEL

A few days after Miss Zawadzka came to visit me again but I wouldn't speak to her, the headmistress walked into our Hebrew lesson with a big smile on her face. She almost cried when she announced in a trembling voice, "In a few days we're going to Israel. Not Palestine, not Eretz Israel, but the State of Israel, our country."

To be honest, I didn't care all that much where I was going. Over the past few years, I'd always been going someplace and it was never anywhere I wanted to be. All the time I was in waiting mode, sometimes not knowing what I was waiting for, only that I was waiting for something that never came. After saying goodbye to someone I had thought was my mother, I waited for her to come visit me at the children's home in Zabrze, but she didn't come. Even the one I had thought was my aunt didn't come. When she came, at last, to visit me at the children's home in France, I no longer wanted to talk to her. I was so mad about having to wait so long for her to show up, that I wasn't able to say anything. I knew that at the end of the visit she would disappear again, and I wouldn't see her for a long time.

Meanwhile, I started waiting for somebody else: my uncle who lived in Israel. After they found him and told me that he lived in a city by the big sea with the sun that shines all year round, I started to draw every day the sea and the shining sun. At first I didn't know what the sea looked like, but the headmistress showed me pictures of Eretz Israel and even a few pictures of the city of Tel Aviv.

On the evening before our journey to Israel, the headmistress told us to pack all our clothes and our things and to be ready out in the yard the next day after breakfast. While I was packing my suitcase, I discovered in one of the pockets the little box with the medallion of the holy mother and the gold chain with the cross that Sophia gave me on my only birthday party. I couldn't recall how old I was on that birthday, but I remembered that everyone gave me presents and Irena even baked me a chocolate cake that was so tasty, I ate more and more of it until I threw up everything. Since we came to Fublaines I never put on the chain with the cross, and it stayed inside the little box in the suitcase, together with the medallion, and I almost forgot about them. Now I took out the medallion and the cross, put them in the palm of my hand and stared at them for a long time. They reminded me of Sophia and Irena, but I was still mad at them for not coming to visit me for such a long time, and now I didn't know what to do with these things that reminded me of the home and even the family I once had. When all the other girls in the room finished packing and left, I tucked the chain with the cross and the medallion of the holy mother under my mattress. They belonged to Mariana Timinska and I was Rachel Zonshein now, a completely different girl. I didn't want to take with me to Israel something that didn't belong to me any more. I only put in the suitcase the old, torn teddy bear, which I could no longer remember who gave it to me and when, and the doll I got from Mr. and Mrs. Olszakowsky for my only birthday celebration.

I took out the pictures Sophia had given me before I boarded the train that took me far away from her. I recalled how she told me then that the people in the picture were my real parents and my real grandmother. Over the past two years, I would look every night at the woman in the white dress and the big smile who was holding a baby a little reminiscent of me, and the tall man in the visor hat and soldier's uniform, and the older woman with the serious face. Now I felt that I knew them. They were my family, after all. I couldn't understand how come my real mother looked so happy and yet I'm so sad now. But the eyes of the man in the soldier's uniform were a little sad and so I believed that he really was my father. I tried to forget the words written in back of the pictures, the words Mr. Olszakowsky read to me on the train that took us from our town, because every time I remembered them I became even sadder, but I couldn't forget them completely. I put the pictures between the pages of a little book of Psalms they handed out to us back in Zabrze, and I wrapped the little book with a new shirt they gave me in Fublaines because all the clothes I came in were too small already. Now I placed the shirt with the book at the center of the suitcase and around it I arranged nicely all the rest of my clothes and bedding. Those pictures were the only thing left to me from my family.

The next morning big trucks arrived, and all the children and all the counselors boarded them and we started on our way. I wasn't sorry to leave this place, because I knew I was going to my uncle in Israel, to a place with a big sea where the sun is shining year-round. For almost two days, we rode in the trucks until finally we reached the harbor of a city called Marseille. Big ships were bobbing on the blue water next to small boats. Some of those ships, our headmistress explained, took part in the war. That was the first time I had seen a real sea and real ships and boats, and I was so excited I could hardly talk. The sea was so beautiful, so blue and radiant; the sunrays danced on the quiet waves and for a moment I felt something my heart didn't recognize at all. I felt a little less sad. I think it was my first time feeling this way. I knew that soon I, too, would be living in a city by the sea where the sun is shining all the time.

In the port of Marseille, there was a mob of children and adults, all of whom had come to make aliyah to Eretz Israel. The headmistress attached me to one of the older girls and told her to keep an eye on me the whole way until we reached Israel. I was six and a half when I went to Israel, and the girl watching me was twelve but looked to me like a little mamma. She was short and silent, and her eyes were sad, and when she spoke it felt as if she was a small woman with a child's voice.

As soon as the ship left the harbor and began to sail on the high seas, I completely forgot all about the uncle waiting for me in Israel, the big city by the sea with the sun that shines year-round, and I just stood by the railing and puked. Thc twelve-year-old girl watching over me tried to help, but besides holding my hand and trying to comfort me, there wasn't much she could do. Congestion on board the ship was terrible; everywhere there were piles of people, children and bundles, crying babies and weird odors. The older girl and I decided to sleep on the top deck, where at least the air was good.

On the seventh day of our journey, we were awakened in the morning to the cries of excitement emanating from all over: "There's the coast! There's Haifa! We've arrived in Israel!" The grownups started hugging and kissing one another and dancing in circles; the children were jumping and screaming, everybody looked happy and thrilled. I looked at the coastline and recognized white houses on the side of a mountain. It was the most beautiful city I had seen in all my life. As soon as I saw it, I stopped feeling the nausea I had been suffering since the ship left Marseille harbor. Only the older girl accompanying me was not as happy as the rest of us. "No one is waiting for me here anyway," she told me in her weak voice.

When we landed in the Haifa harbor and got off the ship, they assembled all the children arriving from France, and after making lists and checking to see that we were all present, they divided us once more into groups. I was weak and tired and felt that the earth was literally moving under my feet, and I almost passed out. But just then the headmistress arrived with a short guy with bright, brown hair, parted meticulously. He wore thick-framed glasses behind which I managed to see big, brown eyes. "Rachel," the headmistress told me excitedly, "this is your Uncle Shimon."

Uncle Shimon gave me his hand, and we shook. He had a big and warm hand, and I think I saw a tear rolling down from his eye, but I didn't say anything.

The uncle took me on a bus to his home in the big city by the sea. He introduced me to my aunt and to the little baby they had a year before. The uncle said I would have to sleep on the living room sofa, and that he hoped it won't bother me. It didn't bother me at all because I was so happy to finally be in my own home, sleep in my own bed, and to no longer have to eat with many other children or shower with many other girls. Most of all I was glad to be with my own family.

The sea really was blue, and the sun was really shining every day in the new city and the oranges my uncle bought in the market were sweet and full of juice. My uncle loved telling me stories about my mother and my grandfather and grandmother, and he showed me their pictures from when they were young, and sometimes he, too, was with them in the old pictures. He even showed me a picture of my mother with Miss Sophia and Miss Irena when they were all young. Only about my father he had almost nothing to say and he didn't have his pictures. The only picture I had from my father was the one I brought with me.

My uncle asked me many questions about the last time I saw them and what I remembered, but I remembered nothing. Sometimes I told him my mother would hold me in her arms and smile a big smile, and that my father had a soldier's stick and hat, but later I realized that I was telling him stories I had made up for myself during the long nights when I would be looking at the pictures I got from Sophia. When my uncle would start asking too many questions, Aunt Penina would tell him in Yiddish to leave me alone. Every time she wanted to tell him something she didn't want me to understand, she switched to Yiddish, but he always answered her in Hebrew.

A short while after coming to Israel I began the first grade. Each day I would come home excited and impatient to share with Uncle Shimon and Aunt Penina everything I learned in school. I was living with my family in the big city by the sea, and I stopped expecting Sophia and Irena to come visit me. It's been a few months since anyone had asked me to pack my suitcase and get ready to leave, and I felt that I was exactly where I needed to be.

One Shabbat my Uncle Shimon took me to eat ice cream by the sea. He said only the two of us were going, without my aunt and the baby. I loved going with my uncle to the beach because he always bought me chocolate ice cream and told me happy stories about my mother and my grandfather and grandmother and didn't ask me about the last time I saw them. Even though I didn't really know them, I loved listening to my uncle's stories about my real family. I was a little surprised that he was taking me for ice cream on the beach because it was almost winter and the sea was stormy. Still, I wasn't cold, definitely not as cold as in Poland or France, where it was always terribly cold in the winter because the homes didn't have heat.

I asked for chocolate ice cream, my favorite, and my uncle bought me a double scoop. We sat down on a big terrace overlooking the water, and at first my uncle kept silent for a very long time. When he started to talk his face became serious and at first I wasn't getting what he was telling me, because I was focusing on the ice cream and on the brilliant dots dancing on the blue water. When I began to understand what he was telling me, I noticed that my ice cream was already dripping on the new clothes my aunt had bought me in the big store not far from our house. "I'm sure you'll have a good time there…" I heard him saying in his quiet voice. "It's for your own good…" he kept on talking, but I wasn't listening any longer. The ice cream continued to drip on me until my uncle took it from my hand and dumped it in the garbage. He wiped the ice cream with a paper napkin but it still left a brown spot on my new, baby blue skirt, and I was mad at him more for the stain than for what he told me. It sounded familiar and made sense that I would have to leave again. "I'm sure you'll find new girlfriends," he said and continued to clean my skirt until the paper napkin was turned into a small, wrinkled ball.

A few days after we went to eat ice cream on the beach Uncle Shimon told me it was time to go. He asked if I wanted him to help me pack the suitcase. I told him I was very good at packing suitcases and that I could manage alone. I was seven already and packed enough suitcases in my life. I rode with my uncle to the Egged central bus station, where tall buses were standing in long columns. My uncle told me the bus to Haifa stood at platform number 1. "From Haifa we'll take the bus to Nahariya," he told me, and I recalled all at once the places where I had lived in recent years. They always promised that the next place would be better. They always said not to worry; I always anticipated something that never happened.

We reached Nahariya at noontime. Throughout the long trip, my stomach was growling and I was sorry I hadn't touched the breakfast my Aunt Penina made me. The bus station in Nahariya had only one platform, and the station was surrounded by piles of sand because, my uncle explained, they were building a second platform.

Nahariya was a small town with low houses and red rooftops. It was very different from the big city where Uncle Shimon lived, and looked more like a small village. "We have to walk a little," my uncle told me and picked up my suitcase. "Look how beautiful, there's the Ga'aton!" he exclaimed when we walked over a tiny spring, but to my eyes it didn't seem beautiful at all. "And here's the water tower!" he said, and I felt how he was trying hard to sound happy. "Neve Ha'Yeled should be right around here."

A gravel path led us to the place my uncle called Neve Ha'Yeled. It was a tall, two-story building, circled by round, cement bows and surrounded by a tall, barbed wire fence. The iron gate was locked, and after Uncle Shimon rang the bell, a boy appeared and let us in. The creaking gate sounded like a howling cat. There was a big grass lawn around the building, with all kinds of trees, and even a small flower garden. The laughter of boys and the singing of girls emanated from inside the building. A tall and handsome man came to greet us. He shook my hand firmly and said to me, "Shalom, I'm Gershon, and you must be Rachel."

I remained silent, a bit confused.

Gershon gave me a big smile, then bent over and whispered, "Tell me, Rachel, do you already know how to swim?"

Chapter 28
SHIMON

After leaving Rachel at the children's home in Nahariya, I kept walking restlessly in the town streets before boarding a bus back to Tel Aviv. I kept reflecting on her indifferent expression, how she didn't cry, didn't say anything, how I felt her little body stiffening when I hugged her. I understood that she was angry. Ever since I had first told her about Neve Ha'Yeled, back in the small café on the promenade, Rachel had turned silent and remote. Even before that day she wasn't exactly talkative, but at least she let me in on her school experiences. Now she wouldn't do even that. She would return from school, put her little book bag next to her bed and sit down by herself on the porch until she was called in for dinner. Penina was also unable to get her to talk, although I'm not sure how much she really tried, and when I came home from work Rachel was already tired and shortly thereafter would fall asleep on the living room couch. I knew I disappointed her, but even worse than that, I felt that I disappointed my parents and especially my sister Zippa, whose last wish it had been to find me and bring Rachel to me.

My decision to send Rachel to the children's home in Nahariya was one of the toughest in my life, but I had no choice; I knew if I wanted to keep my family intact I had to do it. The apartment was tiny and crowded, my pay at the department store was miniscule, and the bonus I received for my service in the world war was not much help. When Penina informed me she was pregnant again, we understood that for the sake of the girl, too, we had to find a better place for her.

A few days after Rachel left our home, I woke up one night awash in sweat. The events of the war once again overtook my dreams.

* * *

The British did not treat the Eretz Israel recruits joining their ranks as soldiers but as manual laborers supporting the fighting forces. After we had been annexed by his majesty's army, we stayed a few months in the Libyan desert, advancing all the time alongside the British combat units. The main task of the Pioneer Corp was to erect and strike camps, dig up fortification ditches, provide porter service loading and unloading military equipment, and other support work. I wasn't put off by the hard work, but as someone who grew up in a European town, the encounter with living conditions in the Libyan desert almost made me go AWOL, even if it meant walking on foot all the way back to Eretz Israel. Tremendous sand storms frequently covered the entire camp, halting all activity for many hours. After every such storm, the auxiliary soldiers from Eretz Israel were forced to remove large sand deposits from the equipment and to rebuild the collapsed camp. In addition, the numerous transportation problems imposed constant shortages of food, water, and supplies.

In January 1941, the British invaded the port of Tobruk, chasing off the Italian forces, and two months later we left the ruined and bombed harbor in a convoy of ships. Only on the high seas did we find out we were headed to Greece, where the British anticipated a German attack. We comprised an enormous force of tens of thousands of soldiers: English, Scottish, Irish, Australian, New Zealanders, Indians, and a few thousand Eretz Israelis, all of us about to join the great war raging through Europe. The idea that

I was about to be fighting the Germans on European soil excited and frightened me in equal measures. My confusion was great. I was in the middle of the Mediterranean, aboard a ship that was part of a large and powerful force, in the opposite direction and under completely different circumstances than the course I had taken only six years before.

My unit spent about two weeks in the port of Piraeus, where we mostly unloaded equipment that arrived in the harbor and transported it to the forces spread across northern Greece. In April of 1941, the entire Balkan was erupting; Bulgaria joined the Axis forces, Yugoslavia was attacked by Germany and its army surrendered, and on the 6th of the month German military forces invaded Greece, too. When the British forces in northern Greece realized they couldn't measure up to the Nazi army, they began a retreat southward to the port of Kalamata in the southern part of the Peloponnesos peninsula, where we were supposed to be boat lifted. But even before we reached the outskirts of Kalamata, we were spotted by the German airplanes which started bombing us ceaselessly. Somehow we managed to reach the harbor while confusion and chaos reigned everywhere. I spent those days of retreat southward experiencing fear, but even worse than that was my disappointment in the "powerful" British army. The soldiers were tired, hungry and dirty, and most of them had abandoned their weapons during the retreat. I was hoping that after the retreat I would continue fighting in a different theater. I didn't imagine any other option.

The British evacuation ships managed to reach the port of Kalamata despite the continuous air raids, and in a few days lifted most of the retreating British forces. On the night of April 28, 1941, the last evacuation ships entered the harbor. Nearly ten thousand British soldiers and some 1500 Eretz Israeli volunteers who remained in the area expecting evacuation were waiting for the ships in the woods and the mountains around the harbor, but instead of entering the port and releasing us from the inferno we were stuck in, the ships turned around and returned to the open seas. We could only guess that because of the great risk of heavy bombing the ships were ordered to go back to Alexandria. Shocked and disappointed, we stared at the ships that were supposed to rescue us disappearing beyond the horizon. At the same time, the vanguard units of the German army were arriving in Kalamata.

On the morning of the 29th of April, following three days of heavy bombing, and when he realized his forces were surrounded, the commander of the remaining British forces in Greece surrendered to the German army. It was a humiliating and depressing event, filled with disturbing question marks. The German soldiers, who have turned into our commanders, pushed us into pens that were constructed outside the city, and for two days conducted detailed questioning which included meticulous listing of all the soldiers that fell into their hands. A few Jewish soldiers, most of them German emigrants who feared being considered traitors by the Germans, could not bear the fear and uncertainty of falling into German captivity, and committed suicide before the Germans had a chance to interrogate them.

When they were done making their lists, the Germans took us on a trip that lasted three months from the camp in Kalamata through another camp in Corinth, from there to a camp in Saloniki, and from there on a cargo train through Yugoslavia and Austria to our final destination. During the journey, we were placed in closed cattle cars that only a day before were used for shipping cement. The Germans packed fifty men in each car, pushed against one another without a drop of water, without food, and almost without air. In the camps where we made stops, we were given miniscule portions of food, and sometimes not even that much. Hundreds of POWs were forced together in a rickety shack or slept inside tunnels, filth was everywhere, and soon we were plagued by lice, which was followed by harsher diseases.

While staying in the transition camps, we were sent to work building bridges and roads that the British had demolished during their retreat a few weeks earlier. At the Saloniki camp, a Yugoslav POW told us that Russia had joined the war, and this news revived us and gave us a little hope that not all had been lost. Despite the rough conditions during the journey, the Jewish soldiers were slowly becoming a cohesive unit, and we even conducted Friday night services. What we couldn't do together during the fighting, we achieved under the harsh prison conditions.

On August 1, 1941, we arrived in Lamsdorf, a small town in Upper Silesia, a region that was annexed to Germany at the beginning of the war, and where our destination, the notorious Stalag 8B POW camp was built.

* * *

For many weeks after Rachel had left our home, I was walking around bothered and restless. I couldn't forgive myself for abandoning this little girl, especially given everything she'd been through. My memories from the POW camp in Silcsia were sharp and clear. I did not forget how we were packed in there, hundreds of men in a lousy and broken down shack, and I was angry at myself that here, in my own home, I was unable to host my little niece, a Holocaust survivor without any other relative in the whole country. My conscience continued to trouble me for a very long time.

Chapter 29
RACHEL

Every morning at Neve Ha'Yeled, including the weekends, started at precisely 6 o'clock. Gershon and his wife Yafa woke us up with classical music they played on Gershon's big gramophone. Summer, winter, spring or fall, we would quickly put on our bathing suits and run along with Gershon down the hundred meters to the beach, swim for half an hour and run back into the warm showers. Those who couldn't swim, like me, had to learn very quickly. After breakfast, we'd go to the local elementary school in town. Besides swimming, Gershon taught us how to play chess, sing Israeli songs, listen to classical music, tie all kinds of knots, and play volleyball. But most of all he liked to read to us the books he considered "the classics." In the afternoon, he and two counselors helped us with our homework, and once a week we would go with them to eat Strauss ice cream at the town center. But despite all that, I still hated Neve Ha'Yeled, and most of the time remained as sad and lonely as I was in Zabrze and in Fublaines.

Four other girls shared my room, two of whom had just recently arrived from Poland. They were stuck to each other the whole day long, and at night before bedtime they would whisper to each other in Polish for the longest time. I had to close my ears real good to avoid hearing what they were saying. I wanted to completely forget that ugly language that reminded me that I once had a real family and a mother and an aunt who took care of me for a really long time and then sent me here. But no matter how hard I tried to forget my Polish, I couldn't, and every night I was forced to hear those two girls telling each other how their mother or their father got shot right before their eyes, and how their little brother and sister cried so much when they, too, were shot, and how they had to flee from one place to another and hide and lie and steal. In Fublaines you weren't allowed to talk before bedtime, and during the day I hardly ever played with the other children, so these girls in Neve Ha'Yeled were the first I heard talking about what happened "there." Sometimes I felt their stories were going to drive me crazy, but I didn't want to ask Gershon to move me to another room because I was afraid the stories there would be even worse. I knew that I, too, was born in Poland, but besides Sophia who told me my whole family was in heaven, and besides the headmistress in Fublaines who told me my parents were killed in the war, no one had ever told me what exactly happened to my father and mother and grandfather and grandmother, and why it happened. Were they also shot? Who were those people killing so many human beings and why did they do it? In my picture with my mother she didn't look like a bad person, so why did they have to kill her?

Some of the children at Neve Ha'Yeled didn't have family to go to and on the weekends they would stay with Gershon and Yafa. On Friday nights Gershon conducted Kabbalat Shabbat, Yafa cooked us special food, and Shabbat mornings in wintertime they sometimes let us skip the morning swim. We had free time on Shabbat, and I liked spending most of the day in my room, reading books that Gershon brought especially for me from the Nahariya library. Since Uncle Shimon didn't drive a car, he would call every Shabbat to ask how I was, and to tell me about Aunt Penina and the new baby they had in the meantime. Once in a while he would visit me in the middle of the week and bring me presents—sometimes new clothes and other times a book he bought in Tel Aviv. He always asked me many questions about the children and my lessons, and I would tell him only what I thought would make him happy. Shimon explained that Neve Ha'Yeled was considered an excellent place and that Gershon was known as a "great educator," plus it was free because the place belonged to the Youth Aliyah organization. I would listen to him, but I felt angry at him, too, because he sent me to a remote and lonely place like others had done before him.

During vacation days most of the children would go to their families or their relatives, but even though I had a place to go, I preferred to stay with Yafa and Gershon and the kids with no place to go. Only during summer vacation would Uncle Shimon arrive and take me to spend an entire week in his house. I loved going back to Tel Aviv, going to the movies with Shimon, seeing all the stores and all the people who always looked so busy, but toward the weekend I would want to go back to Nahariya and in the end I was glad when Shimon accompanied me on the bus back to Neve Ha'Yeled.

Toward the end of the sixth grade, all the kids in my class started telling one another where they were going to study next year. There was no high school in Nahariya, and they had to identify a boarding high school for the Neve Ha'Yeled kids who graduated the sixth grade and didn't have family to go back to. I didn't know if my uncle and aunt in Tel Aviv would want me to come live with them, and I was afraid to ask. I waited for them to bring it up.

On one of the last days of the school year, Uncle Shimon came to visit me. We went to have Strauss ice cream in a small café, sat down on two tall chairs and looked at the Ga'aton. Uncle Shimon drank black coffee and kept wiping his glasses, and then, at last, he said, "Rachel, I think it's time you found out what happened to your parents."

While Shimon was telling me everything he knew, I felt I was about to start crying, but somehow I held back. I thought about the two girls who shared my room in my first year at Neve Ha'Yeled and how much their stories scared me. But what Uncle Shimon was telling me was much worse. I felt sorry for my mother who was forced to hide, escape, be apart from her family and finally give me up, her year-old baby. I thought about my father and my grandfather and grandmother who were killed in such a horrible fashion. I felt strange longings for people I didn't know at all, maybe because I knew they loved me the way no one in the world did, nor ever will.

Finally, Shimon told me about Sophia and Irena, who took care of me after my whole family was killed, and I started to have dim memories of them. I asked him if I could meet them some day. "Israel does not have diplomatic relations with Poland," he explained, "the regime in Poland is very tough, and they can't come here now. Maybe in a few years you'll be able to meet them."

"You're so lucky to have made aliyah to Israel before the war," I told him. Suddenly I realized that if Shimon had not gone to Eretz Israel I may have been left without a relative in the whole world.

"It's true, but did you know I, too, was in the war?"

"Really?" Shimon had never told me about it

"Shortly after the war in Europe began I enlisted in the British army that was fighting the Germans. We were an auxiliary force of Eretz-Israeli soldiers supporting the British. And I served in the Pioneer Corp."

"Where did you fight?" The idea that Shimon had fought the Nazis was surprising and frightening.

"We came by boat to Greece, but the Nazis invaded Greece with such force that the British army had to surrender."

"Were you afraid?"

"Very." Shimon was silent for a while, and it appeared that it was hard for him to remember those war experiences. "I was taken to a POW camp called Stalag 8B, exactly two months before you were born."

"Really, you were captured by the Germans?" I couldn't believe how close I had come to losing my only blood relative.

"Yes, I was in German captivity, and I stayed alive. Imagine, you have such a brute for an uncle!" he tried to joke.

"How long were you there?"

"Too long," Uncle Shimon said, and his face became serious.

Chapter 30
SHIMON

I had great trepidations before deciding to tell Rachel what had happened to her family in the war. I didn't know how a 12-year-old girl would deal with such a terrifying reality, but Rachel was mature for her age in all respects, and now, when she was about to move to yet another place, I felt obliged to tell her. She so reminded me of Zippa, until sometimes when she spoke I imagined I was hearing my sister's voice. Like her mother, she was intelligent, sharp, clever and whimsical. Her Hebrew was beautiful and correct, and when we conversed, I never stopped wondering how proud her grandparents and parents would have been if they saw her.

After I had told her about her family, I felt that we formed a special bond that hadn't been there before. I wasn't planning to tell her about my experiences in German captivity, but now the words were just streaming out of me. Her questions showed interest and curiosity, and for me this was actually the very first opportunity ever to tell anyone about my time as a POW. I never told even my wife Penina all these details.

***

Stalag 8b was a huge camp into which the Germans siphoned tens of thousands of POWs they captured on the different fronts.

A huge flag with a swastika flew at the entrance, and we were welcomed by the camp commandant who informed us that "the same law applies to the Palestinian captives as to the British. You are now under the rule of the Geneva Convention. The German Wehrmacht is responsible for you, and you are subject to its authority."

I received a bed with a straw mat and a blanket in one of the dozens of long sheds that packed the camp grounds, and everything, including our meal service, was done in an orderly fashion. But despite the "calming" words of the German camp commandant, as the Jewish captives in the hands of the Germans we spent our first few days in the camp in a state of great insecurity and complete uncertainty regarding our future. And, indeed, after the Germans' promises on the first day to live up to the rules of the International Red Cross and obey the Geneva Convention, on the third day we were already divided into work gangs and sent each morning for hard labor that lasted from dawn till dark. Those labors were performed in several different locations and included building dams, mining coal, chopping wood and performing various tasks in factories around Lamsdorf. A few of us were even sent in late August 1941, to build a new POW camp for Russian soldiers. We deduced from that that the war on the eastern front was not progressing in a direction favorable to our side.

We were forced to work on Shabbat, on Jewish holidays and even on Yom Kippur, but Sunday was a day off, and we were allowed to play games and exercise. A substantial social and educational program began to flourish in the camp in the evenings and on Sundays. We discovered among us more than a few people able to teach Hebrew and other languages, the history and geography of Eretz Israel, Zionism, literature and social studies. We established a library using books we ordered via the Red Cross; we published a local newspaper, and of course we observed as best we could the Jewish holidays. Every Friday night we had a Kabbalat Shabbat, and we even established an improvised synagogue, run be a friendly priest from New Zealand.

We received the first rumors about the condition of the Jews in Europe from the first Russian captives who began to arrive in Lamsdorf during the winter of 1941. They were mostly civilians kidnapped for forced labor and could tell us about the deportation of Ukrainian Jewry, the identification tags Jews were forced to wear in German-occupied territories, and the decline of their living conditions in Russia, as well as, to the best of their knowledge, in Poland.

The next time I heard testimonies about the situation was in January of 1942 when I went out with a group of prisoners to work in constructing a new railroad near the town of Gleiwitz. Dry, blood freezing winds were blowing in the open area where we were working, the temperature went down to 30 below zero, and I felt that my bones were about to crack like matchsticks. On one of those days, some distance from us, there appeared a group of a few hundred workers in tattered clothes marked with five stars of David each: on the chest, the back, the sleeves and the left knee. A German soldier was lording over them, screaming incessantly, and the minute he walked a small distance away, I took advantage of the opportunity and came close to the workers. It turned out that they were Jews who had been kidnapped from various places in Poland (to my disappointment—or to my delight, I couldn't decide—none of them was from Shedlitz). From them, I learned about the establishment of ghettos in the cities, about the Judenrat, about sudden abductions in broad daylight, and about the killing of innocent Jews, including women and children. Those Jewish workmen suffered from a lack of food and clothing, and whenever possible we'd slip them food, cigarettes, and occasionally even a few clothes.

During the fall of that year, a group of prisoners returned to the Lamsdorf camp after working for a period of time at a metal factory near Katowice. During their work there, the group members met with Jewish forced laborers who told them that Aktions were taking place all across Poland. The Jews were being assembled in the town squares and shipped en masse to "camps."

The Jewish workmen couldn't tell us what exactly was taking place inside those camps, but according to rumors that were spreading through the Polish towns from which they came, it amounted to the elimination of the Jewish population in Poland. Additional testimony reached us in early 1943 when a group working in the coal mines of Jaworzno returned to Lamsdorf. Those workers told us that on their way to work at the mines they spotted a large camp with tall chimneys sticking out of it. Those chimneys were billowing thick smoke all the hours of the day, and when they asked the German foreman in charge of them what was this camp, he burst out laughing and said, "This is Auschwitz, someday you'll hear a lot about this place."

As to the Jewish forced laborers we saw once in a while around Lamsdorf or at the work sites where we'd be taken, those started to disappear from view, until by the beginning of 1944 none were seen anywhere.

By then I had spent close to three years in the camp. I had no idea if and when I would be released. The distress over my family haunted my sleep, which was so tortured and fraught with nightmares to begin with. It had been nearly a decade since I parted with my parents and my sister Zippa at the Shedlitz train station, and now I felt completely inept at being so close to them and still helpless to attain even a sliver of information on their whereabouts.

On January 10, 1945, we heard over the London radio that the Red Army had conquered Częstochowa and was progressing westward at a gallop. Little by little the Russians also plucked Gleiwitz, Sosnowiec and Bendin, all the places where we spent time in work camps over our years in captivity. It was obvious that the German officers and enlisted men in our camp were becoming ever more nervous and tense. In the course of the past year, the German Army was being defeated severely on all fronts, and the prisoners at Lamsdorf were receiving clear news about the advances of the allies on one end of Europe, and of the great accomplishments of the Red Army on the other. The camp prisoners developed different methods of listening to radio broadcasts from England, and despite the repeated searches by the Germans, they didn't always manage to discover our hidden units.

On the evening of January 15, 1945, all the camp dwellers were instructed to report to the front gate the next morning at seven. We weren't told where they were taking us, and all that was left for us to do was speculate about our destination. None of those speculations was very encouraging. The heavy snow that covered the entire area, and the fierce cold, didn't boost our optimism.

On the morning of January 16, close to fifty thousand prisoners were assembled, in groups of several hundred, each organized in three rows, and we began our march westward. The defeated Germans, who fled Poland in a rage, made us endure a path of agony, which I couldn't fathom how most of us came through alive.

For three months, we marched close to 850 kilometers in the heavy snow while most of us didn't wear decent shoes. The meat tins we took with us from the camp were completely frozen when we tried to eat them. The bread arrived every few days on open carts, completely waterlogged. Most days the Germans gave us a quarter of a loaf of bread and a bit of sausage, which was supposed to suffice for the entire day. Some days they gave no food at all, and we were forced to try our luck in nearby fields, where we usually found beets, kohlrabi, or potatoes. The only thing that saved us from a certain death were the Red Cross cars which arrived once or twice during the journey and handed out a little food, which obviously wasn't enough to satiate our hunger, but kept us alive. For drinking we'd thaw in tin cans the snow that lay on the fields throughout most of our journey.

The German soldiers' hands were very light on the trigger, and they often lost their bearings and would start screaming hysterically, or would obliterate prisoners for ridiculous violations like smoking a cigarette. They usually threw the bodies of the dead in the ditches along the road. During the dark and long nights we lit up campfires that warmed our exhausted bodies a little, and if we got lucky we'd spend the night in a warehouse or an abandoned barn, on a soft bed of straw or inside a chicken coop. The further west we got, the more frequent the air raids were becoming, and at every break we had to dig up shelter ditches for the German officers.

Many German refugees, mainly women, children and the elderly, were fleeing the Russians from Silesia in those days. They were easily as frightened and hungry as we were, and the British soldiers often gave them a little food. They had an easier time relating mercifully to German refugees than we, Eretz Israeli soldiers, did, having fed these past few years on grisly rumors and testimonies about the condition of Jews in Europe.

On the morning of April 12, 1945, we arrived in the town of Ziegelheim, Germany, forty kilometers south of Leipzig. At noontime, we started to hear the rumble of tanks coming at us. The German soldiers who were guarding us disappeared as if swallowed by the earth. The tanks coming toward us bore the flags of the United States. We started hugging and crying like children.

That was the happiest day of my life.

The Americans transferred us to a British unit, and in the beginning of May 1945, shortly before Germany's official surrender, we were flown to Newcastle, England. It was my first time flying on a plane, and the sights I was seeing were at once thrilling and gloomy. Bombarded cities, abandoned villages, and endless caravans of people and vehicles making their way all across Europe, streaming like long rivers in every direction. We remained a few weeks in a military camp in Newcastle, where the British set up a "recuperation camp," and then they drove us to Liverpool and boarded us on the good ship Britannica, which took us to Port Said, where there was a large British base. From Port Said, we continued by train to Nitzanim, and from there to the Saraphend base from which I had departed almost five years earlier, in August 1940, the place where my war began.

A little before I parted company with my numerous friends who had been with me through the hell of Stalag 8b and then the March of Death until the arrival of the American tanks, I was approached by an Australian fellow I befriended on the journey. "Why are you going back to Palestine?" he asked me in his typical Australian naiveté. "What exactly is waiting for you over there?"

"It's my country," I answered him.

"I live on a farm not far from Sidney. My family has been raising cattle and sheep for many years. You can live with us, and work. If you wish, you could live in Sidney, too. The Australian government will take care of anyone who fought on the British side."

"My friend," I began to respond, but I couldn't quite find the words to convey to this amiable Australian what the two words Eretz Israel meant to me. He reminded me of Herbert Shlonsky, the sporting goods store owner in Shedlitz who tried to persuade me to stay and work in his store rather than make aliyah to Eretz Israel. Suddenly I was reminded of the play Golden Boy, which British prisoners performed in the Stalag, and a phrase from it that, for some reason, stayed with me. "You're looking at today; I'm looking at tomorrow," I told my Australian friend.

He patted me on my shoulder, gave me a broad smile, and before running back to his buddies, he hugged me warmly and said, "Good luck, my friend."

I returned to Tel Aviv in mid-June, 1945. The sky was blue and the sun shone in its fullest glory. Mr. Ephraim Zelnik, from whom I used to rent a tiny apartment on Sheinkin Street, was weeping when he hugged me.

"I knew you'd be back, so I never rented your room," he said in a voice drenched in tears.

Chapter 31
RACHEL

It was almost evening when Shimon finished telling me about my family and the years he spent in German captivity.

"Thanks for listening to me," he said quietly.

"Thanks for telling me," I answered.

"I hope you're not angry at me for sending you to Neve Ha'Yeled. Please understand, things were really untenable in those years…"

"I'm not angry at all," I told him. When I thought of all the things that happened to Shimon, I felt a pang in my heart. Suddenly I understood that my quiet and dedicated uncle, who came by bus to visit me almost every week, was bearing a heavy load of memories from a family that was annihilated, from years of German captivity, and, in addition, guilt feelings for not being able to raise me in his home the way my mother requested. "I'm sure my mother wouldn't have been angry at you, either," I added after a moment. He hugged me strongly, and I felt that he was shivering a little, despite the heavy heat.

"You realize we haven't discussed where you should be going to school next year."

"True."

"I was thinking you'll do best on a kibbutz," he suggested quietly.

I had no idea what it would be like to live on a kibbutz, but many kids from Neve Ha'Yled said they were moving to a kibbutz the next year, and Gershon and Yaffa told us many stories about the kibbutz pioneers. I asked myself when I would finally find a place where I would feel well enough to want to stay.

"I think it's a good idea," I said.

"There are many good things in our country, and the kibbutz is one of them. These people came here and made the desert bloom. The Jewish National Fund, too, has done nice things in this country. When I came back from captivity, there was just one letter waiting for me at home, from the JNF. I carry it with me wherever I go ever since." He took a letter out of his blue bag and handed it to me.

26 Sivan, 5705, June 6, 1945
Dear Comrade,

Together with the entire Hebrew community in the land we extend a warm welcome to you upon your return from captivity and share in your happiness as you're stepping on the homeland soil for which you have been yearning on your path of wandering and toil.

The JNF is deeply grateful to the Hebrew soldier for his labor to redeem the land, and is proud of its eternal bond with our men and women in uniform wherever they may be, whom, apart from our efforts to prepare for them a land base for dwelling and settlement upon their return from battle, we've also included in our activities and delivered to them from afar the message of our liberated land.

To our great chagrin, we haven't been able to stay in touch with our brethren in captivity, although we've been made aware that even in prison you remembered the JNF and acted on its behalf.

When you return, you'll discover a Jewish community that has expanded in every area of life, with a broader settlement territory that we've expanded to regions a Jewish foot has not stepped on for many generations. Our community has accumulated much power. At the same time, unfortunately, you'll find that we've been disappointed and concerned regarding the political status of our enterprise here and the way the enlightened world views the state of our nation's remnants in Diaspora.

Still, don't let your spirits fall. We shall overcome this loss of sympathy with the victims and the terrible suffering of our nation. The Jewish Holocaust, our just demands, the glorious enterprise we've created, will serve as our foundations, and the vision of our complete redemption will not fail.

Upon your return to Eretz Israel we wish you a renewed integration in its life and the labor of its resurrection, and may we all live to see the fulfillment of the vision of our redemption soon.

We will plant a tree in your name as a sign of blessing and gratitude in Victory Forest, enclosed please find a document of confirmation.

Respectfully,
The board of the Jewish National Fund in Eretz Israel

After reading that letter, I felt great pride in my uncle. He was captured in war, managed to survive, and even the State of Israel was honoring him. My uncle is a hero, I thought.

Near the end of summer vacation my Uncle Shimon arrived in Neve Ha'Yeled to take me to a kibbutz he nicknamed "the kibbutz on a hilltop." Gershon and Yaffa bought me a new suitcase as a goodbye gift, and the evening before they helped me pack all my belongings in it. "It's for your visits to your Uncle Shimon," Gershon said in his deep voice. I recalled the first day I came with Shimon to Neve Ha'Yeled, I was a lonely seven-year-old girl who'd packed her suitcase too many times and was forced to part with anyone who'd ever loved her, first her real parents, then her new mother and aunt, then Uncle Shimon, and now Gershon and Yaffa, who, even though they had many other children to look after, still made everyone in Neve Ha'Yeled feel that he or she were an only child.

In early September 1953, Uncle Shimon and I took a noisy bus to my new home. "I'm sure you'll fall in love with the kibbutz on the hilltop," he said to me excitedly, but I could hardly hear him. The bus windows were open, and hot wind blew through my hair. I didn't want to arrive in the new place with messy hair, so I held my hair tight around my head the whole ride, so it wouldn't get blown. "They've got orchards and coops and a barn, too," Shimon continued to describe the place in his delicate voice, which I could barely hear now. "I'm sure you'll make many new friends."

Finally, the bus stopped by the entrance to the kibbutz. We got off and went to the gate, next to which stood a eucalyptus tree with a thick trunk, and I tried to figure out how many children were needed to hold hands in a circle around that trunk. Shimon and I went into the kibbutz and started walking on a wide dirt road that climbed up a hill. It really is a kibbutz on a hilltop, I thought to myself. The strong odor of compost hit me as we proceeded. To our left stood rows of cowsheds with chubby cows that kept eating and chasing off flies with their tails. To our right were numerous clucking chickens in long coops. So Uncle Shimon was right about that part, too. I was wondering why the kibbutz people decided to locate their cows and chickens by the entrance, of all places, and couldn't think of a logical answer. We continued to climb up the hill and passed by a tall and wide water tower, much taller and wider than the one in Neve Ha'Yeled. Next to it stood wooden sheds, crammed together, very similar to the pictures I had seen in my school books describing the various forms of settlement in Eretz Israel. The odors of the cowsheds and the coops were instantaneously replaced by the intoxicating aroma of citrus trees. A green grove spread before my eyes all the way to the horizon, and among the tree branches I could spot tiny, unripe fruits. In Neve HaYeled, there were many different citrus trees, of which I liked the clementines the best. Every fall we'd pick them, to eat at tea time. The fragrance of ripe clementines a minute after you finished peeling them was my favorite, and their taste was my second most favorite, after chocolate, of course. Now I breathed in the clean and clear aroma of the kibbutz on the hilltop. I had the strange feeling that I was breathing in the smell of freedom.

At the entrance to the high school stood a group of boys and girls who were singing cheerful songs that reminded me of the songs Gershon and Yaffa sang with us around the campfire on our long camping nights. The boys were handsome and tanned, the girls had long braids, and everybody was wearing blue shorts, white shirts, and sandals. I slowed down as we approached the singing youths and felt Shimon's hand on my shoulder.

Two girls came up to me, holding a large bouquet of flowers. They handed it to me with big smiles and one of them said, "You must be Rachel, welcome." Then they took me to the living quarters. When we got there, I paused for a moment at the entrance. Above the door they hung a big sign, especially for me, that said, in colored capital letters: Welcome to Kibbutz Alumah!

Epilogue
SOPHIA

Warsaw, January 9, 1985
Beloved Rachel,

I thank you so much for your holiday greetings as well as for the beautiful pictures you sent. You have wonderful and beautiful sons, and that's the greatest treasure in life.

Forgive me for not writing for such a long time. A few days ago I was shocked to discover that your own long letter was dated from two years ago, and I apologize for it. Your letter made me very happy; you wrote it with great sensitivity, and I thank you very dearly for that. I've waited for so long for this kind of letter, written with feelings and from the heart, as we are so close to one another despite the distance and the passage of time. Very close, considering my friendship with your mother and with you. I remember you as a sweet, little girl, and how we shared with you in all the hardships of living under German rule.

I haven't written for a long time because I didn't want to write an ordinary letter. I made up my mind to write you a detailed letter about many things of interest to you from your distant past. It wasn't easy to recall those awful days, but I mustered all my strength and returned to the years whose memory has become a bit dim, but which will never be forgotten.

I'll start with your mother Zippa's journal. A few years after the war, Irena was visited by a Jew who was saved somehow from the death camps. He brought with him a notebook in which your mother documented her last days and the destruction of the Jewish community of Shedlitz. Irena and I read the journal and were petrified by its contents. It was a blood curdling, eyewitness testimony about an event that is still incomprehensible, particularly in light of what we know today about the Holocaust. Of course, your mother wrote about you as well, about the suffering you were forced to endure in those days, and how she finally decided to hand you over to the Zawadzky family.

After we read the journal we understood—Irena and I—that for the sake of History we were obligated to turn it over to an authority for proper study and documentation. We delivered it to the committee that was established in the 1950s in Poland to investigate war crimes, and after they had examined it for several years, they returned it to us. We'd be glad to mail you the journal, but I must caution you that its content is not easy to digest. Today, when you're already a mature woman, I believe you will be able to come to terms with the terrible reality your mother described.

After the cursed Aktion (the expulsion of the Jews from the ghetto), your mother took her life in her hand, and in boundless self-sacrifice managed to pass through the barbed wire fences (your father, Jacob, being a Jewish policeman, probably aided her). That night she transferred you to the Zawadzky family who lived nearby (since Irena Zawadzka was also a good friend of your mother's). Your mother placed you in the arms of Mrs. Sabina Zawadzka, Irena's mother, with a letter requesting that she raise you in the spirit of loving others. She also requested that we seek out Shimon when it became possible to send you across the border.

During the time of the occupation, we had to be very careful, since there were many stool pigeons out there, happy to assist the Germans in locating Jewish children hidden by Polish families. If the Germans caught them, they beat them mercilessly and took cruel revenge of both the Jews and their benefactors. I relied in every aspect of concealing you on Mrs. Lucina Rychleski, with whom I became acquainted during the war. A short while after your mother managed to flee from the ghetto and a shelter was found for her, she decided to return in order to search for your father and your grandparents, but they were no longer among the living.

Irena and I followed all the necessary procedures to enter you in an orphanage in Shedlitz as an anonymous orphan, in order that you may be removed from there eventually, to be legally adopted by Mrs. Zawadzka. Except that in the meantime, while you were staying at the orphanage, you contracted a bad case of pneumonia, from which you recovered only due to the devoted care of Sabina and Irena. Mrs. Zawadzka was a dear soul, humble and noble, and you owe her a lot. She passed away a few years ago. Irena was also very close to you, I'll tell you about her later on in this letter.

After a few months, we decided to take you out of Shedlitz because too many people were showing an interest in you and were becoming suspicious. During the occupation, I was running schools in different places in the Lublin area and north of it. I would take you along, and people thought you were the illegitimate daughter of a friend of mine. That's where you grew up, under harsh and primitive conditions; you grew up together with Janek, the son of my friend Katja who worked with me in those schools. I took care of you for two years as if you were my own daughter, we didn't discriminate in the least between you and Janek, everything he received, you received, too. I managed to issue for you a birth certificate using the name of a Catholic girl, which is why you became Mariana Timinska. But we usually called you Marisha or Lalechka, Dolly, the name your father, Jacob Zonshein gave you.

After the liberation of eastern Poland in '44, I took a new job that forced me to travel a lot, so I took you back to Shedlitz. You stayed a few months with the Zawadzky family and played a lot with Stephanek, the son of Irena's brother Kazimir. Afterward, you stayed a period of time in my parents' house, where they took care of you with devotion and bottomless love. You also began attending kindergarten then, which you liked a lot.

One day, a short time after we celebrated your fourth birthday, some gentleman from the Jewish Committee of Shedlitz showed up and said that the Jewish community was taking on the responsibility and the care for Jewish orphans and arranging their transfer to Palestine. At first I refused to give you up, but after I contacted Shimon and he wrote that he wished for you to come live with him in Palestine, and in light of your mother's request in her last letter, I decided to hand you over.

My father rode with you to the office of the Jewish community in Warsaw and turned you in, and from there you went out into the big world. In the meantime, there were still a lot of complications and the delivery of Jewish children became stranded in France because the English were not allowing Jews into Palestine. While you were staying at an orphanage near Paris, Irena visited you there, since she was staying in France for her studies. She discovered you in a sad and depressed state; you didn't grace her with a single word during her visit, even though you knew her very well. My sad girl, you had to adjust so many times to new conditions, new schedules, new people —and then, so many times, conditions would force you to part with them. You must be made from hardy and positive stock, since despite everything that you endured you kept your faith in the kindness of people, because it was your mother's wish—together with a wish for a good life for you.

These days I'm the grandmother of three grandchildren already, sharing my strength and my time with them. Michael is four and a half and Anja is two and a half, and they're now with my eldest daughter in Canada. My granddaughter Susana is three and living in Warsaw. It goes without saying that I'm not left with too much free time for thinking.

Irena, too, like me, lives in Warsaw, and we see each other very often. She still teaches French, just like she's been doing all her life. Irena never married. A few years after the war she suffered a nervous breakdown, after which she became even weaker and more sensitive than she used to be – Irena always was a delicate soul, which was one of the reasons your mother and I loved her so much. During her breakdown she imagined that the Germans were returning to Poland, and so she destroyed parts of your mother's journal, especially the parts about your mother's escape from the ghetto and the people who helped her. She's regretting every single day the damage she caused. Over the years, she's suffered several other psychological events and we always took care of her with love and devotion.

I was delighted to hear that you're planning a visit to Poland. We'll come to greet you, Irena, Jadzia, Hanka—all of your mother's girlfriends. We'll receive you heartily and will introduce you to the country of your birth; we'll try to make it a pleasant experience. I was happy to tell from your business card that you serve as a manager. Your sons must be very proud of their mother, as am I.

I send you big kisses and wish you all the best in the new year—you, your sons, and Shimon and his family, too. Please tell Shimon I was touched by the photograph from his seventieth birthday. I hadn't imagined he had such a big family. May they all enjoy only the best. I'm also fast approaching that age, but my family isn't quite that big.

In closing, I thank you for approaching the Yad Vashem organization for a certificate of gratitude for us, but I don't believe we deserve any award. I did what I did, and likewise Sabina and Irena Zawadzka, because of our love for your mother and because it was the most natural thing to do. I would do it all over again if I had to.

Hugging and kissing you warmly,
Sophia Glazer-Olsakowska

AFTERWARD

Some ten years ago I visited a couple of friends of mine in San Francisco. One night the wife told me excitedly about a journal written by the husband's maternal grandmother in the ghetto in Poland. The grandmother, whom he never met, was a young woman of twenty-seven at the time, and she described in her journal the last days of the Shedlitz Ghetto, that terrible time when the 15 thousand Jews of Shedlitz were led to their death, and how she had to hide with her baby girl in an attic, at the beginning of the mass deportation of Jews to Camp Treblinka. The story of the journal of Zippa Jablon-Zonszajn, my friend Gal Ben Shaul's grandmother, was for me the answer I had been seeking for many years, since my own childhood, about the past of his mother Rachel.

At age 12, Rachel arrived at Kibbutz Ma'abarot and joined the Aluma group at the Ramot Chefer regional school. She excelled in all the areas of her high school studies (much like her mother Zippa), even though she wasn't a native of Israel. After her military service, she married a kibbutz member and had two children from him—Still, Rachel soon found herself alone once again, following the failure of her marriage. Her eldest son, Gal, was born a mere 36 hours after I was born, in the early winter of 1963. Since then my mother and Rachel became close friends.

After she had completed her university studies, she held several executive positions at the helm of the Kibbutz Ma'abarot Industries. Once her youngest son completed his military service, Rachel made a brave decision to leave the kibbutz. She resided in Tel-Aviv and later in Hertzelia, and reached a top position with the produce exporter Agrexco. In the early 1990s, she was asked to manage the company's New York branch, and she moved to the city she revered with all her heart.

Over the years she became, despite our age difference, my friend, too. Our friendship grew during my many visits to New York in the 90s, and then she would occasionally talk about herself. But the one thing she never discussed with anyone was her past.

Her closest relative, Uncle Shimon, with whom Rachel maintained a close and warm relationship over the years, passed away in 1995. But that wasn't the only blow Rachel received that year. On January 1, 1995, her younger son Yariv was killed at age 26 in a tragic accident in South America – a loss from which Rachel never recovered.

When America was attacked on September 11, 2001, Rachel and her older son, Gal, were kept in a Swiss airport, waiting for their delayed flight to New York, having just returned from Shedlitz, Poland, where Rachel had introduced Gal to both Sophia and Irena. They finally made it back to the States; Rachel returning to her New York home and Gal continuing to San Francisco. A few days later, Rachel flew to San Francisco and while on board the plane she began to sense that something was wrong with her. A few days later she was diagnosed with an aggressive brain cancer.

Less than two years later, when Rachel was dying, she decided to disseminate her mother's journal among her closest friends. From the journal pages that remained intact, collected in a simple folder and translated into Hebrew in the 1980s by a veteran kibbutz member, there emerged an entire epic of a Jewish family that lived in peace and humility in a typical Polish town until the day their entire world was shattered. Zippa described with sensitivity, gentleness and clarity the atrocities of deportation, the constant terror, and her parting with everything she had ever loved. Her descriptions touched my heart, perhaps because, as a young mother myself, I was deeply affected by the story of a mother fighting to save her baby daughter.

Rachel passed away on April 30, exactly on Holocaust Day, 2003, and her mother's journal has never left my side. Eventually, I realized that her story had set root inside me. But the deeper I dug into the story and was searching for those individuals who could tell it to me, the more aware I became that those who might be able to help me were dwindling away. In order to be able to interview those few key characters, I had to act at once, before it was too late.

A month after I decided to begin writing this book, I found myself on a plane to Poland. My first few days in Warsaw were a total shock for me; I wasn't sure what I wanted from myself or from the story, and I had a hard time being away, for the first time in my life, from my two little girls. And then I met Mrs. Sophia Glazer-Olsakowska. This elderly, bent lady, who had just turned 92, hosted me in her small and humble apartment on the outskirts of Warsaw, where she had been living since the end of WW2, and in simple, honest words, in a clarity that is rare in people her age, told me the story of her wondrous friendship with Zippa Zonshein. When she spoke of Rachel, she called her "my wartime daughter." The story was completed the next day, by Miss Irena Zawadzka, whose tendency to be emotional was evident even at her very old age. The memories brought them back to that unusual triangle of two young Polish Christian and one Jewish girlfriends, whose friendship survived the ultimate evil.

In the following days I went to Shedlitz, too, visited the places where the story took place, dug through the town's dusty archives and interviewed people I had never imagined I would speak to. At that stage I already knew there was no going back; I wanted to memorialize this story. I had to write this book.

I credit the late Sophia Glazer-Olsakowska and Irena Zawadzka with giving me the opportunity to tell the story of Zippa and her daughter Rachel, but the story of Zippa and Rachel would not have been complete without the wondrous ability of Sala Feigenbaum, Rachel's cousin, to introduce me in her unique way to the tales of the various Jablon family members. Rachel's past had been for me—and for others—a mystery for many years, and if not for those kind ladies who opened their hearts to me, it would have been forgotten, like so many other stories no one's left to tell.

I'm grateful to Gal Ben Shaul for his support, and especially for giving me his blessings to embark on this journey, and to Aaron Jablon (Shimon's son) for his great support. A great big thank you to my publisher Rony Zafrir for his patience and attention and for his perfect execution. The author Lilach Galil edited the book professionally and efficiently, but also with great warmth and sensitivity, and I am deeply grateful to her.

My thanks also to the dept. of "The Righteous Among The Nations" at Yad Vashem, the Central Zionist Archive, the Institute of Oral Documentation at Hebrew University, the Archive of Religious Zionism, and the archive of the Theater Department at Tel Aviv University. Finally, it would be impossible to conclude the English language edition without expressing my gratitude to the translator, Yori Yanover, who performed his work with admirable talent and professionalism.

Please consider leaving a review of the book on its Amazon page.

Amira Keidar
Ma'abarot, May 2010

"This is your Mamma, my little doll, your Mamma who couldn't raise you and who wishes that never in your life will you feel the absence of your Mamma, and that life will bring you happiness and goodness, and whatever you want out of life. These are the blessings of your wretched Mamma. Shedlitz, August 1942."

"You are now in your father's arms; you loved playing with that hat of his and the cane. At eleven months, he saved you from certain death and then said goodbye to you. I bless you that you'll have in your life everything that he now wishes for you. Shedlitz, August 1942."

"Dear, beloved Dolly! This is your grandmother; remember her well because she loved you very, very much and gave her life to save you from certain death. The whole town knew about her great love for you, and I wish you will have in your life everything that she wishes for you. We can't show you your grandfather, but he, too, loved you very, very much. Shedlitz, August 1942."